# DODGE
## 1968-1979
### TUNE-UP · MAINTENANCE

By
**JIM COMBS**

**ERIC JORGENSEN**
Editor

**JEFF ROBINSON**
Publisher

# CLYMER PUBLICATIONS

World's largest publisher of books
devoted exclusively to automobiles and motorcycles

**12860 MUSCATINE STREET · P.O. BOX 20 · ARLETA, CALIFORNIA 91331**

Copyright ©1977, 1979 Clymer Publications

*All rights reserved. No part of this publication may
be reproduced, stored in a retrieval system, or transmitted,
in any form or by any means, electronic, mechanical,
photocopying, recording or otherwise,
without the written permission of Clymer Publications.*

FIRST EDITION
Published February, 1977
SECOND EDITION
*Revised by Jim Combs to cover 1977-1979 models*
First Printing April, 1979
Second Printing June, 1980
Third Printing August, 1981

Printed in U.S.A.

ISBN: 0-89287-143-1

**Chapter One**
**General Information**

**Chapter Two**
**Troubleshooting**

**Chapter Three**
**Periodic Maintenance**

**Chapter Four**
**Lubricants and Fluids**

**Chapter Five**
**Ignition Tune-up**

**Chapter Six**
**Carburetor and Fuel Pump**

**Chapter Seven**
**Cooling System**

**Chapter Eight**
**Brakes and Front Wheel Bearings**

**Chapter Nine**
**Clutch Adjustment**

**Chapter Ten**
**Shock Absorbers**

**Chapter Eleven**
**Emission Control Systems**

**Chapter Twelve**
**Starter and Alternator**

**Supplement**
**1977 and Later Service Information**

# CONTENTS

### CHAPTER ONE
### GENERAL INFORMATION . . . . . . . . . . . . . . . . . . . . . . . . 1

    Manual organization      Service hints
    Identification numbers     Tools
    Parts replacement

### CHAPTER TWO
### TROUBLESHOOTING . . . . . . . . . . . . . . . . . . . . . . . . . . . 7

    Principles     Fuel system
    Starter     Exhaust emission control
    Charging system     Clutch
    Engine     Brakes
    Ignition system

### CHAPTER THREE
### PERIODIC MAINTENANCE . . . . . . . . . . . . . . . . . . . . . . . 14

    Routine checks     Periodic checks

### CHAPTER FOUR
### LUBRICANTS AND FLUIDS . . . . . . . . . . . . . . . . . . . . . . 34

    Engine lubrication     Manual transmissions
    Cooling system     Automatic transmission
    Power steering     Rear axle
    Chassis lubrication     Brake fluid
    Manual steering gear

### CHAPTER FIVE
### IGNITION TUNE-UP . . . . . . . . . . . . . . . . . . . . . . . . . . . . 38

    Tune-up sequence     Breaker points
    Compression test     Ignition timing
    Spark plug replacement     Valve lash adjustment (6-cylinder only)
    Cable resistance check     Tune-up specifications

### CHAPTER SIX
### CARBURETOR AND FUEL PUMP . . . . . . . . . . . . . . . . . . 54

    Curb idle adjustment     Fuel pump checks

## CHAPTER SEVEN

## COOLING SYSTEM . . . . . . . . . . . . . . . . . . . . . . . . . . . 66

Accessory drive belts
Cooling system flushing
Cooling system cleaning
Pressure cap
Radiator hose
Fans

## CHAPTER EIGHT

## BRAKES AND FRONT WHEEL BEARINGS . . . . . . . . . . . . . . . . 72

Drum brakes
Front wheel bearing lubrication
Wheel cylinders
Brake adjustment
Hydraulic system bleeding
Disc brakes

## CHAPTER NINE

## CLUTCH ADJUSTMENT . . . . . . . . . . . . . . . . . . . . . . 96

Free play adjustment
Gearshift interlock rod

## CHAPTER TEN

## SHOCK ABSORBERS . . . . . . . . . . . . . . . . . . . . . . . . 105

Front shock absorber removal
Rear shock absorber removal
Front shock absorber installation
Rear shock absorber installation

## CHAPTER ELEVEN

## EMISSION CONTROL SYSTEMS . . . . . . . . . . . . . . . . . . . 110

Description and service
Manifold heat control valve
Air injection system (air pump)
Vapor saver system
Exhaust gas recirculation system
Electric assist choke system
Orifice spark advance control system
Coolant controlled idle enrichment
  system
Catalytic converter
EGR maintenance indicator

## CHAPTER TWELVE

## STARTER AND ALTERNATOR . . . . . . . . . . . . . . . . . . . 123

Starter
Alternator

## SUPPLEMENT

## 1977 AND LATER SERVICE INFORMATION . . . . . . . . . . . . . 124

Periodic maintenance
Lubricants and fluids
Ignition timing
Tune-up specifications
Idle speed adjustment
Fuel pump checks
Clutch free play adjustment
Shock absorbers

## INDEX . . . . . . . . . . . . . . . . . . . . . . . . . . . . . . . 141

CLYMER

# DODGE
## 1968-1979
### TUNE-UP · MAINTENANCE

# CHAPTER ONE

# GENERAL INFORMATION

This book provides information and procedures for maintaining and tuning all 1968-1979 U.S.-built Dodges.

## MANUAL ORGANIZATION

This chapter provides general information.

Chapter Two provides methods and suggestions for finding and fixing troubles fast. Troubleshooting procedures discuss typical symptoms and logical methods to pinpoint the trouble.

Chapter Three explains all periodic lubrication and routine maintenance required to keep your car in top running condition. Chapter Four recommends fluids and lubricants to be used.

Chapters Five and Six include recommended ignition and carburetor tune-up procedures, eliminating the need to constantly consult chapters covering the various subassemblies.

Subsequent chapters provide procedures for servicing specific systems such as the cooling system, clutch, and electrical system. If a procedure is impractical for the home mechanic, it is so indicated. Such procedures are usually more economically and quickly done by a dealer or other competent repair shop. Specification concerning a particular system are provided in the applicable chapter.

The main body of this book contains information regarding 1968-1976 models. A supplement at the back of the book contains information for 1977-1979 models.

Some of the procedures in this manual specify special tools. In all cases, the tools are illustrated in actual use or alone. A well-equipped mechanic may find he can substitute other similar tools he has on hand or can fabricate his own.

The terms NOTE, CAUTION, and WARNING have specific meanings in this manual. A NOTE provides additional information to make a step or procedure easier or clearer. Disregarding a NOTE could cause inconvenience, but would not cause damage or personal injury.

A CAUTION emphasizes areas where equipment damage could result. Disregarding a CAUTION could cause permanent mechanical damage; however, personal injury is unlikely.

A WARNING emphasizes areas where personal injury or even death could result from negligence. Mechanical damage may also occur. WARNINGS *are to be taken seriously*. In some cases serious injury or death has been caused by mechanics disregarding similar warnings.

## IDENTIFICATION NUMBERS

Several identification numbers are important when ordering spare parts or identifying the automobile for registration purposes. The vehicle number is on the top of the instrument panel at the left front edge. See **Figure 1**. The engine serial number is stamped on a pad on the side of the cylinder block. Use these numbers when ordering parts.

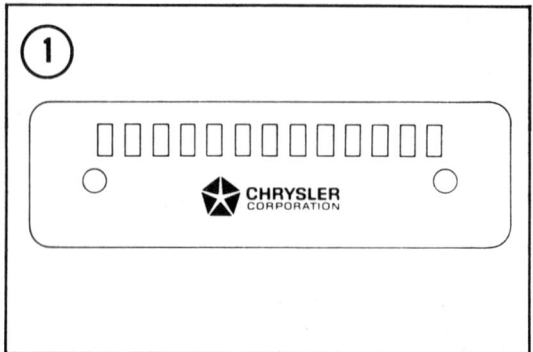

## PARTS REPLACEMENT

Dodge has made frequent changes during the period covered by this book; some minor, some relatively major. When you order parts from a dealer or other parts distributor, always order by year, engine and chassis numbers. Write the numbers down and carry them in your wallet. Compare new parts to old before purchasing them. If they are not alike, have the parts man explain the difference.

## SERVICE HINTS

Observing the following practices will save time, effort, and frustration, as well as prevent possible injury.

Throughout this manual keep in mind two conventions. "Front" refers to the front of the car. The front of any component such as the engine or transmission is that end which faces toward the front of the car. The left and right side of the car refers to a person sitting in the car facing forward. For example, the steering wheel is on the left side. These rules are simple, but even experienced mechanics occasionally become disoriented.

When working under a car, do not trust a hydraulic or mechanical jack alone to hold the car up. Always use jackstands.

Disconnect the battery ground cable before working near electrical connections and before disconnecting wires.

### CAUTION
*Never run the engine with the battery disconnected; the alternator could be seriously damaged.*

Tag all similar internal parts for location and mark all mating parts for position. Record number and thickness of any shims as they are removed. Small parts such as bolts can be identified by placing them in plastic sandwich bags and sealing and labeling the bags with masking tape.

Protect finished surfaces from physical damage or corrosion. Keep gasoline and brake fluid off painted surfaces.

Frozen or very tight bolts and screws can often be loosened by soaking with penetrating oil, then sharply striking the bolt head a few times with a hammer and punch (or screwdriver for screws). Avoid heat, unless absolutely necessary, since it may melt, warp, or remove the temper from many parts.

Avoid flames or sparks when working near a charging battery or flammable liquids such as brake fluid or gasoline.

No parts, except those assembled with a press fit, require unusual force during assembly. If a part is hard to remove or install, find out why before proceeding.

Cover all openings after removing parts to keep dirt, small tools, etc., from falling in.

When assembling two parts, start all fasteners, then tighten evenly.

Read each procedure in its entirety while looking at the actual parts *before* beginning. Many procedures are complicated and errors can be disastrous. When you thoroughly understand what is to be done, follow the procedures step-by-step.

## TOOLS

For proper servicing, you need an assortment of ordinary hand tools. As a minimum, these include:

a. Combination wrenches
b. Socket wrenches
c. Plastic mallet
d. Small hammer
e. Snap ring pliers
f. Gas pliers
g. Phillips screwdrivers
h. Slot (common) screwdrivers
i. Feeler gauges
j. Spark plug gauge
k. Spark plug wrench

# GENERAL INFORMATION

Some of the procedures in this manual specify special tools. In all cases, the tools are illustrated in actual use or alone. A well-equipped mechanic may find he can substitute other similar tools he has on hand or can fabricate his own.

Troubleshooting and engine tune-up require a few more specialized tools which are described in the following sections.

Quality and price vary considerably. Adequate light-duty equipment can be purchased for the cost of 3 or 4 tune-ups. Professional tune-up and troubleshooting equipment can cost several hundred dollars. As is the case with most tools, cost is usually a fair indicator of quality.

In the following paragraphs, each of the above items of equipment is described and its purpose discussed.

## Dwell Meter

A dwell meter (**Figure 2**) measures the distance in degrees of distributor cam rotation from the time the breaker points close until they open again, while the engine is running. Since this angle is determined by the breaker point gap setting, dwell angle is an accurate indication of breaker point gap.

Many tachometers intended for tuning and testing incorporate a dwell meter. The manufacturer's instructions should be followed to measure dwell with these combination instruments.

## Tachometer

A tachometer is a necessity for tune-up work, as ignition timing and carburetor adjustments must be made at specified idle speeds. The best instrument for this work is one that has 2 ranges: a low range of 0-1,000 to 0-2,000 rpm for setting low or "curb" idle, and a high range of 0-4,000 or more rpm for setting fast idle and checking ignition timing at faster engine speeds. Tachometers with only one extended range (0-6,000 to 0-8,000 rpm) lack accuracy at lower speeds. The instrument should be capable of detecting changes of 25 rpm on the low range.

## Timing Light

This instrument is required for accurate engine timing adjustment. The light is connected to flash each time the No. 1 cylinder fires, making the position of the timing mark visible at that instant. When the engine is properly timed, the timing marks will appear to be aligned.

Suitable timing lights range from inexpensive neon bulb types ($3-5) to powerful xenon strobe lights ($20-50). See **Figure 3**. Neon timing lights are difficult to see and must be used in dimly lit areas. Xenon strobe timing lights can be obtained for either AC or DC operation, and the DC types can be operated from the car's battery.

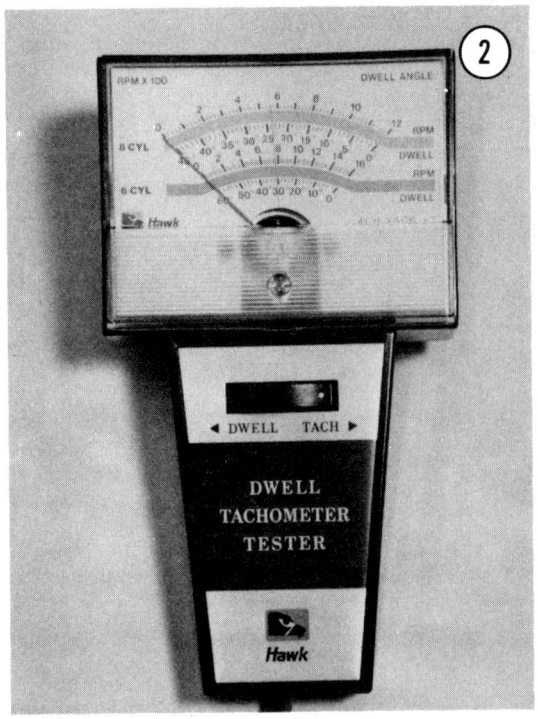

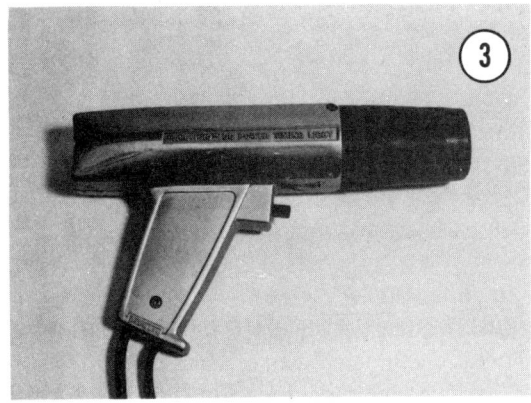

## Compression Tester

The compression tester measures the pressure built up in each cylinder as the engine is turned over. The results, when properly interpreted, can indicate general cylinder and valve condition. Many compression testers have long flexible extensions as accessories (**Figure 4**). See Chapter Five for compression test procedures.

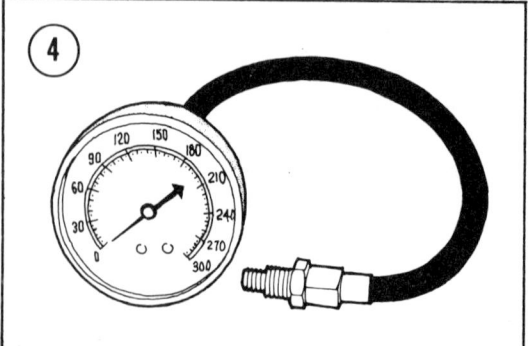

## Vacuum Gauge

The vacuum gauge (**Figure 5**) is one of the easiest instruments to use, but one of the hardest for the inexperienced mechanic to interpret. Test results, when interpreted with other findings, can give valuable clues to possible troubles.

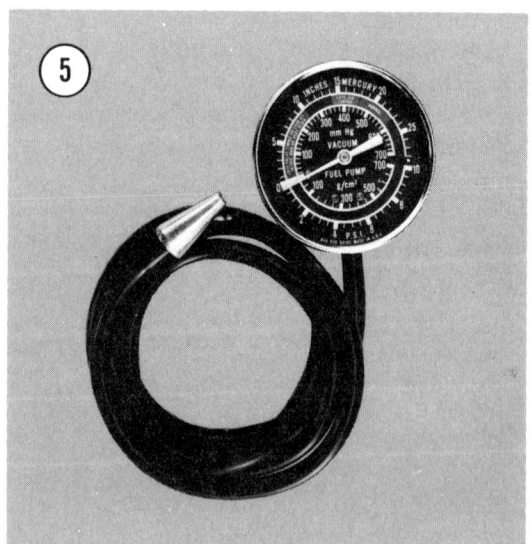

**Figure 6** shows a number of typical vacuum gauge readings with interpretations. Results should be compared with other test results, such as compression, before reaching conclusions.

## Fuel Pressure Gauge

This instrument is needed for evaluating fuel pump performance. Usually a vacuum gauge and a fuel pressure gauge are combined into one instrument.

## Voltmeter, Ammeter, and Ohmmeter

A good voltmeter is required for testing ignition and other electrical systems. An instrument covering 0-20 volts is satisfactory and it should also have a 0-2 volt scale for testing relays, points, or individual contacts where voltage drops are much smaller. Accuracy should be $\pm\tfrac{1}{2}$ volt.

An ohmmeter measures electrical resistance. This instrument is useful in checking continuity (for open and short circuits) and testing fuses and lights.

The ammeter measures electrical current. Ammeters for automotive use should have scales covering 0-50 amperes and 0-250 amperes. These are useful for checking battery starting and charging currents.

Several inexpensive VOM's (volt-ohm-milliammeter) combine all 3 instruments into one which fits in any tool box. See **Figure 7**. The ammeter ranges are usually too low for automotive work, though. Combination instruments designed especially for engine diagnostic work are available, however, and they are not excessively expensive (from $35 up).

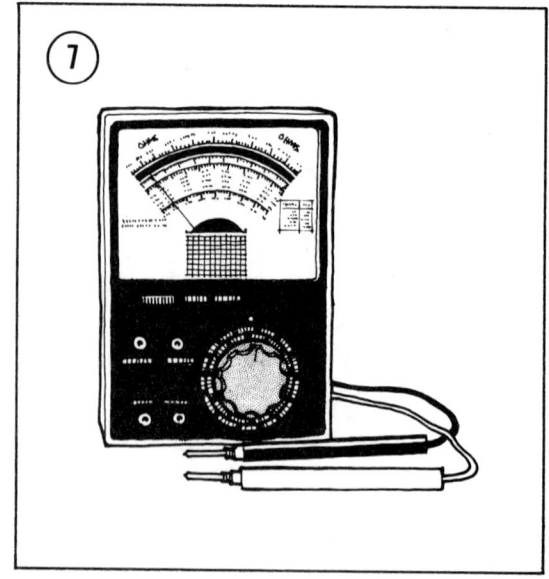

# GENERAL INFORMATION

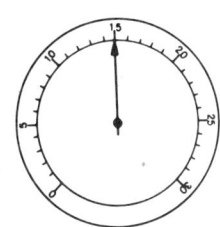

**1. NORMAL READING**
Reads 15 in. at idle.

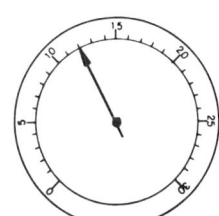

**2. LATE IGNITION TIMING**
About 2 inches too low at idle.

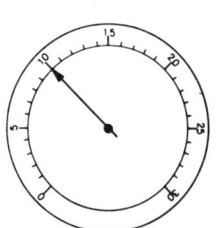

**3. LATE VALVE TIMING**
About 4 to 8 inches low at idle.

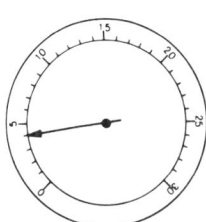

**4. INTAKE LEAK**
Low steady reading.

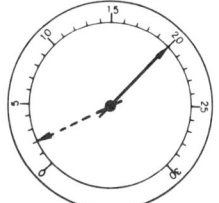

**5. NORMAL READING**
Drops to 2, then rises to 25 when accelerator is rapidly depressed and released.

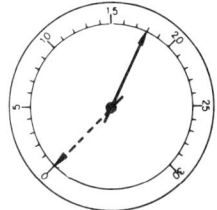

**6. WORN RINGS, DILUTED OIL**
Drops to 0, then rises to 18 when accelerator is rapidly depressed and released.

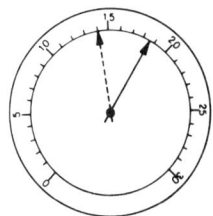

**7. STICKING VALVE(S)**
Normally steady. Intermittently flicks downward about 4 in.

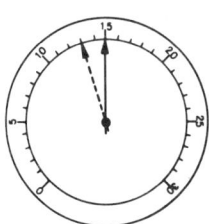

**8. LEAKY VALVE**
Regular drop about 2 inches.

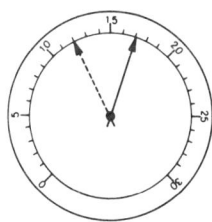

**9. BURNED OR WARPED VALVE**
Regular, evenly spaced down-scale flick about 4 in.

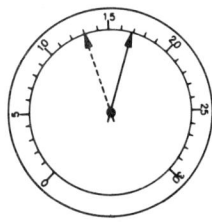

**10. WORN VALVE GUIDES**
Oscillates about 4 in.

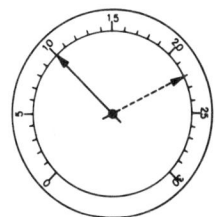

**11. WEAK VALVE SPRINGS**
Violent oscillation (about 10 in.) as rpm increases. Often steady at idle.

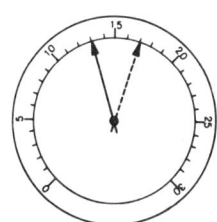

**12. IMPROPER IDLE MIXTURE**
Floats slowly between 13-17 in.

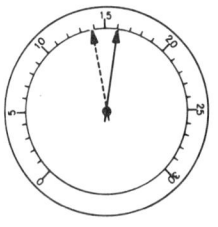

**13. SMALL SPARK GAP or DEFECTIVE POINTS**
Slight float between 14-16 in.

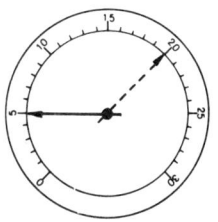

**14. HEAD GASKET LEAK**
Gauge floats between 5-19 in.

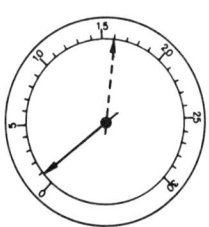

**15. RESTRICTED EXHAUST SYSTEM**
Normal when first started. Drops to 0 as rpm increases. May eventually rise to about 16.

## Hydrometer

Hydrometer testing is the best way to check battery condition. Use a hydrometer with numbered graduations from 1.100-1.300 rather than one with color-coded bands. To use the hydrometer, squeeze the rubber ball, insert the tip into a battery cell, and release the ball (**Figure 8**). Draw enough electrolyte into the instrument so that the weighted float is riding freely in the liquid. Note the number on the float in line with the liquid surface level: this is the specific gravity of the cell. Return the electrolyte to the cell from which it was taken and continue to test all cells.

Specific gravity gives an indication of cell condition. A fully charged cell will read 1.275-1.380, while a cell in good condition may read 1.250-1.280. A cell in fair condition reads from 1.225-1.250, and anything below 1.225 is practically dead. If the cells test in the poor range, the battery requires recharging. The hydrometer may also be used for checking the progress of the charging operation. A reading from 1.200 to about 1.225 indicates a half charge, while 1.275-1.380 indicates full charge.

### CAUTION
*Always disconnect both battery cables before hooking up charging equipment.*

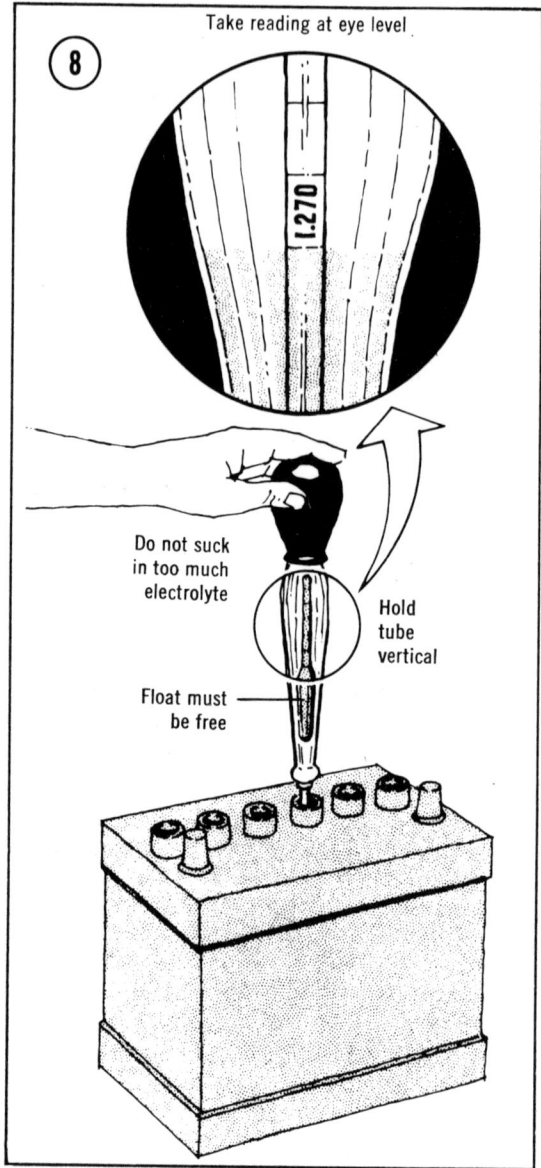

## Exhaust Analyzer

Of all the instruments described here, the exhaust analyzer is the least likely to be owned by a home mechanic. This instrument samples exhaust gases at the tailpipe and measures the thermal conductivity of the exhaust gases. Since different gases conduct heat at varying rates, thermal conductivity of the exhaust is a good indication of gases present.

This instrument is required for accurately checking the effectiveness of exhaust emission control (carburetor) adjustments. While the exhaust analyzer is relatively expensive to buy, some equipment rental dealers have them available for a modest fee.

# CHAPTER TWO

# TROUBLESHOOTING

Effective troubleshooting is simply a logical approach to diagnosing engine failure or malfunction. The first step is to define the symptoms. Subsequent steps consist of a series of tests and analyses to localize and identify the cause of the trouble, starting with the most likely areas.

In the case of the automobile engine, it should be remembered that operation depends upon an uninterrupted fuel supply, air, a reliable ignition (electrical) system, and proper compression. Failure of any one of these will invariably result in engine failure or poor performance.

## TROUBLESHOOTING PROCEDURES

While no accurate statistics are available, it has been estimated that as many as 90% of all automobile engine starting failures can be attributed to the ignition and other electrical problems. The remaining 10% can be blamed on fuel system and other problems. While this may appear to be an exaggeration, the experienced mechanic, when trying to discover an unknown reason for engine failure, will usually suspect the electrical system.

In spite of the odds, however, more than a few mysterious engine failures can be solved very rapidly by a quick glance at the fuel gauge. The car may simply be out of gas.

Troubleshooting can be a relatively simple matter if it is done logically. A haphazard approach may eventually find the problem, but in terms of wasted time and unnecessary parts replacement, it can be very costly. The troubleshooting procedures in this chapter analyze typical symptoms and show logical methods of isolation. These are not the only methods. There may be several approaches to a problem, but all good methods have one thing in common— a logical, systematic approach.

During the years covered by this book, Chrysler Corporation used a large number of different size engines. These engines were used in a large number of combinations with various manual and automatic transmissions, carburetors, and distributors. Various emission control devices have also been used. Because of these factors, it would be impossible to provide specific checkout procedures for all of the numerous combinations. Instead, the troubleshooting procedures given below have been purposely kept general in order to cover the largest possible combinations of engine-transmission-carburetor-distributor.

If you do not fully understand how a procedure applies to your particular car, or how a component should be checked, the problem should be referred to your dealer or to a mechanic who has had specific experience with your engine combination.

## STARTER

Starter system troubles are fairly easy to isolate. The following are common symptoms and cures.

1. *No cranking action*—Verify that transmission selector is in NEUTRAL or PARK, or that clutch pedal is depressed on manual transmission. Make a quick check of battery, battery terminals, and cables. Recharge battery if discharged. If battery is partially discharged, solenoid will usually produce a clattering noise. If battery terminals are badly corroded, clean them with baking soda solution, remove cable connectors, clean contacting surfaces of terminals and connectors with a wire brush, and reconnect the cables, making certain all connections are tight. Check cables for continuity. If starter motor spins and drive pinion engages ring gear but does not drive it, starter clutch is slipping. Remove starter motor to replace drive assembly.

Note whether solenoid plunger is pulled into solenoid when starter circuit is closed (ordinarily the plunger makes a loud click when it is pulled in). If plunger is pulled in, the solenoid circuit is not the problem and the trouble is in the solenoid switch, starter motor, or the starter motor circuit. Remove starter motor for repairs to either motor or switch.

If plunger does not pull into solenoid, solenoid circuit is open or solenoid is at fault. Connect jumper wire between solenoid relay terminal and terminal on solenoid switch. If starter works, solenoid is OK and trouble is in neutral start switch, ignition switch, or in the wires and connections between the switches.

Some late models are equipped with seat belt/starter interlock systems. If battery, cables, and connections are OK, and no solenoid click is heard when starter circuit is closed, the problem may be a malfunction in the interlock system.

If starter still fails to operate, remove it and have it tested.

2. *Cranking speed abnormally low* — Low cranking speed can be caused by partially discharged battery, defective battery cables, defective solenoid switch, defective starter motor, or by an internal engine condition.

Make a quick test of battery and recharge if required. Check cables for continuity and condition and replace if faulty or doubtful. Clean corrosion from battery terminals and cable connectors, if present.

NOTE: *If battery is low, check generator belt tension.*

If battery and cables check out OK, test solenoid switch and cranking motor as outlined in Step 1 above. If these items are working properly, an internal engine condition may exist.

NOTE: *The use of motor oil which is too heavy for prevailing temperatures may cause abnormally slow cranking action.*

3. *Starter engages, but will not disengage when ignition switch is released*—This condition is usually caused by either a sticking solenoid or a defective ignition switch. A sticking solenoid can sometimes be temporarily remedied by lightly tapping the solenoid with a piece of wood or a rubber mallet. After the problem is isolated, replace the faulty part.

4. *Loud grinding noise when starter runs*—This may mean that the gear on the pinion and/or flywheel ring gear is not meshing properly, or it may mean that the starter clutch is broken. The solution is to remove the starter and find and replace the defective parts.

5. *Starter engages (clunks) but does not crank engine*—This is usually caused by an open circuit in the solenoid armature or field coils, or by a short or ground in the starter motor field coil or armature. The solution is to check out both systems to isolate the problem and then to repair or replace the faulty component.

## CHARGING SYSTEM (ALTERNATOR/REGULATOR)

When troubleshooting the charging system the following precautions should be observed:

# TROUBLESHOOTING

a. Do not polarize the alternator.
b. Do not short across or ground any of the terminals in the charging system unless specifically directed to do so in a procedure.
c. Never operate the alternator with the output terminal open circuited.
d. Make sure the alternator and the battery are of the same ground polarity.
e. When connecting booster cables or a charger to the battery, connect negative terminal to negative terminal and positive terminal to positive terminal.

1. *Telltale warning lamp constantly on*—Check alternator drive belt for proper tension. Check condition of battery with hydrometer. Check and clean all electrical connections in charging system. If trouble still persists, have the charging system checked.

2. *Battery requires frequent additions of water or lamps require frequent replacement*—The system is probably overcharging the battery. Have the voltage regulator checked or replace it.

> NOTE: *Models since 1970 have used non-adjustable electronic voltage regulators. Older models use mechanical regulators.*

3. *Noisy alternator*—Check for loose alternator mounting. If this is not the problem, check alternator bearings.

## ENGINE

These procedures assume that the starter motor cranks the engine normally. If not, refer to *Starter* section in this chapter.

1. *Engine will not start*—Could be caused by ignition system or fuel system. First determine if high voltage is arriving at spark plugs by disconnecting one of the spark plug wires. Hold the exposed wire terminal ½ in. or so from ground (any exposed metal in the engine compartment) with an insulated screwdriver. Turn ignition switch on and crank engine. If sparks do not jump from wire terminal to ground, or if sparks are very weak, the trouble may be in the ignition system. See *Ignition System* troubleshooting procedure in this chapter to further isolate the trouble. If a good strong spark is present, the trouble may be in the fuel system. See *Fuel System* troubleshooting procedure, this chapter.

2. *Engine misses steadily*—Remove one spark plug wire at a time and ground the wire. If engine miss increases, that cylinder was working properly. Reconnect wire and check other spark plugs. When a wire is disconnected and the engine miss remains the same, that cylinder is not firing. Check spark as described in Step 1. If no spark occurs for one cylinder only, check distributor cap and spark plug wire. If spark occurs properly, check spark plug and then check compression and intake manifold pressure to isolate the problem.

3. *Engine misses erratically at all speeds*—Intermittent trouble like this can be hard to find. The trouble could be in the ignition system, the exhaust system (exhaust restriction), or in the fuel system. Carefully follow the troubleshooting procedures for all 3 systems until the trouble is isolated.

4. *Engine misses at idle only*—Trouble probably exists in ignition system. Follow *Ignition System* troubleshooting procedure carefully. Trouble could also exist in carburetor idle system. Check idle mixture adjustment (Chapter Six) and verify that anti-dieseling solenoid (if so equipped) is functioning properly. Check also for restrictions in the idle linkage.

5. *Engine misses at high speed only*—Troubles could exist in either the fuel system or the ignition system. Check fuel filter and lines for obstructions, fuel pump output delivery, and accelerator pump operation, as described in the *Fuel System* troubleshooting procedure in this chapter. Also check spark plugs and wires. See *Ignition System* troubleshooting procedure.

6. *Low performance at all speeds, poor performance*—Trouble usually exists in ignition or fuel systems. Check each using the appropriate troubleshooting procedure.

7. *Excessive fuel consumption*—This problem can be caused by any or a combination of a wide variety of seemingly unrelated problems. Check for clutch or automatic transmission (some types) slippage, brake drag, defective

wheel bearings, and poor front end alignment. Also check the ignition and fuel systems, using the appropriate troubleshooting procedure.

8. *Oil pressure gauge reads low (or warning light is constantly on)*—This may mean low or complete loss of oil pressure. Stop the engine immediately and coast to a stop with clutch disengaged or transmission in NEUTRAL. This may be caused simply by low oil level or an overheating engine. Check oil level and belt tension. Check for shorted oil pressure sender with an ohmmeter or other continuity tester. Listen for unusual noises which might indicate bad bearings, etc. Do not operate the car until the cause of the low oil pressure has been discovered and corrected.

## IGNITION SYSTEM (CONVENTIONAL)

The following procedures assume that the battery is good enough to crank the engine at a normal rate.

1. *No spark to one plug (only)*—The only possible causes are a defective distributor cap or spark plug wire. Examine distributor cap for moisture, dirt, cracks, carbon tracking caused by flash-overs, etc. Replace if necessary. Check spark plug wire with an ohmmeter. If the reading is abnormally high (over 20,000 ohms) or infinity, replace the wire.

2. *No spark to any plugs*—This could be caused by trouble in the primary or secondary ignition circuits. First, remove the coil wire from the center post of the distributor. Use an insulated screwdriver to hold the bare wire terminal about ¼ in. from ground and crank the engine. If sparks are produced, the trouble is in the distributor. Remove the distributor cap and check for burns, moisture, dirt, carbon tracking, pitting of contacts, or cracks. Check rotor for excessive burning, pitting, or cracks. Replace either or both if necessary.

If the coil did not produce sparks, check the secondary (center) wire for continuity with an ohmmeter. If the wire is good, turn engine over so breaker points are open. Examine them for excessive gap, burning, pitting, or looseness. Replace and/or adjust points if necessary. With the points still open, check voltage from the minus terminal of the coil to ground with a voltmeter or test light. If voltage is present, the coil is probably bad. Have it checked or substitute a coil known to be good.

If voltage is not present, check wire connections to coil and distributor. Temporarily disconnect the wire from the coil minus terminal and measure from minus terminal to ground. If voltage is present, the distributor is shorted; examine breaker points and connecting wires carefully. If voltage is still not present, measure plus terminal of coil. Voltage on plus terminal, but not on minus terminal, indicates a defective coil. No voltage on plus terminal indicates an open wire between minus terminal and battery.

3. *Weak spark*—If spark is so weak it cannot jump from the wire ¼-⅓ in. to ground, check condition of the battery. Other causes are bad breaker points, bad condenser, incorrect breaker point gap, or dirty or burned rotor or distributor cap. Also check for worn distributor cam lobes.

4. *Missing*—This is usually caused by fouled or damaged spark plugs, plugs of the wrong heat range, or incorrect plug gap. Clean and regap the spark plugs (or replace and gap them). This trouble also can be caused by weak spark or incorrect engine timing.

## IGNITION SYSTEM (ELECTRONIC)

The Chrysler Electronic Ignition System was used on some 1972 models and on all 1973-1976 models. The electronic distributor utilizes a magnetic pulse to interrupt current flow through the primary circuit, which induces a high voltage in the secondary circuit. This causes a spark plug to fire. This system, which replaces conventional breaker points, is not adjustable. The entire ignition system rarely requires any maintenance other than inspection (and replacement, if required) or wiring and the cleaning and changing of spark plugs. Timing, which is initially set at the factory, rarely requires adjustment, but should be checked at intervals. See Chapter Three.

In troubleshooting a malfunctioning engine equipped with the Chrysler Electronic Ignition

# TROUBLESHOOTING

Service, verify that the fuel and carburetion system is functioning properly before troubleshooting the ignition system.

A special Electronic Ignition tester (Chrysler Part No. C-4166) and adapter circuit (Part No. C-4166-1), or tester (Part No. C-4166-A) with integrated adapter circuit, is required for properly testing the distributor. As this tool is not readily available to the home mechanic, isolating faults and making repairs to the Chrysler Electronic Ignition System distributor should be referred to your dealer. In an emergency, the following procedure may be used.

1. *Engine will not start (fuel and carburetion good)*—Check the resistance of the dual ballast resistor (**Figure 1**). Normal ballast resistance at 70-80°F (21-25°C) should be 0.50-0.60 ohm, and auxiliary ballast should be 4.75-5.75 ohms. Replace if faulty. Also check for a carbonized tower on the ignition coil. Check coil primary and secondary resistances. Primary should be 1.60-1.79 ohms for a Prestolite coil and 1.41-1.55 ohms (1972-1974) or 1.41-1.62 ohms (1975-1976) for an Essex coil.

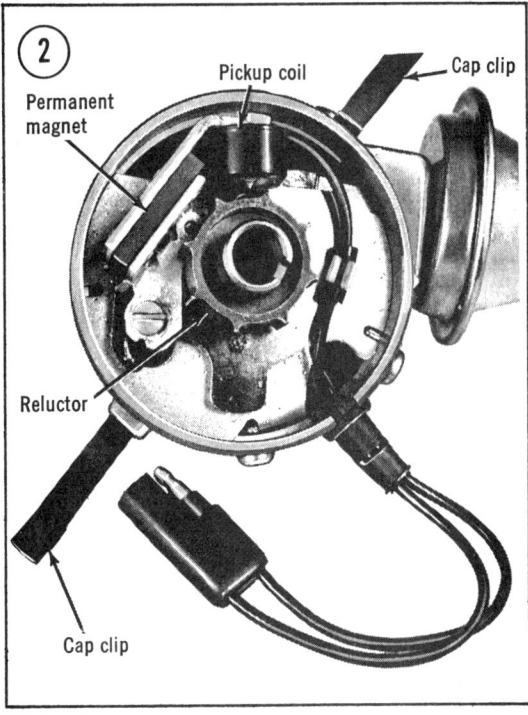

**CAUTION**
*Do not force the gauge, as damage could result.*

Check all wiring and connectors for brittle insulation and faulty connections. If the above checks fail to isolate a problem, replace the control unit (**Figure 3**).

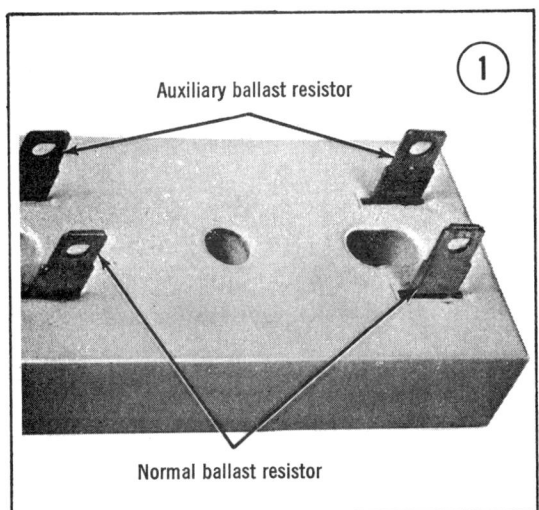

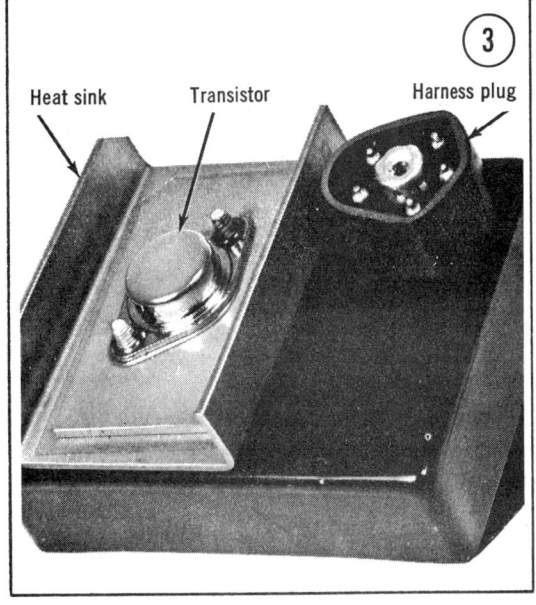

Secondary resistance should be 9,400-11,700 ohms for a Prestolite coil and 8,000-11,200 ohms for an Essex coil. Check the resistance of the pickup coil (**Figure 2**). This should be between 400 and 600 ohms. Also check the pickup airgap. The gap should be 0.008 in. Reset if a 0.010 in. feeler gauge will slip between the pickup coil core and an aligned reluctor blade.

2. *Engine surges severely (carburetion good)*—Inspect for faulty wiring and/or poor connections. Disconnect the vacuum advance; if surging stops, replace pickup. Check the ignition for an intermittent short or open circuit.

3. *Engine misses (carburetion good)*—Check spark plugs; clean or replace and regap, if indicated. Check spark plug wires with an ohmmeter. Replace if resistance is infinity or more than 30,000 ohms (if under 25 in. long) or 50,000 ohms (cables over 25 inches long). Check coil for carbonized tower and have coil checked on a coil tester. Disconnect vacuum advance; if miss stops, replace pickup. If none of the checks above reveal the problem, replace the control unit.

## FUEL SYSTEM

Fuel system troubles must be isolated to the carburetor, fuel pump, fuel filter, or fuel lines. The following procedures assume the ignition system has been checked and properly adjusted.

> NOTE: *Verify that adequate fuel is present in the fuel tank before proceeding.*

1. *Engine will not start*—First determine if fuel is being delivered to the carburetor. Remove the air cleaner, look into the carburetor throat, and depress the accelerator several times. There should be a stream of fuel from the accelerator pump discharge each time the accelerator is depressed. If not, check fuel pump delivery, float valve and float adjustment, fuel filter, and fuel pump and lines. If necessary, rebuild or replace carburetor.

2. *Rough idle or engine miss with frequent Stalling*—Check carburetor idle mixture and idle screw and/or solenoid adjustments. See Chapter Six.

3. *Engine diesels when ignition is cut off*—Check carburetor adjustments, particularly the idle stop or "anti-dieseling" solenoid (if so equipped).

4. *Stumbling when accelerating from idle*—Check idle speed adjustment. Also check fuel filter.

5. *Engine misses or stumbles at high speed or lacks power*—This indicates possible fuel starvation. Check fuel filter and fuel pump pressure and capacity (see procedures in this chapter). If this does not solve problem, clean carburetor main jet and float needle valve.

6. *Black exhaust smoke*—Black exhaust smoke means a badly overrich fuel/air mixture. Verify that automatic choke is working properly. Check idle mixture and idle speed settings (see Chapter Six). Check for excessive fuel pump pressure, leaky float, or worn float needle valve.

### Fuel Pump Pressure Testing

1. Install T-fitting in fuel line near carburetor.
2. Connect fuel pressure gauge to fitting, using a short tube.
3. Operate engine at curb idle speed (see Tune-up decal in engine compartment or Table 1, Chapter Six). Fuel pressure should be 3½-5 psi (6-cylinder engines) or 3½-8½ psi (8-cylinder engines), depending on model, with float needle valve closed. If pressure is considerably above or below limits stated, fuel pump should be replaced.

### Fuel Pump Capacity Testing

1. Disconnect fuel line near carburetor.
2. Fit a rubber hose over end of fuel line so fuel can be directed into a graduated container with about one quart capacity.
3. Start engine and run for 30 seconds. There is sufficient fuel in float chamber for this.
4. Stop the engine. The fuel pump should have delivered at least one pint of fuel in 30 seconds.

## EXHAUST EMISSION CONTROL

The following symptoms assume you have adjusted the ignition and carburetion (Chapters Five and Six), and you have checked the results on an accurate exhaust analyzer.

1. *CO content too low*—Ensure that idle speed is not too low. Check idle mixture adjustment (too lean). Check carburetor jets and channels. Clean and/or replace as necessary. Check engine condition with compression and vacuum tests.

# TROUBLESHOOTING

2. *CO content too high*—Check idle mixture adjustment (too rich). Check for sticking air cleaner warm air flap, and sticking or defective automatic choke. Check carburetor jets and channels. Clean and/or replace as necessary. Check engine condition with compression and vacuum tests.

3. *Hydrocarbon level too high*—Make sure throttle valve closes completely. Check spark plug gap and condition. Check breaker points. Check ignition timing (too early). Check valve clearance (too small). Check valve condition wtih compression test.

## CLUTCH

All clutch troubles except adjustments require transmission removal for isolation and repair.

1. *Slippage*—This condition is most noticeable when accelerating in high gear at relatively low speed. To check slippage, park car on a level surface with the handbrake set. Shift to second gear and release clutch as if driving off. If clutch is good, engine will slow and stall. If clutch slips, continued engine speed will give it away.

### CAUTION
*This is a severe test which should be performed only when clutch slippage is suspected. It should not be a periodic test.*

Slippage results from insufficient clutch pedal free play, oil or grease on the clutch disc, worn pressure plate, or weak springs. Also check for binding in the clutch linkage which may prevent full engagement.

2. *Drag or failure to release*—This trouble usually causes difficult shifting and gear clash, especially when downshifting. The cause may be excessive clutch pedal free play, warped or bent pressure plate, broken or loose linings, or burns on the main shaft splines.

3. *Chatter or grabbing*—Worn or misaligned pressure plate or binding clutch linkage.

4. *Other noises*—Noise usually indicates a dry or defective release (throwout) or pilot bearing.

Check the bearings and replace if necessary. Check all parts for misalignment and uneven wear.

## BRAKES

1. *Brake pedal goes to floor*—This can be caused by excessively worn linings, air in hydraulic lines, leaky brake lines and wheel cylinders, and leaky or worn master cylinder. Check for leaks and thin linings. Bleed and adjust the brakes. If problem still is present, rebuild or replace wheel cylinders and/or master cylinder.

2. *Spongy brake pedal* — This is normally caused by air in hydraulic system. Bleed hydraulic lines and adjust brakes.

3. *Brakes pull to one side*—Check brake adjustment. Also check for contaminated or damaged brake linings (front leaks), leaky wheel cylinders, loose calipers, frozen or seized cylinder pistons, and pinched or restricted hydraulic lines or hoses. If brake system checks out, have wheel alignment checked. Worn or partially deflated tires also can cause a problem.

4. *Brake squeal or chatter*—This can be caused by worn linings and/or out-of-round brake drums. Other causes are new linings without chamfered ends, loose linings, and dirt or rocks inside drums.

5. *Dragging brakes*—Check brake adjustment, including handbrake. Also check for weak or broken shoe return springs, swollen rubber parts (due to brake fluid contamination), and obstructed master cylinder bypass port. Clean or replace defective parts.

6. *Hard brake pedal*—Check linings for fluid or other contamination. Also check for restricted brake lines and hoses.

7. *High speed fade*—Check for distorted or out-of-round brake drums and contaminated linings. Make sure recommended brake fluid (Mopar or DOT-3 fluid) is used. If in doubt, drain, refill, and bleed entire system.

8. *Pulsating pedal*—Check for distorted or out-of-round brake drums. Check for excessive brake disc runout.

# CHAPTER THREE

# PERIODIC MAINTENANCE

An automobile represents a sizeable investment to the average owner. One of the best ways to protect this investment is a carefully followed maintenance program. Such a program is especially important if the vehicle is used in remote areas or is operated under severe service conditions.

A few basic maintenance checks should be made at every gas stop. Other tasks should be performed at regular intervals. The program described in this chapter was compiled from Chrysler Corporation service recommendations. See Chapter Four for the proper lubricants to be used.

## GAS STOP CHECKS

At each gas stop the following items should be checked:

1. Coolant level
2. Battery electrolyte level
3. Windshield washer fluid level
4. Engine oil level

Many—but not all—service station attendants make the checks as a matter of routine. To be on the safe side, you may want to develop the habit of looking over the attendant's shoulder, or even doing the task yourself. Even though the tasks are simple, they are important. They can also provide a warning of the need for other maintenance.

### Coolant Level

> **WARNING**
> *Driving in heavy traffic, at high altitudes, or in extremely hot weather may build up excessive pressure in the cooling system. If there is any evidence of steam, do not attempt to remove radiator cap until engine has cooled.*

If the vehicle is equipped with a "Coolant Reserve" system, the radiator is normally completely full. It is not necessary to remove the radiator cap for coolant inspection. Instead, check the level in the reserve tank. At normal engine operating temperature the fluid level should be at the one quart level. See **Figure 1** for a typical installation. Add coolant, if required, by removing the reserve tank cap and filling to the one quart level.

If not equipped with a Coolant Reserve system, inspect coolant level by carefully removing the radiator cap. If the engine is hot, observe the CAUTION above. Carefully cover the radiator cap with a cloth and turn the cap to the left to the first stop. Allow any residual steam to es-

# PERIODIC MAINTENANCE

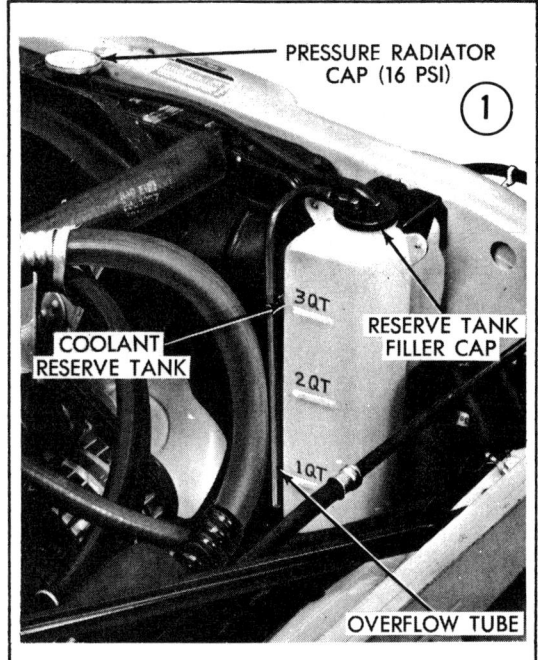

cape through the overflow tube, then remove the cap. Coolant level should be maintained 1¼ in. below the bottom of the filler neck. Overfilling will result in loss of coolant.

> NOTE: *If the radiator requires frequent additions of coolant, leakage or system blockage is indicated. See Chapter Seven for remedial procedures.*

**Battery Electrolyte Level**

The electrolyte level in each cell should be maintained at the bottom of the filler hole well.

> CAUTION
> *Do not overfill, as loss of electrolyte could result.*

If the electrolyte level is low, add mineral-free (distilled) water to fill to the level recommended above.

> CAUTION
> *Never add electrolyte ("battery acid") to an old battery.*

**Windshield Washer Fluid**

The windshield washer is an important safety feature, and an adequate supply of fluid should be present in the reservoir at all times. A quick check of the reservoir while performing other under-the-hood services should become a habit. Refill the reservoir with water if it is less than half full. If an additive is used, follow the manufacturer's instructions.

**Engine Oil Level**

Engine oil level should be checked as the last step in fuel stop under-the-hood service. This will allow the oil in the upper part of the engine to drain back into the crankcase. Check the oil level by removing the dipstick, wiping it clean, reinserting the dipstick until it is firmly seated, and then removing it again and reading the oil level as shown on the dipstick lower end.

The oil level should be maintained between the ADD OIL and FULL marks on the dipstick. Oil should be added whenever the level drops below the ADD OIL mark. Add only enough to bring the level no higher than the FULL mark.

> CAUTION
> *Overfilling the engine with oil can cause engine damage.*

## PERIODIC MAINTENANCE

A recommended periodic maintenance program is given in **Table 1**. Lubrication, which is included in the table, is discussed in detail in Chapter Four. The schedule is intended only as a guide. If your vehicle is operated under any of the following conditions, the maintenance intervals should be cut in half:

1. Trailer towing
2. Police, taxi, or limousine operation
3. Operation in very dusty areas
4. Operation (50% or more) in heavy city traffic in temperatures above 90°F
5. Prolonged idling
6. Very short trips (less than 10 miles) with no long trips

Following is a brief explanation of each item contained in Table 1. Use only those services that apply to your vehicle.

1. *Battery*—Check fluid level at least once a month and restore to bottom of filler hole neck. *Do not overfill.* Use only water with low mineral

## CHAPTER THREE

Table 1 MAINTENANCE SCHEDULE

See legend at end of table.

| Service | Interval in months and/or miles | 1968 | 1969 | 1970 | 1971 | 1972 | 1973 | 1974 | 1975 | 1976 |
|---|---|---|---|---|---|---|---|---|---|---|
| 1. Battery | 1 | C | C | C | C | C | C | C | C | C |
| 2. Cooling system | 1 | C | C | C | C | C | C | C | C | C |
| 3. Engine oil | 3 (4,000) | R | R | R | R | R | R | R | | |
| Engine oil | 6 (5,000) | | | | | | | | R | R |
| 4. Oil filter | 6 (8,000) | R | R | R | R | R | R | R | | |
| Oil filter | 12 (10,000) | | | | | | | | R | R |
| 5. Power steering | 3 (4,000) | C | C | C | C | C | C | C | | |
| Power steering | 6 (5,000) | | | | | | | | C | C |
| 6. Carburetor air filter | 3 (4,000) ① | — | — | — | — | — | — | — | | |
| Carburetor air filter | 12 (12,000) ① | | | | | | | | — | — |
| Carburetor air filter | (15,000) ② | | | | | | | | | |
| 7. Tire rotation | ⑩ | S | S | S | S | S | S | S | S | S |
| 8. Choke shaft, fast idle cam, pivot pin | 6 | I ③ | I ③ | I ③ | I ③ | I ③ | I ③ | I ③ | I ③ | I ③ |
| 9. Manifold heat control valve | 6 (15,000) | S ③ | S ③ | S ③ | S ③ | S ③ | S ③ | S ③ | S ③ | S ③ |
| 10. Transmission | 6 | C | C | C | C | C | C | C | C | C |
| 11. Rear axle | 6 | C | C | C | C | C | C | C | C | C |
| 12. Manual steering | 6 | C | C | C | C | C | C | | | |
| 13. Steering linkage | 6 | — | — | — | — | — | — | — | — | — |
| 14. Suspension — ball joints | 6 | — | — | — | — | — | — | — | — | — |

# PERIODIC MAINTENANCE

Table 1  MAINTENANCE SCHEDULE (continued)

See legend at end of table.

| Service | Interval in months and/or miles | 1968 | 1969 | 1970 | 1971 | 1972 | 1973 | 1974 | 1975 | 1976 |
|---|---|---|---|---|---|---|---|---|---|---|
| 15. Steering linkage and ball joints | 36 (36,000) | L | L | L | L | L | L | L | L | L |
| 16. Universal joints | 6 | — | — | — | — | — | — | — | — | — |
| 17. Brake master cylinder | 6 | C | C | C | C | C | C | C | C | C |
| 18. Brake hoses | 6 | — | — | — | — | — | — | — | — | — |
| 19. Headlight aiming | 6 | S | S | S | S | S | S | S | S | S |
| 20. Hood latch and safety catch | 6 | I,L | I,L | I,L | I,L | I,L | I,L | I,L | I,L | I,L |
| 21. Drain and refill cooling system | 12 | S | S | S | S | S | S | S | S | S |
| 22. Crankcase ventilation system / Crankcase ventilation system | 12 (15,000) | R | R | R | R | I,S ④ | I,S ④ | I,S ④ | I,S ⑤ | I,S ⑤ |
| 23. Crankcase inlet air filter / Crankcase inlet air filter | 6 / 12 | | | — | — | I,S | I,S | I,S | I,S | I,S |
| 24. Throttle linkage | 12 | L | L | L | L | L | L | L | L | L |
| 25. Brakes ③ | 12 (12,000) | I,S | I,S | I,S | I,S | I,S | I,S | I,S | I,S | I,S |
| 26. Exhaust gas recirculation system / Exhaust gas recirculation system | 12 (12,000) / 15,000 | | | | | | — | — | — | — |
| 27. Front wheel bearings / Front wheel bearings | 12 (12,000) / 24 (24,000) | I,L | I,L | I,L | I,L | I,L | I,L | I,L | I,L | I,L |
| 28. Fuel vapor canister | 12 (12,000) | | | | | S | S | S | S | S |
| 29. Spark plugs / Spark plugs / Spark plugs / Spark plugs | (5,000) / (12,000) / (18,000) / (30,000) | I ⑦ | I ⑦ | I ⑦ | I ⑦ | R | R | R | R ⑨ | R ⑨ |

**Table 1  MAINTENANCE SCHEDULE** (continued)

| Service | Interval in months and/or miles | 1968 | 1969 | 1970 | 1971 | 1972 | 1973 | 1974 | 1975 | 1976 |
|---|---|---|---|---|---|---|---|---|---|---|
| 30. Distributor (conventional) | (12,000) | I, S | I, S | I, S | I, S | | | | | |
| Distributor (conventional) | (24,000) | | | | | I, S | | | | |
| 31. Fuel filter | 24 | | | | | | | | | |
| | (24,000) | R | R | R | R | R | R | R | | |
| | (15,000) | | | | | | | | R | R |
| 32. Brake pedal linkage, bushings | 24 | | | | | | | | | |
| | (24,000) | L | L | L | L | L | L | L | L | L |
| 33. Clutch torque shaft bearings | 36 | | | | | | | | | |
| | (36,000) | L | L | L | L | L | L | L | L | L |
| 34. Engine idle speed timing, idle mixture | 12 | | | | | | | | | |
| | (12,000) | I, S | I, S | I, S | I, S | I, S | I, S | I, S | | |
| | (15,000) | | | | | | | | I, S | I, S |
| 35. Distributor cap, ignition wiring rotor (pre-1973) | 12 | | | | | | | | | |
| | (12,000) | I, R ⑧ | I, R ⑧ | I, R ⑧ | I, R ⑧ | I, R ⑧ | | | | |
| Distributor cap, ignition wiring | (15,000) | | | | | | I, R ⑧ | I, R ⑧ | I, R ⑧ | I, R ⑧ |
| 36. Gearshift linkage | 6 | | | | | | | | | |
| | (6,000) | L | L | L | L | L | L | L | L | L |
| 37. Orifice spark advance control | 24 | | | | | | | | | |
| | (24,000) | | | | | I | I | I | | |
| Orifice spark advance control | (15,000) | | | | | | | | I | I |
| 38. Catalyst over temperature control | (15,000) | | | | | | | | I, S ⑧ | I, S ⑧ |

**Legend:**

C = Check fluid level
R = Replace
I = Inspect and/or clean
L = Lubricate
S = Service

① = Change every 24 months
② = Change every 30,000 miles
③ = Apply solvent
④ = Replace every 24 months
⑤ = Replace every 30,000 miles
⑥ = Replace linings if necessary
⑦ = Replace if required
⑧ = If required
⑨ = Replace at 15,000 miles if leaded gas is used
⑩ = Every 2nd oil change

# PERIODIC MAINTENANCE

content. Check specific gravity with a hydrometer at least once a year or every 12,000-15,000 miles. Check more often if battery requires frequent water. Clean posts and cable terminals with a wire brush and tighten terminals. Coat connections with a light coat of grease or petroleum jelly.

2. *Cooling system*—Check fluid level at every gas stop or at least once a month. Drain system once a year, preferably in the fall. Flush system with water and refill with a solution of permanent anti-freeze (ethylene glycol based) sufficient to provide protection to at least —20°F (—29°C) or lower if required by anticipated temperatures. See Chapter Seven for additional procedures.

3. *Engine oil*—Check level at every gas stop (see procedure above), and drain and replace oil at the intervals shown in Table 1 for your vehicle. See Chapter Four for oil type and quantity. Oil additives are not recommended.

4. *Oil filter*—Change the oil filter with every second oil change or at the intervals shown in Table 1. Change filter with every oil change if the vehicle is consistently operated under any of the severe conditions described in the introducduction of this section. See **Figures 2, 3, and 4** for typical oil filter installations.

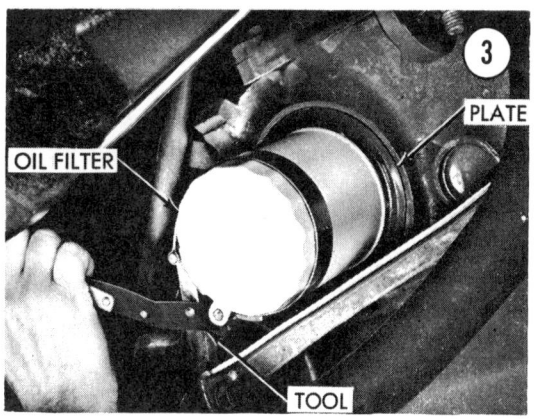

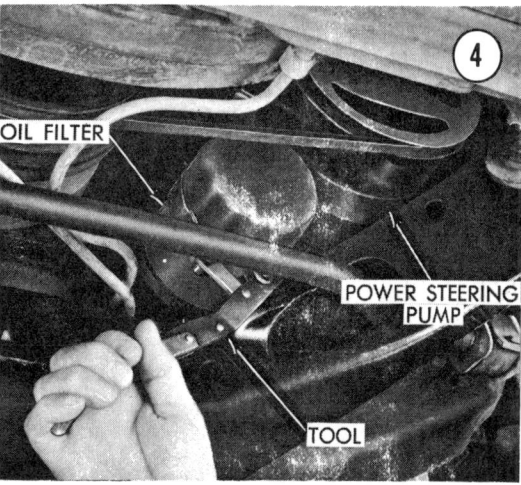

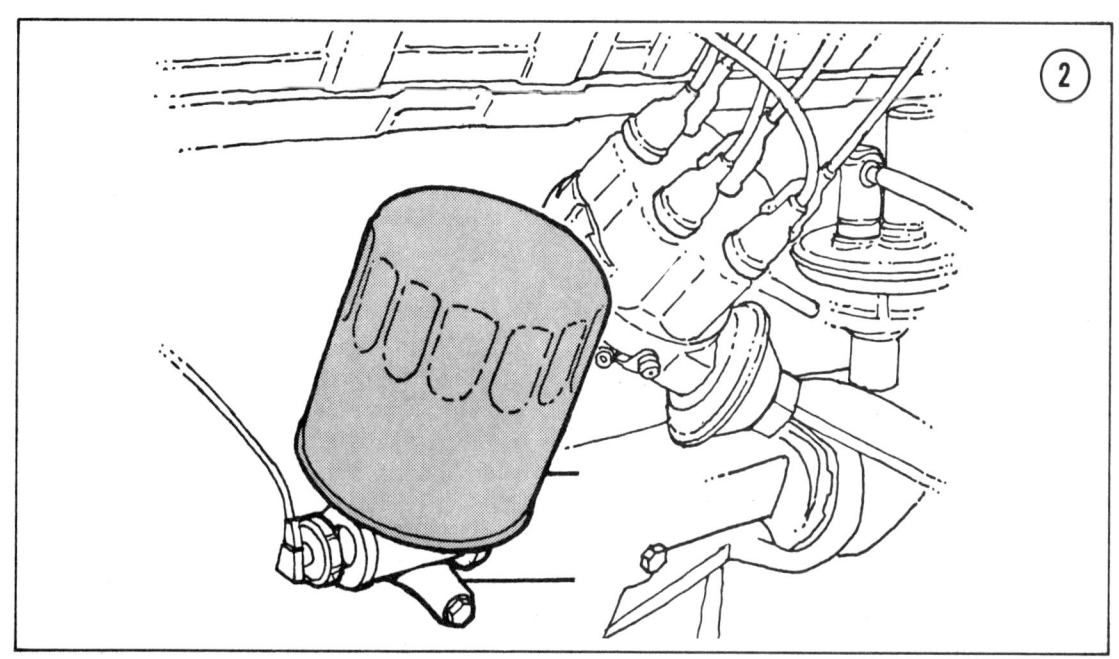

5. *Power steering*—Check the fluid level in the power steering pump at the interval indicated in Table 1. On the ".94" pump used on some 1967-1973 models (**Figure 5**), the fluid level should be maintained in the zone indicated on the dipstick. This also applies to all 1974-1976 models (**Figure 6**). On the "1.06" pump used in 1967-1973 models (**Figure 7**), the level (when fluid is hot) should be maintained ½-1 in. below the top of the filler neck (1½-2 in. when cold).

#### CAUTION
*Use only Power Steering Fluid, Chrysler Part No. 2084329 or equivalent. Do not use automatic transmission fluid as it will cause damage to the system.*

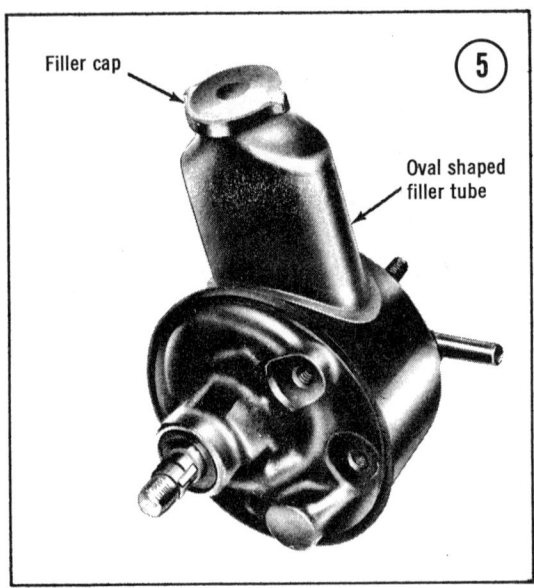

6. *Carburetor air filter*—Inspect and clean the paper filter element at the intervals shown on Table 1. See **Figure 8** for typical installation. If element is saturated with oil over more than half its surface, replace it. Otherwise replace elements every 2 years (1967-1974 models) or every 30,000 miles (1975-1976 models). Use compressed air on inside screen to clean element (**Figure 9**). Hold air nozzle at least 2 in. away.

#### CAUTION
*Do not apply compressed air to outside of filter element as this will imbed particles in the filter paper. After cleaning, inspect element for pin holes and replace element if puncture holes are are present.*

7. *Tire rotation*—Rotate tires and have them checked for balance at every second oil change. The rotation should follow the diagram shown in **Figure 10** for the most uniform tread wear. If only 4 tires are to be rotated, follow the diagram shown in **Figure 11**. Examine the tires at every oil change for unusual wear patterns. If unusual wear is present, the cause should be determined and corrected. See **Figure 12** for wear patterns and their most probable causes.

8. *Choke shaft, fast idle cam and pivot pin*—Every 6 months apply Chrysler Combustion Chamber Conditioner (Part No. 2933500) or an equivalent solvent to the choke valve shaft

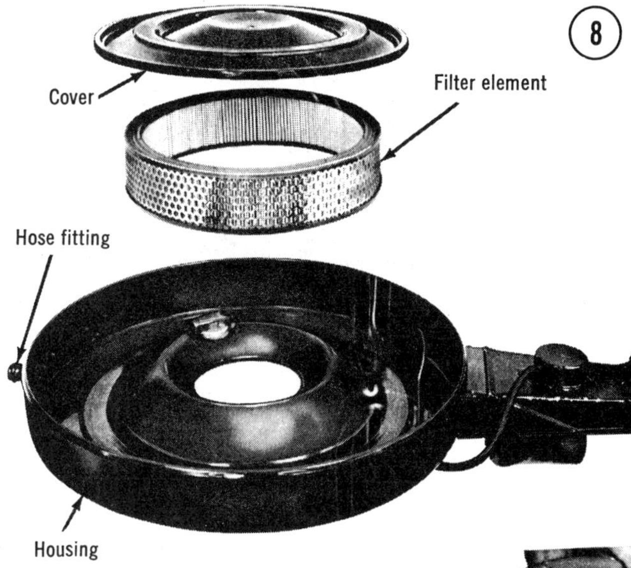

# PERIODIC MAINTENANCE

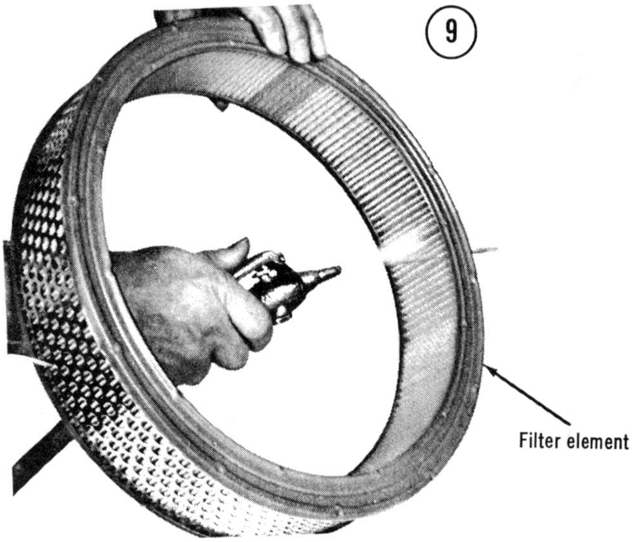

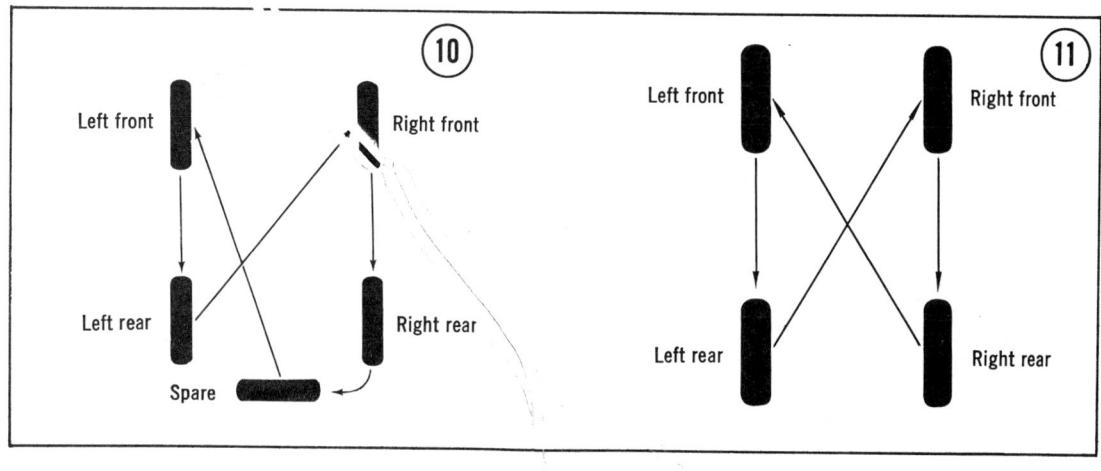

⑫

**Underinflation**—Worn more on sides than in center.

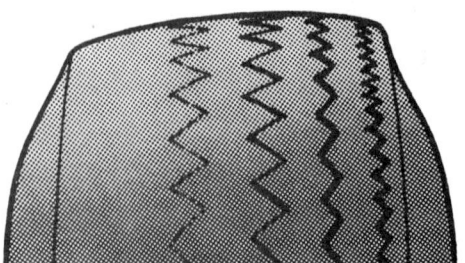

**Wheel Alignment**—Worn more on one side than the other. Edges of tread feathered.

**Road Abrasion**—Rough wear on entire tire or in patches.

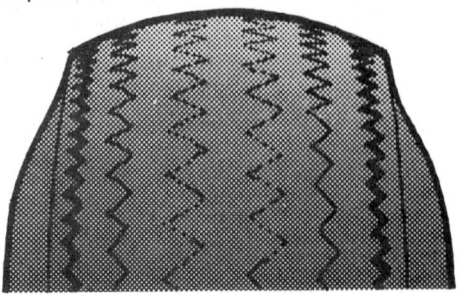

**Overinflation**—Worn more in center than on sides.

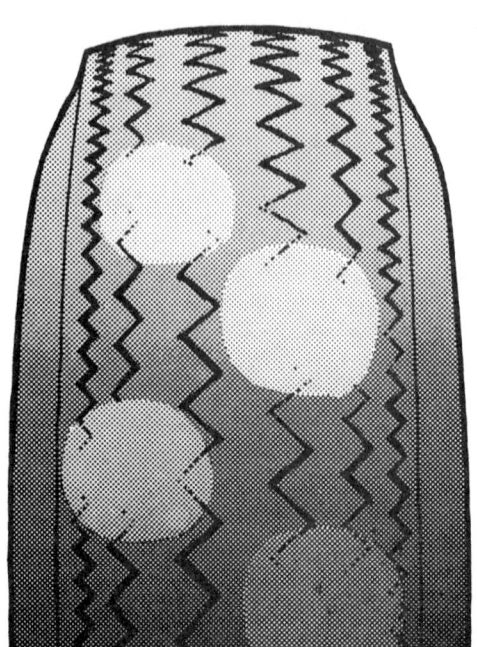

**Wheel Balance** — Scalloped edges indicate wheel wobble or tramp due to wheel unbalance.

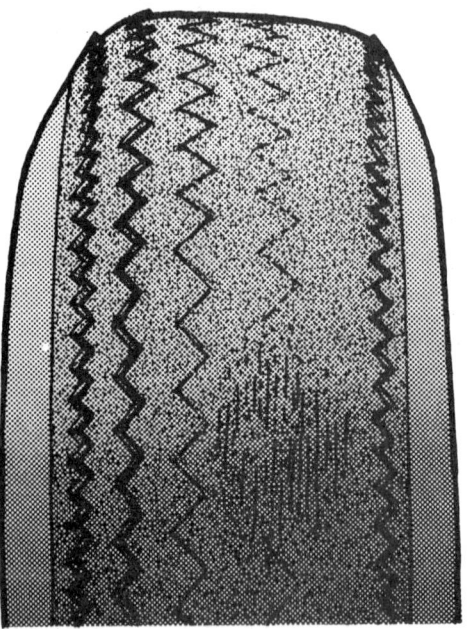

**Combination**—Most tires exhibit a combination of the above. This tire was overinflated (center worn) and the toe-in was incorrect (feathering). The driver cornered hard at high speed (feathering, rounded shoulders) and braked rapidly (worn spots). The scaly roughness indicates a rough road surface.

# PERIODIC MAINTENANCE

(both ends) where it passes through the air horn (**Figure 13**). Move shaft back and forth to flush out deposits. Start engine and run at idle until excess solvent is removed. Apply same solvent to fast idle cam and pivot pin to remove deposits that could cause sticking.

9. *Manifold heat control valve*—At the interval shown in Table 1, apply a penetrating fluid (part No. 3419129 or equivalent) to the manifold heat control valve shaft and bushings. See **Figures 14, 15, and 16** for typical locations. Allow solvent to soak in for a few minutes, then operate valve shaft until it moves freely.

### CAUTION
*Apply solvent to cool manifold only. Do not use motor oil for this purpose.*

10. *Manual transmission*—On manual transmission, check fluid level every 6 months and add fluid if required. See Chapter Four for type. Level should be even with bottom of the filter plug (**Figure 17**). Normally, the fluid installed at the factory need not be changed for the life of the vehicle. If the vehicle is used for commercial type operation or trailer towing, drain and refill every 36,000 miles. If objectional gear rattle occurs during idle or acceleration, the

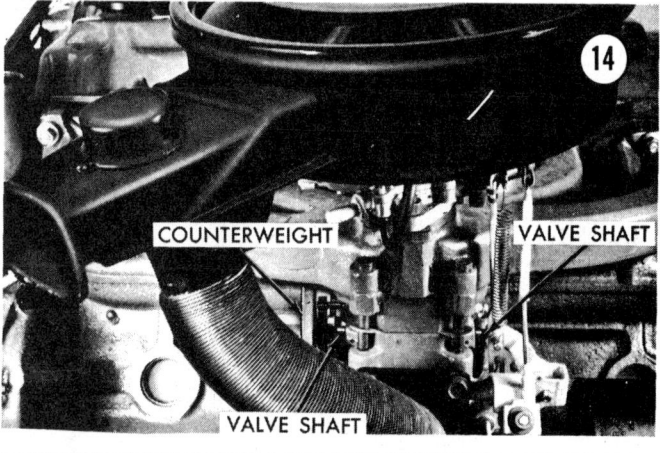

**CHAPTER THREE**

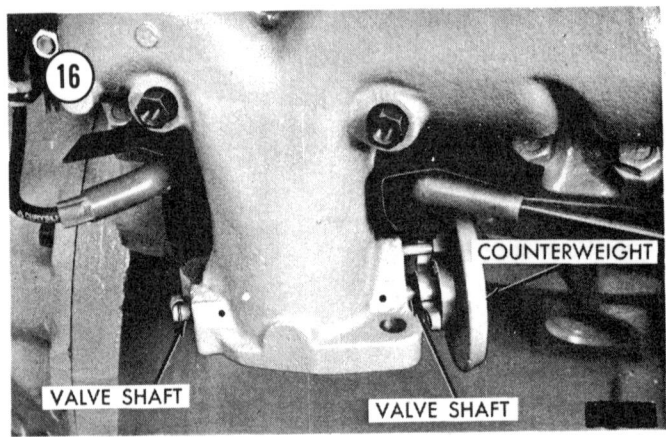

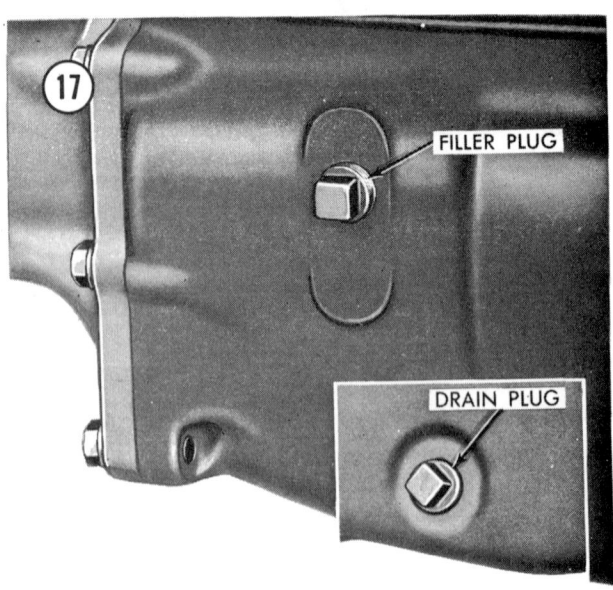

# PERIODIC MAINTENANCE

factory fluid may be drained and replaced with multipurpose gear lubricant, SAE 90 or SAE 140.

10a. *Automatic transmission*—On automatic transmissions, check fluid level every 6 months with engine idling at normal operating temperature. Be sure to set parking brake firmly. After engine has idled for 2 minutes, move shift lever through all gears, pausing momentarily in each, ending in NEUTRAL. Clean cap and top of filler tube, then remove transmission cap and dipstick. When fluid is hot, level should be at or slightly below—*never above*—the FULL mark (**Figure 18**). Add or remove fluid as required. Fluid and filter changes and band adjustments are not required for normal passenger car service. Vehicles subjected to severe use or operating conditions (trailer towing, etc.) and vehicles powered by 440 cu. in. engines with three 2-barrel carburetors require fluid and filter changes and band adjustments every 24,000 miles. See Chapter Four for recommended fluid.

11. *Rear axle*—Check the fluid level every 6 months, using **Table 2** as a guide. Add fluid if required. See Chapter Four for type.

Normally, rear axle lubricant does not require periodic changing. However, if vehicle is used in severe service, such as towing a trailer, check every 3 months or 4,000 miles and change every 36,000 miles. See Chapter Four for specified lubricant.

12. *Manual steering gear*—Check lubricant level every 6 months. Lubricant should cover worm gear. Add oil, if required (**Figure 19**). See Chapter Four for recommended lubricant. 1974 and later models do not require lubrication.

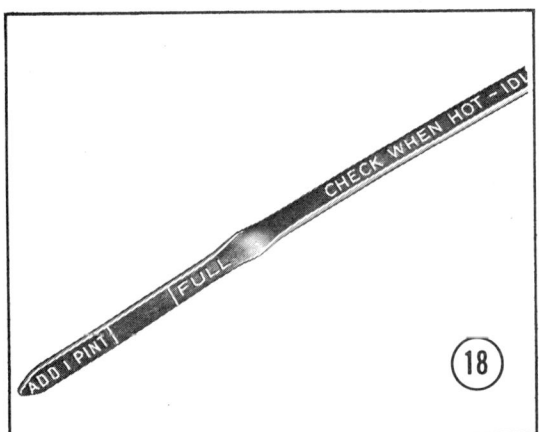

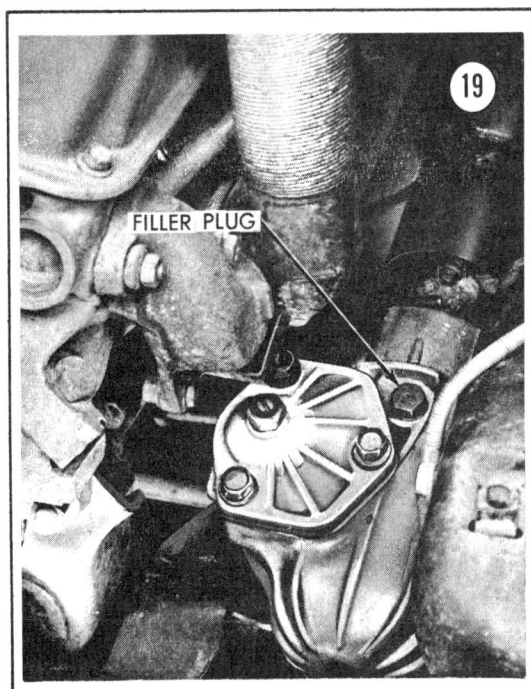

Table 2   REAR AXLE LUBRICATION

| Axle Size | Filler Location | Capacity (Pints) | Lubricant Level |
|---|---|---|---|
| 7¼ | Cover | 2.1 | Bottom of filler hole to ⅝ in. below |
| 8¼ | Right side | 4.4 | ⅛ in. to ¼ in. below filler hole* |
| 8¾ | Right side | 4.4 | Bottom of filler hole |
| 9¾ (through 1973) | Cover | 5.5 | Bottom of filler to ½ in. below |
| 9¼ (1974-1976) | Cover | 4.5 | ⅜ in. to ½ in. below filler hole* |
| * Do not fill to bottom of filler as this overfills axle. | | | |

13. *Steering linkage*—Inspect every 6 months and replace damaged joints and seals. Lubricate every 3 years or 36,000 miles, whichever comes first. If vehicle is subjected to severe service, lubricate every 18 months or 18,000 miles. To lubricate, remove plugs and install grease fittings. Fill and flush joints with lubricant (see Chapter Four). Take care to avoid damage to seals. See **Figures 20, 21, and 22**.

14. *Suspension ball-joints*—Inspect every 6 months and replace damaged joints or seals. Lubricate every 3 years or 36,000 miles, whichever comes first. See **Figures 23, 24, 25, and 26**. Cut intervals in half if vehicle is subjected to severe service. Take care to avoid damage to seals.

15. *Steering linkage and suspension ball-joints* See Steps 13 and 14.

16. *Universal joints*—Inspect every 6 months for leakage or damaged seals (**Figures 27 and 28**). Replace joint if leakage or damage is evident. Periodic lubrication is not required.

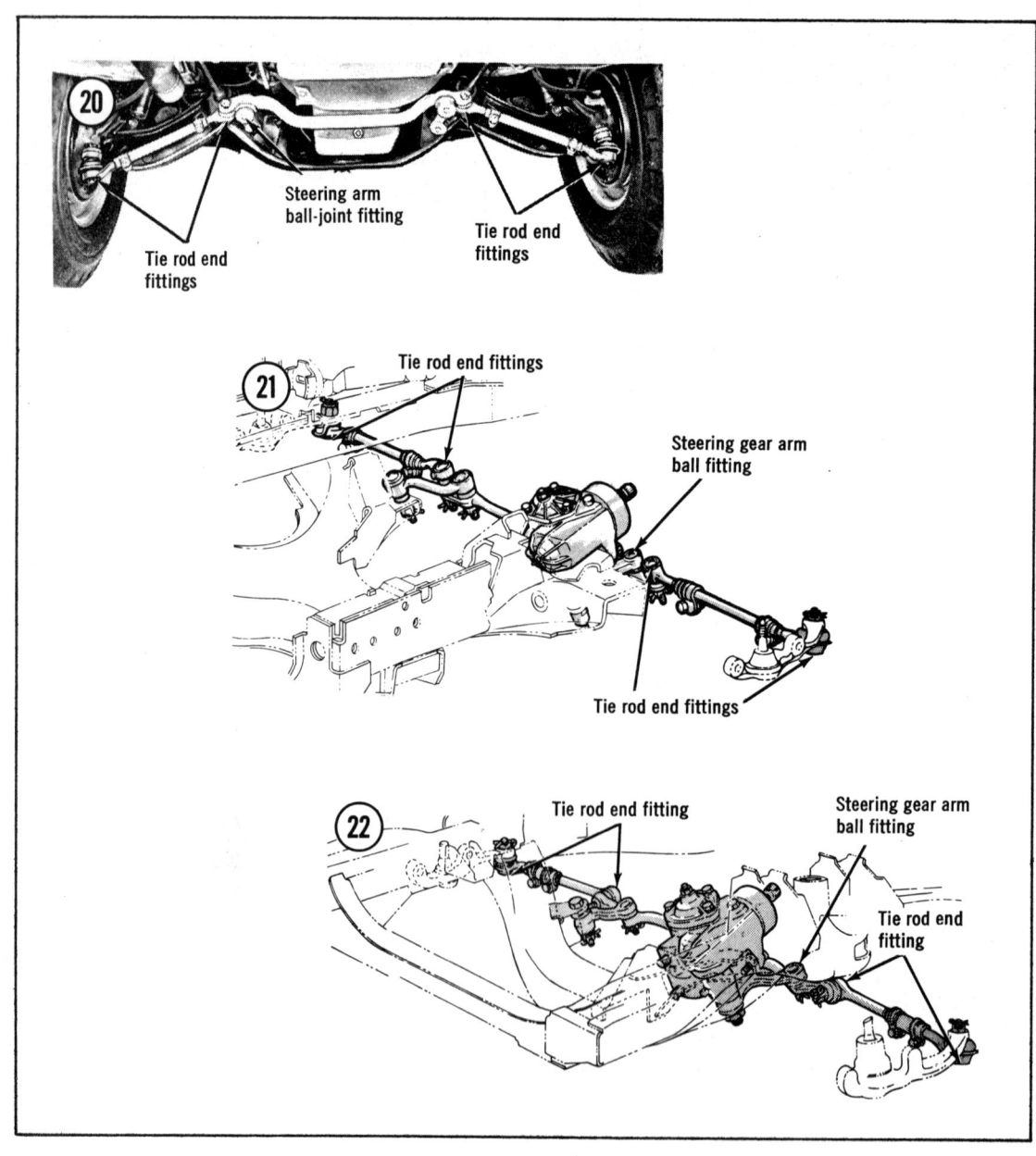

# PERIODIC MAINTENANCE

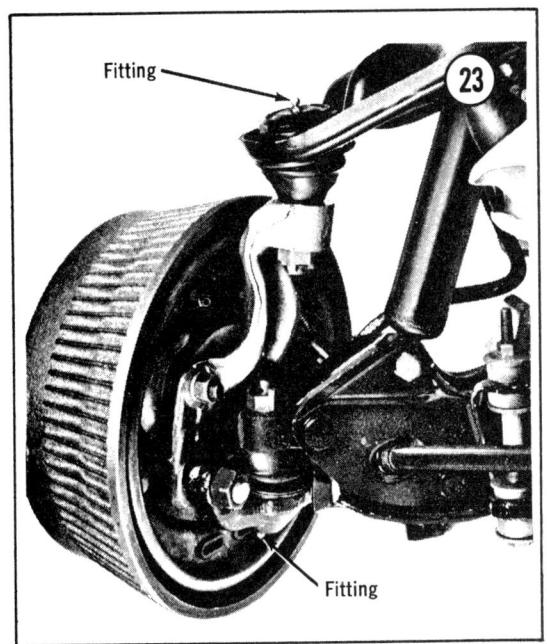

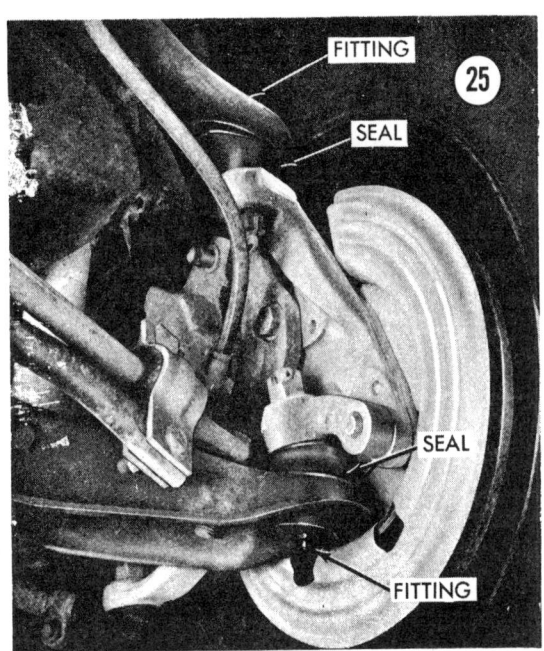

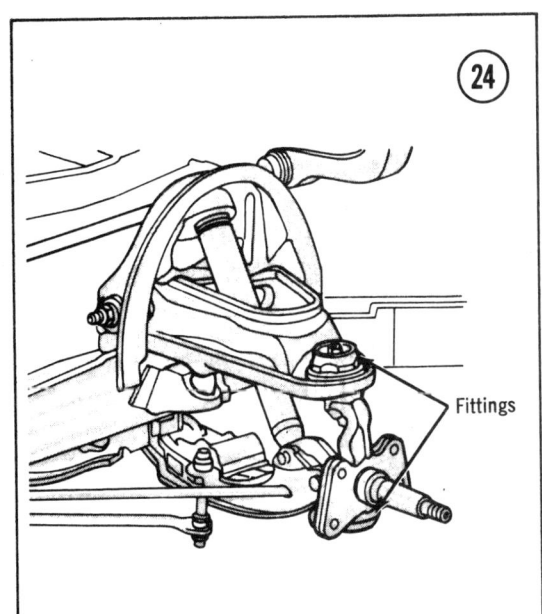

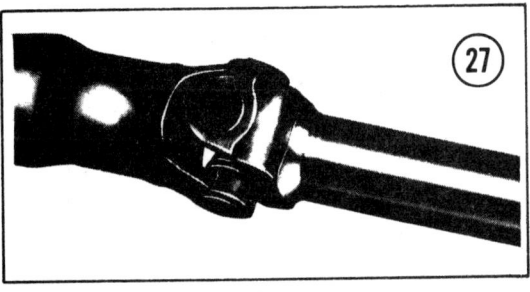

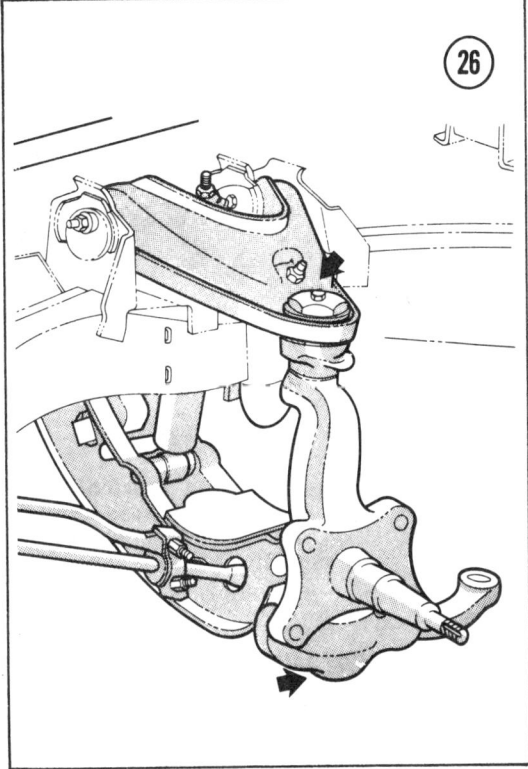

17. *Brake master cylinder*—Check fluid level every 6 months and fill to within ¼ in. of top of reservoir if required. To check, clean cover, push clamp to one side, and remove cover

CHAPTER THREE

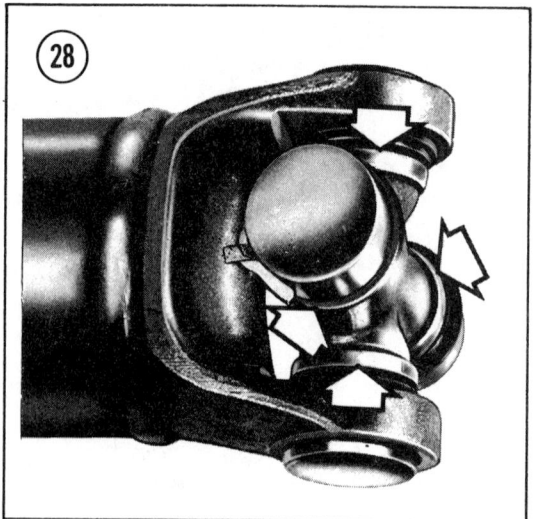

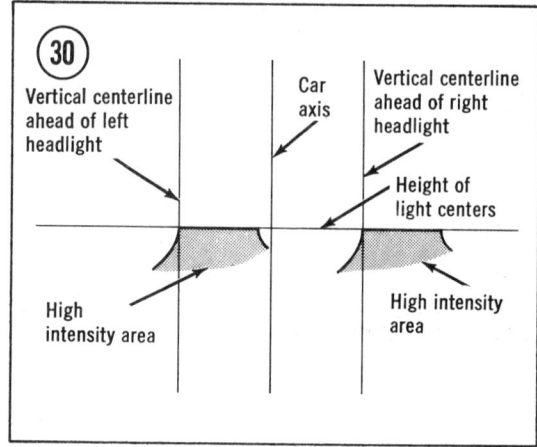

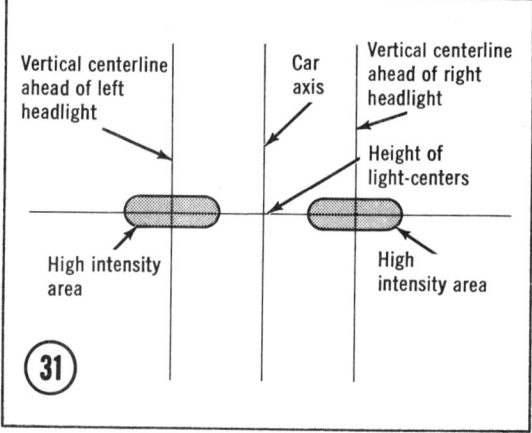

(**Figure 29**). With disc brakes, fluid level will drop as brake pads wear down. If car is equipped entirely with drum brakes, no noticeable drop in level should occur. In the latter case, if fluid is low, check for leak in hydraulic system. Use only brake fluid conforming to DOT 3.

18. *Brake hoses*—Check every 6 months for severe cracking, pulling, scuffing, or worn spots. Also check for twisting and interference with the wheel, tire, or chassis. All damaged tubing should be replaced. See Chapter Eight for procedure.

19. *Headlight aiming*—Have the headlights checked and reaimed, if required, every 6 months. Headlight patterns should be adjusted to conform with **Figures 30** (low beam) and **31** (high beam).

20. *Hood latch and safety catch*—Inspect, clean, and lubricate (chassis lubricant) every 6 months.

21. *Cooling system*—Drain and refill once a year. See 2 above and Chapter Seven for details.

22. *Crankcase ventilation system*—Every 12 months, replace (1968-1971 models) or inspect, check the operation of, and clean (1972-1976) the crankcase ventilation valve (**Figure 32**). In the latter case, replace every 2 years. Inspect and clean all connecting hoses.

23. *Crankcase inlet air filter*—Inspect and clean at the interval shown in Table 1 by washing in kerosene or similar solvent (**Figure 33**).

# PERIODIC MAINTENANCE

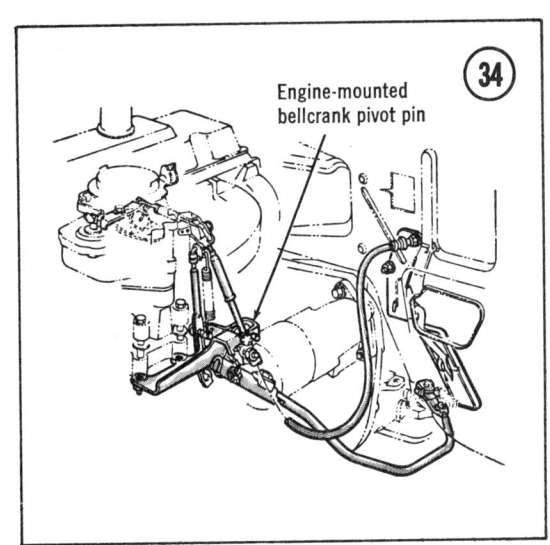

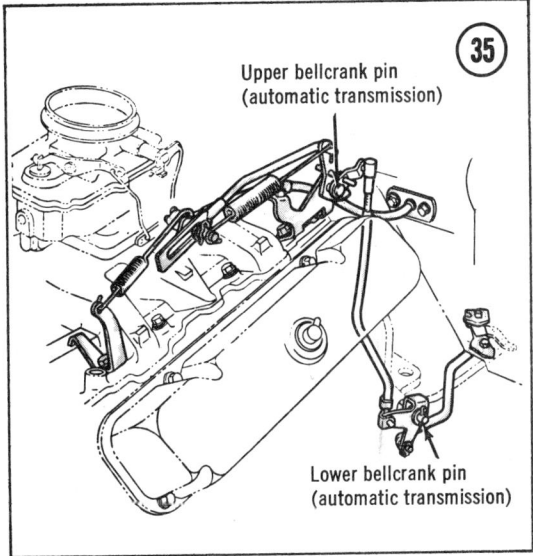

24. *Throttle linkage* — Lubricate every 12 months, using multipurpose grease. See **Figures 34 and 35** for typical installations. *Do not* lubricate ball-joints or throttle control cable.

25. *Brakes* — Inspect linings and/or pads every 12 months or 12,000 miles, whichever comes first. Adjustment is not required (except on special taxi models). Replace linings or pads if required (see Chapter Eight). On drum brake models, lightly lubricate contact areas on brake shoe supports, using a high temperature lubricant (Chrysler part No. 2932524 or equivalent).

26. *Exhaust gas recirculation system*—After the first 24,000 miles, and every 12,000 miles thereafter, inspect floor jet (on models so equipped, 1972 and later) for deposit buildup (**Figure 36**). With engine off and air cleaner removed, hold choke and throttle valve open. Inspect floor jets visually, using a flashlight. If passage in jet is open, condition is satisfactory. If passage is closed, remove, clean, and replace jet.

NOTE: *Take care not to damage jet or enlarge orifice. Install a new jet if necessary. Torque to 25 ft.-lb. (3.5 mkg).*

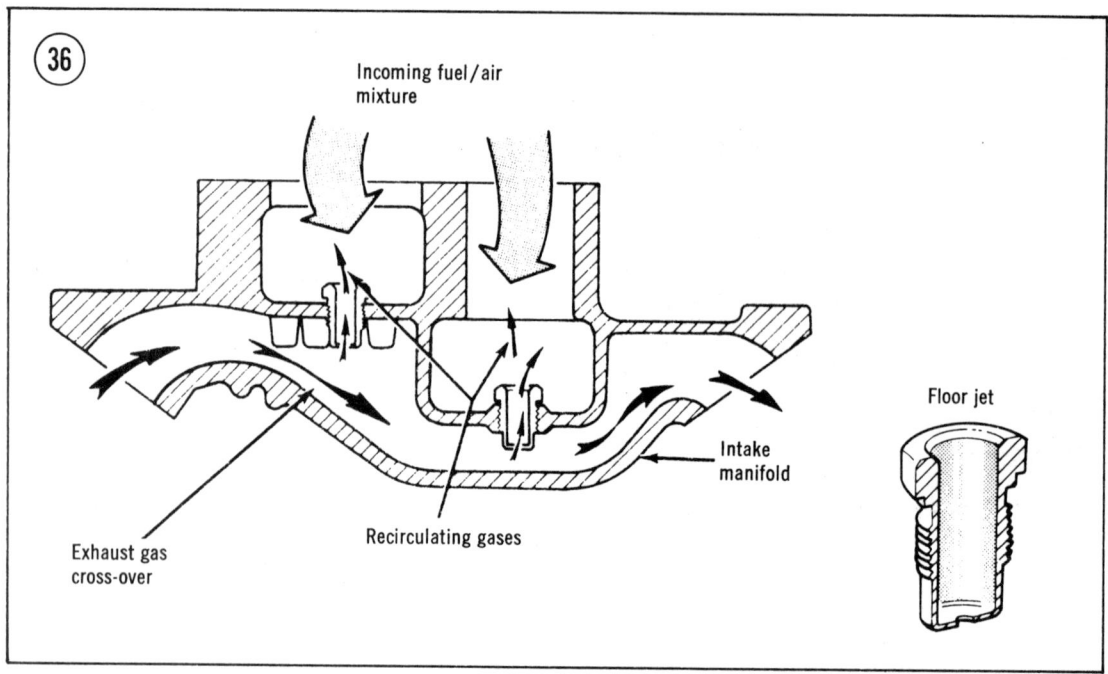

27. *Front wheel bearings*—Inspect and lubricate at the interval shown in Table 1. See Chapter Eight for procedure. See Chapter Four for proper lubricant.

28. *Fuel vapor canister* — On models so equipped, inspect canister and replace the filter element every 12 months or 12,000 mlies, whichever comes first (**Figure 37**).

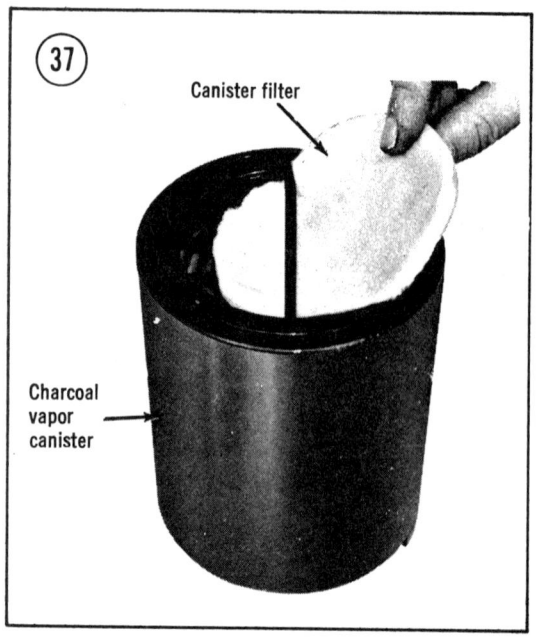

29. *Spark plugs*—Inspect and replace plugs at the intervals shown in Table 1. On 1967 models, plugs may be cleaned and reused if condition warrants, but should be replaced at least every 10,000 miles. Make certain plugs are gapped to 0.035 in. (0.889mm).

30. *Distributor service (conventional)*—At the interval shown, or whenever contact points are changed, wipe old lubricant from cam and apply a thin film of new lubricant (Chrysler part No. 1473595 or equivalent). Also add one drop of light engine oil to felt rotor wick (**Figure 38**).

#### CAUTION
*Avoid over-lubrication, as excess can spread to contact points and cause damage to the points and degraded engine performance.*

31. *Fuel filter*—Replace at the interval shown in Table 1, or more often if operating under dusty or other severe conditions. When replacing filter, check all connections for leaks.

32. *Brake pedal linkage bushings*—Lubricate every 2 years or 24,000 miles (at the points shown in **Figures 39, 40, and 41,** typical), using Lubriplate or equivalent.

33. *Clutch torque shaft bearings*—Every 3 years or 36,000 miles, whichever comes first,

# PERIODIC MAINTENANCE

31

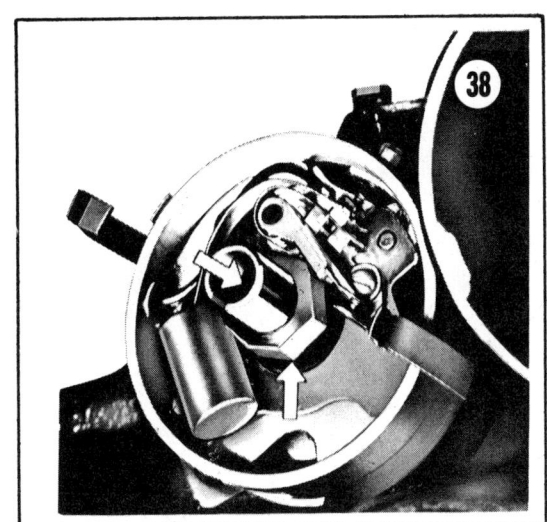

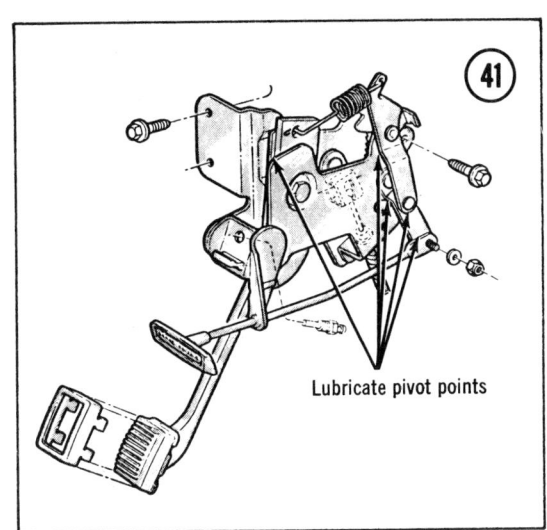

Lubricate pivot points

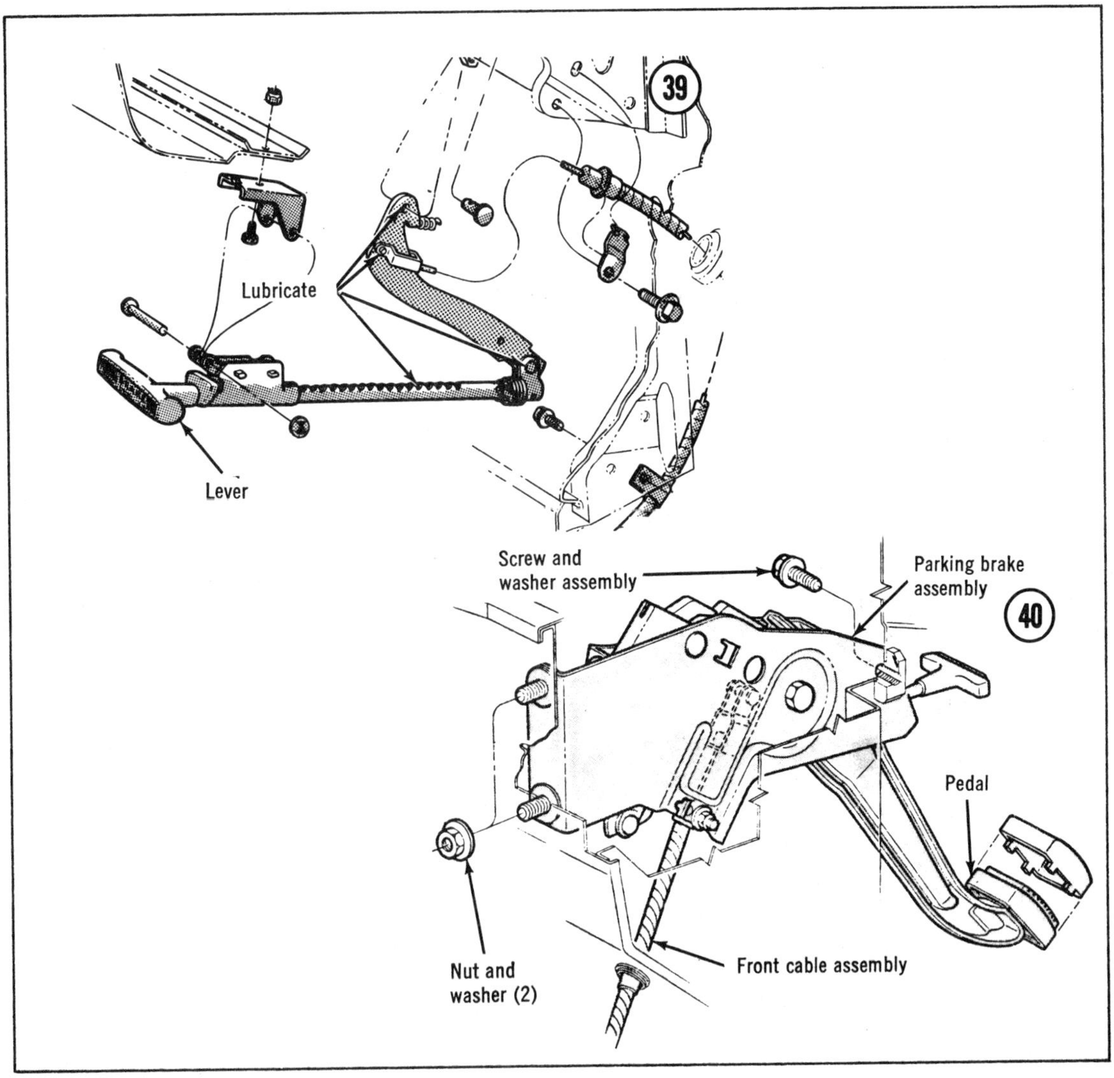

Lubricate

Lever

Screw and washer assembly

Parking brake assembly

Pedal

Nut and washer (2)

Front cable assembly

inspect and lubricate clutch torque shaft bearings (**Figure 42**). After disassembly, clean in solvent, inspect bearings for wear, and replace damaged bearings and/or ball studs. When reassembling, coat inside surfaces at ends of shaft, inside and outside bearing surfaces, and ball studs with multimileage lubricant (Chrysler No. 2525035 or equivalent).

34. *Engine idle speed, timing, and idle mixture*—Check and adjust as required, using the procedures given in Chapters Five and Six. Replace joints and set dwell angle (if so equipped) at the same time. Perform these services at the intervals indicated in Table 1.

35. *Distributor cap, ignition wiring, rotor (if so equipped)*—Inspect at the intervals shown in Table 1 and replace if required. See Chapter Five for procedures.

36. *Gearshift linkage*—Every 6 months or 6,000 miles, lubricate column mounted gearshift linkage as shown in **Figure 43** (typical) and floor mounted gearshift linkage as shown in **Figure 44** (typical), using multipurpose grease. See Chapter Four.

37. *Orifice spark advance control*—Inspect valve at the interval indicated in Table 1 for

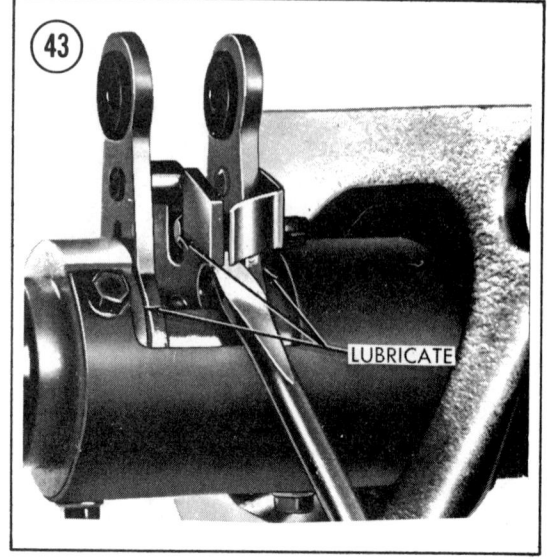

deposits which could cause plugging or sticking. Replace if necessary.

38. *Catalytic overtemperature protection system*—Every 15,000 miles, 1975-1976 models equipped with catalytic converters should be inspected for proper operation of the overtemperature protection system. See Chapter Eleven for procedures.

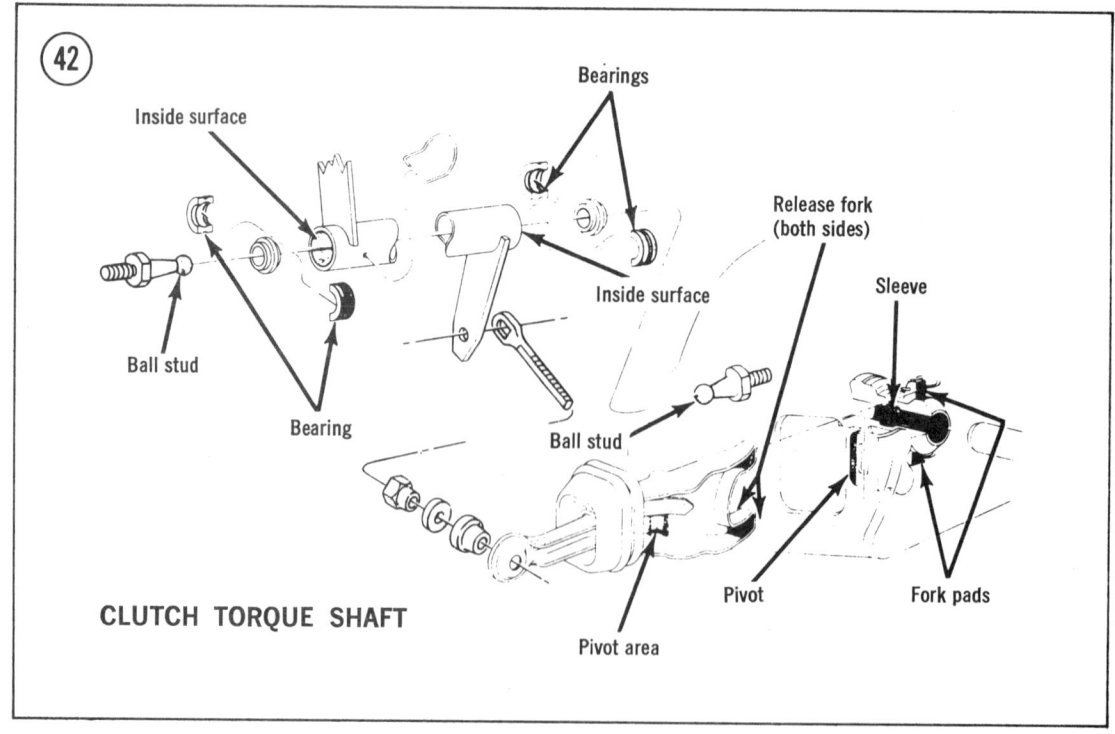

CLUTCH TORQUE SHAFT

# PERIODIC MAINTENANCE

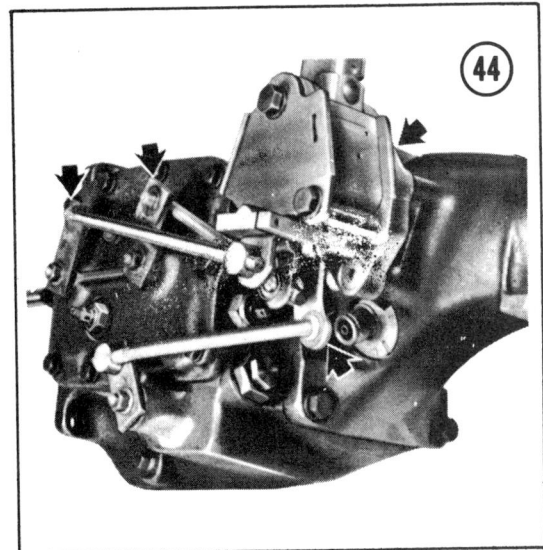

## Parts Not Requiring Lubrication

Some parts require no lubrication because they have been permanently lubricated at the factory. Others should not be lubricated because lubricants will cause breakdown and/or failure of the component. Rubber bushings, for instance, should not be lubricated because lubricants not only will cause rubber to fail but also will destroy the necessary friction characteristics of the bushings. Parts which should not be lubricated include:

1. Alternator bearings
2. Automatic transmission linkage
3. Clutch adjustment and pedal pushrod end
4. Clutch release bearings
5. Drive belts
6. Fan belt idler pulley
7. Rear springs and wheel bearings
8. Rubber bushings of any kind
9. Starter bearings
10. Throttle control cable and linkage ball-joints
11. Upper and lower control arm bushings
12. Water pump bearings

# CHAPTER FOUR

# LUBRICANTS AND FLUIDS

The selection of lubricants and fluids is an important part of automobile care. The use of improper lubricants can lead to unnecessary wear and early breakdown of parts. The lubricants and fluids described in this chapter are those recommended by Chrysler Corporation for all Chrysler-built vehicles. A summary of the recommended lubricants and fluids is contained in **Table 1**.

## ENGINE LUBRICATION

### Crankcase Capacity

All Chrysler-built engines in this book require 4 quarts of engine oil, plus one additional quart if the filter is changed, with the following exceptions:

1. 1968-1971 426 cu. in. Hemi engines—6 quarts plus one quart at filter change.
2. 1970-1972 440 cu. in. High Performance engines—6 quarts plus one quart at filter change.
3. 1970-1971 440 cu. in., three 2-barrel carburetor engines—6 quarts plus one quart at filter change.
4. 1975-1976 400 and 440 cu. in. High Performance engines—5 quarts plus one quart at filter change.

### Engine Oil and Filter

Engine oil should meet the requirements of the American Petroleum Institute (API) classification "For Service SE," and the fact should be clearly stated on the oil container. The "weight" or Society of Automotive Engineers (SAE) grade of the oil should be chosen with the expected temperatures and anticipated driving conditions in mind. **Table 2** shows the SAE grades recommended by Chrysler Corporation for all engines except the 1971 and earlier 426 cu. in. Hemi engine.

For 426 cu. in. Hemi engines, Chrysler recommends SAE 10W40 if the temperature is consistently above +32°F (0°C) and 10W30 if it is consistently below +32°F (0°C).

Any V8 engine used for maximum performance service (competition, etc., or very rapid acceleration) should be serviced with SAE 30 or SAE 40 oil. SAE 20W40 and 20W50 also may be used.

For normal operation, oil additives should not be used. However, if the car is operated infrequently or on short trips only, or has just been overhauled, anti-rust, anti-scuff additive such as Chrysler part No. 3419130 may be used.

Since 1972, all Chrysler engines have been equipped at the factory with short oil filters. The short type filter must be used on the 1973-

# LUBRICANTS AND FLUIDS

**Table 1  RECOMMENDED LUBRICANTS AND FLUIDS**

| Requirement | Recommended |
|---|---|
| 1. Engine oil change | 1. Engine oil labeled "For SERVICE SE." (See Chart in text for SAE grade). |
| 2. Cooling system | 2. Permanent ethylene glycol-type anti-freeze in proper solution for anticipated temperatures. |
| 3. Power steering | 3. Power steering fluid, part No. 2084329, or equivalent. |
| 4. Manual steering gear (1973 and earlier) | 4. Multi-purpose gear oil, SAE 90. Part No. 2933565 or equivalent. |
| 5. Front suspension ball joints | 5. Multi-mileage lubricant, part No. 2525035, or equivalent.* |
| 6. Steering linkage ball joints | 6. Multi-mileage lubricant, part No. 2525035, or equivalent* |
| 7. Rear axle, including Sure Grip | 7. Chrysler hypoid lubricant, part No. 2933565 or equivalent. |
| 8. Manual transmission | 8. DEXRON automatic transmission fluid, on 3-speed and 1971 and later 4-speed. Multi-purpose gear lubricant, SAE 90 or SAE 140 also may be used to minimize gear rattle. SAE 140 multi-purpose gear lubricant per MIL-L-2105B on 1970 and earlier 4-speed. SAE 80 or 90 or DEXRON automatic transmission fluid may be used in cold weather only. |
| 9. Automatic transmission | 9. DEXRON automatic transmission fluid. |
| 10. Brake fluid | 10. Fluid marked as conforming to DOT 3 only. |
| 11. Front wheel bearings | 11. Multi-mileage lubricant, part No. 2525035 or equivalent.* |
| 12. Throttle linkage | 12. Multi-mileage lubricant, part No. 2525035 or equivalent.* |

*National Lubricating Grease Institute Grade 2EP.

1976 Dart equipped with 318, 340 and 360 cu. in. engines, and on all 400 or 440 cu. in. engines equipped with air pump or power steering pump. Either a short or long filter may be used on all other engines.

## Oil Changes

Engine oil does not "wear out." Instead, it becomes diluted by fuel vapor leaking by the pistons and piston rings, and by the condensation of water vapor on the cylinder walls and crankcase. The detergents which provide the engine cleaning capability of the oil also tend to carry dirt and other contamination in suspension.

Leakage of fuel or fuel vapors into the crankcase occurs mostly during warm-up periods, when fuel is not always thoroughly vaporized and burned. Water vapor enters the crankcase through normal crankcase ventilation (especially on pre-1970 models) and through exhaust gas blow-by. When the engine is not completely warmed up, the water vapor tends to condense, combine with the condensed fuel and exhaust gases, and form acid compounds. When the temperature in the crankcase is hot enough to prevent condensation, no harm is done. In extremely cold climates, however, the engine does not, as a rule, warm up sufficiently to prevent acid formation (especially on short runs). The acid can cause serious etching or pitting and thus cause very rapid wear on piston pins, bearings, and other moving parts. Fortunately, modern engines are equipped with a number of automatic devices which minimize the danger of crankcase dilution.

The thermostat mounted in the cylinder head water outlet restricts the flow of water to the radiator until a pre-selected temperature is

### Table 2  RECOMMENDED ENGINE OIL

| Expected Temperature | SAE Grade |
|---|---|
| Consistently above +32°F (0°C) | 10W-30<br>10W-40<br>10W-50<br>20W-40<br>20W-50<br>30 |
| All-year operation,<br>no lower than —10°F (—23°C) | 5W40<br>10W30<br>10W40<br>10W50 |
| Consistently below +10°F (—12°C) | 5W20<br>5W30<br>5W40 |
| Between —10°F and +32°F<br>(—23°c and —0°C) | 10W |

Note: SAE grades 5W20, 5W30, and 5W40 are not recommended at any temperature if the car is driven in competition or other types of maximum performance operation.

reached. This cuts down on the amount of time required for the engine to reach an efficient operating temperature. This, in turn, cuts down on the time that engine temperatures are low enough to allow condensation.

Engines also have a water bypass in the cooling system which allows limited circulation until the thermostat opens. This helps to eliminate hot spots during warm-up, and also helps prolong engine life.

A thermostatic heat control on the exhaust manifold directs hot exhaust gases against the center of the intake manifold during the warming period. This greatly aids in the vaporization of fuel.

The automatic choke (if so equipped) reduces the likelihood of unvaporized fuel entering the combustion chambers and leaking into the crankcase.

An efficient crankcase ventilation system helps draw off fuel and other vapors and aids in the evaporation of fuel and water.

From the above discussion, the need for regular oil changes can be seen, especially if the vehicle is used exclusively on short trips or in extremely cold temperatures. See Chapter Three for the recommended oil change frequency.

## COOLING SYSTEM

When adding or replacing coolant, use only ethylene glycol anti-freeze in a solution of at least 50%. If temperatures below —20°F (—29°C) are anticipated at any time during the year, a correspondingly stronger solution should be used. For the proper solution, follow the anti-freeze manufacturer's instructions.

## POWER STEERING

Use only petroleum fluids especially formulated for minimum effect on rubber hoses. Chrysler Corporation recommends Power Steering Fluid, part No. 2084329, or equivalent. Never use automatic transmission fluid.

## CHASSIS LUBRICATION

Mopar Multi-Mileage Lubricant, part No. 2525035, or an equivalent that meets the requirements of the National Lubricating Grease Institute (NLGI) Grade 2EP, is recommended for front suspension and steering linkage ball-joints, front wheel bearings, and clutch and throttle linkage.

## MANUAL STEERING GEAR

The manual steering gear on 1974 and later models is permanently lubricated at the factory and periodic lubrication is not required. On 1973 and earlier models, use a multipurpose gear oil, SAE 90, such as Special Sure-Grip Lubricant, part No. 2585318, or Chrysler Hypoid Lubricant, part No. 2933565, or an equivalent.

## MANUAL TRANSMISSIONS

Chrysler Corporation recommends the use of Dexron Automatic Transmission Fluid in all 3-speed and 1971-1976 4-speed manual transmissions. In warm climates, if desired, 3-speed transmissions may be drained and then refilled with multipurpose gear lubricant, SAE 90 (per MIL-L-2105B). If objectional gear rattle develops in a 4-speed manual transmission, it may be drained and refilled with multi-purpose gear lubricant, SAE 140.

# LUBRICANTS AND FLUIDS

On 1970 and earlier 4-speed manual transmissions, a special gear lubricant was used to fill the transmission at the factory. If the level becomes low, replenish with multi-purpose gear lubricant SAE 140, meeting the requirements of MIL-L-2105B. If shifting becomes difficult during cold weather operation, the transmission may be drained and filled with SAE 80 or 90 multipurpose gear lubricant (MIL-L-2105B), or with DEXRON-type automatic transmission fluid. If the automatic transmission fluid is used, it should be replaced with SAE 140 lubricant during warm weather. No other lubricants should be used.

## AUTOMATIC TRANSMISSION

Use only Dexron Automatic Transmission Fluid, part No. 3549660, or equivalent. Special additives are not recommended, except that Chrysler Automatic Transmission Sealer, part No. 2298923, or equivalent, may be used to reduce leakage around seals in high-mileage transmissions.

## REAR AXLE

Use a multipurpose gear lubricant, such as Chrysler Hypoid Lubricant, part No. 2933565, meeting the requirements of American Petroleum Institute (API) Gl-5. If the anticipated temperature will be consistently above —10°F (—23°C) use SAE 90. If it will be as low as —30°F (—34°C), use SAE 80. If temperatures below —30°F (—34°C) are expected, use SAE 75.

## BRAKE FLUID

Use only Mopar Brake Fluid or an equivalent conforming to DOT-3. Use of other fluids could result in brake failure.

# CHAPTER FIVE

# IGNITION TUNE-UP

The tune-up consists of a series of inspections, adjustments, and parts replacements to compensate for wear and deterioration of certain engine components. Regular tune-ups are especially important to the operation of modern high performance engines. Emission control systems, improved electrical systems, and other advances make these engines especially sensitive to improperly operating or incorrectly adjusted parts.

Since proper engine operation depends upon a number of interrelated system functions, a tune-up consisting of only one or two corrections will seldom get lasting results. Instead, a thorough, systematic procedure of analysis and correction will pay dividends in improved performance and operating economy.

**Table 1**, at the end of the chapter, contains tune-up specifications. Before using these specifications, check your engine compartment to determine if a "Vehicle Emission Control Information" sticker is present. If so, use the information contained on the sticker, as it pertains specifically to your engine. If the sticker is missing, determine the displacement of your engine by checking the Vehicle Identification Number Plate (**Figure 1**). On 1968-1976 models, the plate is located on top of the instrument panel, on the left side, and can be read through the windshield from outside the car. The

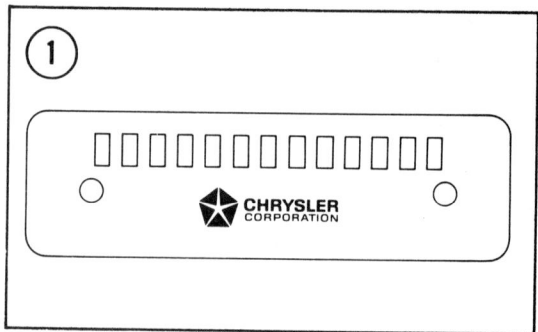

5th digit of the vehicle identification number indicates the engine displacement. See **Table 2** to interpret the code. After determining the displacement of your engine, use Table 1 to obtain the correct tune-up specifications.

## TUNE-UP SEQUENCE

During the period covered by this book Chrysler Corporation produced a number of different size 6- and 8-cylinder engines, which use both conventional breaker point and electronic ignition systems. The sequence of tune-up steps given below may be used for all models, however. Exceptions are noted wherever they occur.

1. Clean battery top and clean and tighten cable connections. Add water if required, and check

# IGNITION TUNE-UP

Table 2  ENGINE DISPLACEMENT CODE

ENGINE DISPLACEMENT IN CUBIC INCHES

| 5th Digit of I.D. Number | 1968 | 1969 | 1970 | 1971 | 1972 | 1973 | 1974 | 1975 | 1976 |
|---|---|---|---|---|---|---|---|---|---|
| A | 170 | 170 | | | | | | | |
| B | 225 | 225 | 198 | 198 | 198 | 198 | 198 | | |
| C | ② | ② | 225 | 225 | 225 | 225 | 225 | 225 | 225 |
| D | 273 | 273 | | | | | | | |
| E | | | ② | ② | ② | ② | | | |
| F | 318 | 318 | 318 | 318 | 318 | 318 | 318 | 318 | 318 |
| G | 383 | 383 | 340 | 340 | 340 | 340 | | | |
| H | 383 ① | 383 ① | | | | | 360 4 bbl | 360 4 bbl | 360 4 bbl |
| J | 426 | 426 | | 360 | 360 | 360 | 360 2 bbl | 360 2 bbl | 360 2 bbl |
| K | 440 | 440 | 383 | 383 | | | 360 4 bbl ① | 360 4 bbl ① | |
| L | 440 ① | 440 ① | | | 400 2 bbl | 400 2 bbl | 400 2 bbl | 400 2 bbl | 400 2 bbl |
| M | ③ | ③ | | | | | | | |
| N | 340 | 340 | 383 ① | 383 ① | | | 400 4 bbl | 400 4 bbl | 400 4 bbl |
| P | 340 ① | | | | 400 4 bbl | 400 4 bbl | 400 4 bbl ① | | |
| R | | | 426 | 426 | | | | | |
| T | | | 440 | 440 | 440 | 440 | 440 | 440 | 440 |
| U | | | 440 ① | 440 ① | 440 ① | 440 ① | 440 ① | 440 ① | 440 ① |
| V | | | 440 3-2 bbl | 440 3-2 bbl | 440 3-2 bbl | | | | |
| Z | | | ③ | ③ | ③ | | | | |

① = High performance engine    ② = Special Order 6    ③ = Special Order 8

the specific gravity of each battery cell with a hydrometer. Refer to Chapter Twelve for battery tests.

2. Tighten intake manifold bolts to 20 ft.-lb. (2.8 mkg) for 6-cylinder and 40-50 ft.-lb. (5.5-6.9 mkg) for V8's.

3. Perform a cylinder compression test. Refer to *Compression Test* later in this chapter.

4. Clean or replace spark plugs, adjust gap to 0.035 in. (0.9mm), and torque to 30 ft.-lb. (4.15 mkg). Use new gaskets (if required).

5. Check spark plug and coil secondary cables for resistance. Refer to *Cable Resistance Check* procedure later in this chapter.

6a. On engines with breaker point ignition systems, inspect points, primary wire, and vacuum advance operation. Replace parts as required. Refer to *Breaker Point Adjustment* procedure later in this chapter for necessary adjustments.

6b. On engines equipped with the Chrysler Electronic Ignition system, inspect primary wire and vacuum advance operation. Distributor adjustments are not required for a routine tune-up.

7. Reset ignition timing. Refer to *Ignition Timing* procedure later in this chapter.

8. Set carburetor idle speed and mixture adjustment. Refer to procedure for your carburetor in Chapter Six.

9. Check fuel pump for pressure and volume. Refer to *Fuel Pump Checks* in Chapter Six.

10. Verify that manifold heat control valve is operating freely. Lubricate bushing and shaft with penetrating lubricant such as Manifold Heat Control Valve Solvent, Chrysler part No. 3419129 or equivalent.

11. If 6-cylinder valve mechanism is noisy or engine still runs rough, adjust valve lash. See procedure later in this chapter.

12. Clean carburetor air filter element with compressed air (refer to Chapter Three). Replace filter every 2 years, or more often if required.

13. Inspect crankcase ventilation system. Refer to Chapter Eleven.

14. Inspect and adjust all engine accessory drive belts. Refer to Chapter Seven.

15. Road test the car.

## COMPRESSION TEST

1. Remove all spark plugs.

   NOTE: *Use compressed air, if available, to remove all foreign matter from spark plug wells prior to removal. If compressed air is not available, use a tire pump or a vacuum cleaner. A small paint brush will also serve.*

2. Remove air cleaner from carburetor and block choke and throttle valves wide open.

3. Remove the distributor primary lead wire from the negative post of the ignition coil.

4. Connect a remote starter button, using the manufacturer's instructions. If a remote starter is not available, have an assistant crank the engine, when required, from the driver's seat.

5. Install a compression gauge in the No. 1 cylinder and crank the engine through at least 4 compression strokes to obtain the highest possible reading. Record the reading and repeat the step for each cylinder in turn.

   NOTE: *The No. 1 cylinder is the one nearest the front of the vehicle. On V-8 engines, observe that one bank of cylinders is offset closer to the front than the other. The No. 1 cylinder is in the closer bank.*

6. Check the readings against the specifications given in Table 1 (end of the chapter). If one or more cylinders is below the minimum limit, the engine needs repairs. If there is more than the allowable variation between the lowest and highest readings, the engine cannot be properly tuned.

   NOTE: *If all readings were above the specified minimum, and the variations between cylinders were within the specified tolerance, the remaining step may be omitted.*

7. Inject about a tablespoon of engine oil through the spark plug hole of each low-reading cylinder. Crank the engine through several compression strokes and then take another compression reading. If compression increases, the problem usually is worn rings. If no improvement is noted, valves are probably burned, sticking, or not seating properly.

# IGNITION TUNE-UP

NOTE: *If 2 adjacent cylinders read low and oil injection does not increase compression, the problem may be a defective head gasket.*

## SPARK PLUG REPLACEMENT

1. Make sure all plugs to be installed are of the proper heat range (Table 1, end of the chapter).
2. Gap plugs to 0.035 in. (0.9mm) for all models, using a round wire-type feeler gauge.

NOTE: *Always adjust gap by bending the negative or side—never the center—electrode. Never adjust by tapping the electrode on a hard surface, as this can damage the procelain insulator.*

3. Inspect the threads in the spark plug hole and clean if necessary.

NOTE: *A 14mm thread chaser can be used to remove corrosion, carbon build-up, or minor flaws from the threads. Coat chaser with grease to catch chips or foreign matter. Use care to avoid cross threading.*

4. Crank engine several times to blow out any dislodged material.
5. Coat spark plug threads lightly with engine oil—a drop from the dipstick will do—and install plug in hole. Torque to 30 ft.-lb. (4.15 mkg).

NOTE: *If torque wrench is not available, tighten as much as possible by hand. Then use wrench to tighten another half turn. Do not overtighten, as excessive torque may change the gap setting.*

6. Reconnect spark plug wires.

## CABLE RESISTANCE CHECK

1. Verify that all "high tension" wires (spark plug and coil cables) are firmly seated in their proper distributor cap "towers" and nipples are in place.

NOTE: *Do not remove wire or nipples from the towers unless testing indicates excessive resistance or broken insulation, or nipples are damaged.*

2. Clean all high tension wires with a cloth moistened with non-flammable solvent. Check wires for brittle or cracked insulation and replace if present.

NOTE: *If an automotive oscilloscope is available, check wires for punctures and cracks, following the scope manufacturer's instructions.*

3. If an oscilloscope is not available, check cables as follows:

   a. Connect one end of a test probe to a good ground in the engine compartment.
   b. Disconnect a wire from one spark plug and insulate the end to prevent grounding.
   c. Start the engine and move the free end of the test probe along the entire length of the wire. At any point where a crack or puncture exists a spark will jump from the wire to the probe end. Coil secondary wire can be checked in the same manner by operating starter. Replace damaged wires.

CAUTION
*On 1975-1976 models equipped with catalytic converters, this test should be completed as rapidly as possible to avoid heat buildup which could damage catalytic converter. Total test time must not exceed 10 minutes.*

4. Check the resistance of each "high tension" wire, using an ohmmeter, as follows:

   a. Remove a spark plug wire and connect it to a suitable adapter.
   b. Lift the distributor cap, with cables intact, from the distributor. *Do not* remove the cables.
   c. Connect an ohmmeter between the adapter installed in Step A and the corresponding electrode inside the distributor cap. If the resistance is more than 30,000 ohms, remove the wire from the cap tower and recheck the resistance. If resistance is still over 30,000 ohms for wires under 25 in. long or over 50,000 ohms for wires over 25 in. long, replace the wire. Repeat the test for all spark plug wires. To test the ignition coil secondary wire, do not dis-

connect the wire but measure from the center terminal inside the distributor cap to either primary terminal on the coil. If resistance is more than 25,000 ohms, remove the wire and remeasure. If resistance is greater than 15,000 ohms, replace the wire. If less, check for a loose connection or a faulty coil.

## BREAKER POINTS

### Replacement and Adjustment

*Single Point Distributor*

1. Remove distributor cap and rotor.

   NOTE: *Do not remove wires from cap.*

2. Loosen point plate lock screw and remove point set and condenser.

3. Remove all old grease from cam with a clean cloth and apply a small amount of fresh lubricant.

4. Install new point set and condenser. Verify that points are properly aligned (**Figure 2**). Bend fixed contact to align. Turn engine over until point rubbing block is resting on the highest point of a cam lobe. Using a feeler gauge of the specified size (Table 1, end of chapter), set the point gap. A slight drag should be felt when the gauge is removed. Tighten the locking screws and recheck the gap.

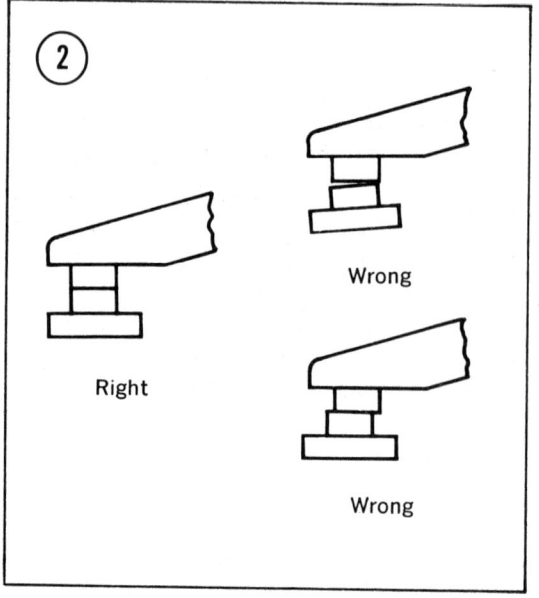

5. Replace distributor cap and rotor and check dwell angle with a dwell meter. See *Distributor Dwell* procedure below. Readjust gap, if required, to obtain specified dwell. See Table 1 at the end of the chapter.

6. Road test vehicle.

*Dual Point Distributor*

1. Remove and install point sets as described above for single point distributors.

2. Set the specified gap (Table 1, end of the chapter) on both sets of points, as described in Step 4 of the procedure above for single point distributors. Make sure the rubbing block is on the highest point of a cam lobe when making adjustments.

3. Place a clean insulator between the contacts on one set of points, replace the rotor and distributor cap, and check the dwell angle, using the procedure given later in this chapter. Verify that dwell angle is as specified (Table 1, at the end of the chapter) for "one set of points."

4. Remove distributor cap and remove the clean insulator from the contacts and place it between the contacts of the other point set. Replace the cap and check dwell as described in Step 3.

5. After dwell has been individually adjusted for both sets of points, remove distributor cap and remove clean insulator. Replace cap and check dwell angle. Verify that angle meets specifications. See Table 1 at the end of the chapter for "both sets of points."

### Distributor Dwell

1. Connect dwell meter and tachometer to engine using the manufacturer's instructions.

2. Turn dwell meter selector switch to the proper setting for the engine being checked (6- or 8-cylinders).

3. Disconnect and plug vacuum advance hose.

4. Operate engine at idle speed and observe dwell meter reading. If not within specification (Table 1, at the end of the chapter), readjust point gap to obtain proper reading.

5. Slowly increase engine speed to 1,500 rpm and observe dwell meter. If reading varies more

# IGNITION TUNE-UP

than 2 degrees from first reading, have distributor checked for wear.

> NOTE: *Dwell variations of more than 2 degrees at speeds above 1,500 rpm do not necessarily indicate distributor wear. Dwell and point gap must be within their respective specified limits at the same time. If this cannot be accomplished, verify that the correct points were installed. If points are correct the distributor should be checked by your dealer or a competent mechanic having access to the specialized equipment needed for checking out the distributor.*

## IGNITION TIMING

1. Locate the timing marks on your engine. They are located on the timing chain cover and the vibration damper at the front of the engine. See **Figure 3** (typical).

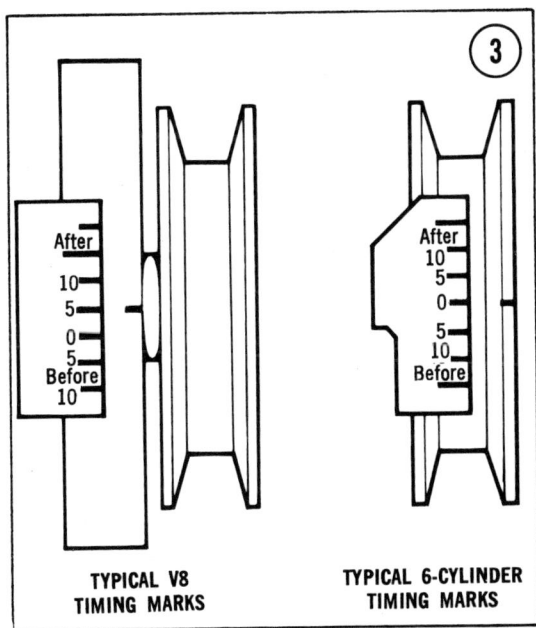

2. Obtain timing specification from sticker in engine compartment, or from Table 1 (end of chapter). Locate the proper mark on the timing indicator and mark with white paint or chalk. Also paint the mark on vibration damper. This will greatly assist in making timing adjustments.

3. Connect a timing light to the No. 1 spark plug, using the manufacturer's instructions.

4. Disconnect and plug the vacuum hose leading to the vacuum advance mechanism on the distributor. A golf tee makes a good plug.

5. Start the engine and operate at the idle speed shown on the Vehicle Emission Control Sticker in the engine compartment, or in Table 1 (end of chapter).

6. Aim the timing light at the timing marks. If the ignition is properly timed the marks will appear to stand still exactly opposite each other under the flashing light.

7. If the timing requires adjustment, loosen the distributor hold-down bolt and turn the distributor body as required to align the timing marks under the flashing timing light. When the timing marks are aligned, tighten the hold-down bolt, recheck the alignment, and stop the engine.

8. Reconnect the vacuum hose to the distributor and remove the timing light.

## VALVE LASH ADJUSTMENT (6-CYLINDER ONLY)

1. Warm up engine to normal operating temperature. Allow engine to idle at curb idle speed for 5 minutes. Remove valve cover.

2. Adjust all tappets to 0.010 in. (intake) and 0.020 in. (exhaust). These settings apply to all 6-cylinder engines. See **Figure 4**.

3. Using a new gasket, install valve cover on cylinder head. Torque to 40 in.-lb. (45.6 cmkg).

4. Install closed ventilation system and evaporation control system, if so equipped.

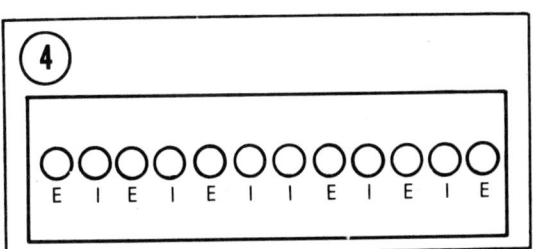

**Table 1  TUNE-UP SPECIFICATIONS**

**1968 MODELS**

| Engine Cyl./Carb. | CID | Trans-mission | Idle Speed Curb | Idle Speed Fast | Comp. (psi) | Points Setting ② | Distributor Dwell Angle ⑤ | RPM | Spark Plugs (Champion) Type | Spark Plugs (Champion) Gap | Timing (°BTC) | Air-Fuel Ratio | Remarks ① |
|---|---|---|---|---|---|---|---|---|---|---|---|---|---|
| 6/1 bbl | 170 | M | 700 | 1,550 | 110-140 ⑥ | 0.020 | 43° | 700 | N14Y | 0.035 | 5 | 14.2:1 | w/o CAP |
| 6/1 bbl | 170 | M | 700 | 1,550 | 110-140 ⑥ | 0.020 | 43° | 700 | N14Y | 0.035 | 5° ATC | 14.2:1 | w/CAP |
| 6/1 bbl | 170 | A | 650 | 1,700 | 110-140 ⑥ | 0.020 | 43° | 650 | N14Y | 0.035 | 5 | 14.2:1 | w/o CAP |
| 6/1 bbl | 170 | A | 650 | 1,700 | 110-140 ⑥ | 0.020 | 43° | 650 | N14Y | 0.035 | 2.5° ATC | 14.2:1 | w/CAP |
| 6/1 bbl | 225 | M | 650 | 1,550 | 110-140 ⑥ | 0.020 | 43° | 650 | N14Y | 0.035 | 5 | 14.2:1 | w/o CAP |
| 6/1 bbl | 225 | M | 650 | 1,550 | 110-140 ⑥ | 0.020 | 43° | 650 | N14Y | 0.035 | TDC | 14.2:1 | w/CAP |
| 6/1 bbl | 225 | A | 650 | 1,550 | 110-140 ⑥ | 0.020 | 43° | 650 | N14Y | 0.035 | 5 | 14.2:1 | w/o CAP |
| 6/1 bbl | 225 | A | 650 | 1,550 | 110-140 ⑥ | 0.020 | 43° | 650 | N14Y | 0.035 | TDC | 14.2:1 | w/CAP |
| V8/2 bbl | 273 | M | 700 | 1,400 | 120-150 ⑥ | 0.017 | 31° | 700 | N14Y | 0.035 | SATC | 14.2:1 | w/CAP |
| V8/2 bbl | 273 | A | 650 | 1,600 | 120-150 ⑥ | 0.017 | 31° | 650 | N14Y | 0.035 | 2.5° ATC | 14.2:1 | w/CAP |
| V8/2 bbl | 318 | M | 500 | 700 | 125-155 ⑥ | 0.017 | 31° | 500 | N14Y | 0.035 | 5 | 14.2:1 | w/o CAP |
| V8/2 bbl | 318 | M | 650 | 1,300 | 125-155 ⑥ | 0.017 | 31° | 650 | N14Y | 0.035 | 5 | 14.2:1 | w/CAP |
| V8/2 bbl | 318 | A | 500 | 700 | 125-155 ⑥ | 0.017 | 31° | 500 | N14Y | 0.035 | 10 | 14.2:1 | w/o CAP |
| V8/2 bbl | 318 | A | 600 | 1,500 | 125-155 ⑥ | 0.017 | 31° | 600 | N14Y | 0.035 | 10 | 14.2:1 | w/CAP |
| V8/4 bbl | 340 | M | 700 | 1,700 | 130-175 ⑥ | 0.017 | 30°③; 40°④ | 700 | N9Y | 0.035 | TDC | 14.2:1 | w/CAP |
| V8/4 bbl | 340 | A | 650 | 1,400 | 130-175 ⑥ | 0.017 | 30°③; 40°④ | 650 | N9Y | 0.035 | 5 | 14.2:1 | w/CAP |
| V8/2 bbl | 383 | M | 650 | 1,600 | 125-155 ⑥ | 0.017 | 31° | 650 | J14Y | 0.035 | TDC | 14.2:1 | w/CAP |
| V8/2 bbl | 383 | A | 600 | 1,600 | 125-155 ⑥ | 0.017 | 31° | 600 | J14Y | 0.035 | 7.5 | 14.2:1 | w/CAP |
| V8/4 bbl | 383 | M | 650 | 1,600 | 130-165 ⑦ | 0.017 | 31° | 650 | J11Y | 0.035 | TDC | 14.2:1 | w/CAP |
| V8/4 bbl | 383 | A | 650 | 1,600 | 130-165 ⑦ | 0.017 | 31° | 650 | J11Y | 0.035 | 7.5 | 14.2:1 | w/CAP |
| V8/4 bbl | 440 | M | 600 | 1,600 | 130-165 ⑦ | 0.017 | 31° | 600 | J13Y | 0.035 | TDC | 14.2:1 | w/CAP |
| V8/4 bbl | 440 | A | 600 | 1,400 | 130-165 ⑦ | 0.017 | 31° | 600 | J13Y | 0.035 | 7.5 | 14.2:1 | w/CAP |
| V8/4 bbl | 440 hp | M | 650 | 1,600 | 130-165 ⑦ | 0.017 | 30°③; 40°④ | 650 | J11Y | 0.035 | 5 | 14.2:1 | w/CAP |
| V8/4 bbl | 440 hp | A | 650 | 1,400 | 130-165 ⑦ | 0.017 | 30°③; 40°④ | 650 | J11Y | 0.035 | 5 | 14.2:1 | w/CAP |
| V8/2-4 bbl | 426 | M | 750F, R | 1800R | 150-205 ⑧ | 0.017 | 30°③; 40°④ | 750 | N10Y | 0.035 | TDC | 14.2:1 | w/CAP |
| V8/2-4 bbl | 426 | A | 750F, R | 1800R | 150-205 ⑧ | 0.017 | 30°③; 40°④ | 750 | N10Y | 0.035 | TDC | 14.2:1 | w/CAP |

① = CAP—Cleaner air package.
② = ± 0.003 in.
③ = One set of points.
④ = Both sets of points.
⑤ = ± 2 degrees.
⑥ = Should not vary more than 20 psi between cylinders.
⑦ = Should not vary more than 25 psi between cylinders.
⑧ = Should not vary more than 30 psi between cylinders.

# IGNITION TUNE-UP

Table 1  TUNE-UP SPECIFICATIONS (Continued)

## 1969 MODELS

| Engine Cyl./Carb. | CID | Trans-mission | Idle Speed Curb | Idle Speed Fast | Comp. (psi) | Points Setting ② | Distributor Dwell Angle ⑤ | RPM | Spark Plugs (Champion) Type | Spark Plugs (Champion) Gap | Timing (°BTC) | Air-Fuel Ratio | Remarks ① |
|---|---|---|---|---|---|---|---|---|---|---|---|---|---|
| 6/1 bbl | 170 | M | 750 | 1,600 | 110-140 ⑥ | 0.020 | 45° | 750 | N14Y | 0.035 | 5° ATC | 14.2:1 | w/CAP |
| 6/1 bbl | 170 | A | 750 | 1,800 | 110-140 ⑥ | 0.020 | 45° | 750 | N14Y | 0.035 | TDC | 14.2:1 | w/CAP |
| 6/1 bbl | 225 | M | 700 | 1,600 | 110-140 ⑥ | 0.020 | 45° | 700 | N14Y | 0.035 | TDC | 14.2:1 | w/CAP |
| 6/1 bbl | 225 | A | 650 | 1,800 | 110-140 ⑥ | 0.020 | 45° | 650 | N14Y | 0.035 | TDC | 14.2:1 | w/CAP |
| V8/2 bbl | 273 | M | 700 | 1,500 | 120-150 ⑥ | 0.017 | 33° | 700 | N14Y | 0.035 | 2.5° ATC | 14.2:1 | w/CAP |
| V8/2 bbl | 273 | A | 650 | 1,600 | 120-150 ⑥ | 0.017 | 33° | 650 | N14Y | 0.035 | 2.5° ATC | 14.2:1 | w/CAP |
| V8/2 bbl | 318 | M | 700 | 1,300 | 125-155 ⑥ | 0.017 | 33° | 700 | N14Y | 0.035 | TDC | 14.2:1 | w/CAP |
| V8/2 bbl | 318 | A | 650 | 1,700 | 125-155 ⑥ | 0.017 | 33° | 650 | N14Y | 0.035 | TDC | 14.2:1 | w/CAP |
| V8/2 bbl | 340 | M | 750 | 1,700 | 130-175 ⑥ | 0.017 | 30°③; 40°④ | 750 | N9Y | 0.035 | TDC | 14.2:1 | w/CAP |
| V8/4 bbl | 340 | A | 700 | 1,700 | 130-175 ⑥ | 0.017 | 30°③; 40°④ | 750 | N9Y | 0.035 | 5 | 14.2:1 | w/CAP |
| V8/4 bbl | 383 | M | 700 | 1,600 | 125-155 ⑦ | 0.017 | 33° | 700 | J14Y | 0.035 | TDC | 14.2:1 | w/CAP |
| V8/4 bbl | 383 | A | 600 | 1,600 | 125-155 ⑦ | 0.017 | 33° | 600 | J14Y | 0.035 | 7.5 | 14.2:1 | w/CAP |
| V8/4 bbl | 383 | M | 700 | 1,700 | 130-165 ⑦ | 0.017 | 33° | 700 | J11Y | 0.035 | 5 | 14.2:1 | w/CAP |
| V8/4 bbl | 383 | A | 650 | 1,700 | 130-165 ⑦ | 0.017 | 33° | 650 | J11Y | 0.035 | TDC | 14.2:1 | w/CAP |
| V8/4 bbl | 383 S | M | 700 | 1,700 | 130-165 ⑦ | 0.017 | 30°③; 40°④ | 700 | J11Y | 0.035 | 5 | 14.2:1 | w/CAP |
| V8/4 bbl | 383 S | A | 650 | 1,700 | 130-165 ⑦ | 0.017 | 30°③; 40°④ | 650 | J11Y | 0.035 | TDC | 14.2:1 | w/CAP |
| V8/2-4 bbl | 426 | M | 750F, R 2,000R | | 150-205 ⑧ | 0.017 | 30°③; 40°④ | 750 | N10Y | 0.035 | 5 | 14.2:1 | w/CAP |
| V8/2-4 bbl | 426 | A | 750F, R 2,000R | | 150-205 ⑧ | 0.017 | 30°③; 40°④ | 750 | N10Y | 0.035 | TDC | 14.2:1 | w/CAP |
| V8/4 bbl | 440 | A | 600 | 1,400 | 130-165 ⑦ | 0.017 | 33° | 600 | J13Y | 0.035 | 7.5 | 14.2:1 | w/CAP |
| V8/4 bbl | 440 hp | M | 700 | 1,700 | 130-165 ⑦ | 0.017 | 30°③; 40°④ | 700 | J11Y | 0.035 | TDC | 14.2:1 | w/CAP |
| V8/4 bbl | 440 hp | A | 650 | 1,700 | 130-165 ⑦ | 0.017 | 33° | 650 | J11Y | 0.035 | 5 | 14.2:1 | w/CAP |

① = CAP—Cleaner air package.
② = ± 0.003 in.
③ = One set of points.
④ = Both sets of points.
⑤ = ± 2 degrees.
⑥ = Should not vary more than 20 psi between cylinders.
⑦ = Should not vary more than 25 psi between cylinders.
⑧ = Should not vary more than 30 psi between cylinders.

**Table 1 TUNE-UP SPECIFICATIONS** (continued)

**1970 MODELS**

| Engine Cyl./Carb. | CID | Transmission | Idle Speed Curb | Idle Speed Fast | Comp. (psi) | Points Setting ② | Distributor Dwell Angle ⑤ | RPM | Spark Plugs (Champion) Type | Gap | Timing (°BTC) | Air-Fuel Ratio | Remarks |
|---|---|---|---|---|---|---|---|---|---|---|---|---|---|
| 6/1 bbl | 198 | M | 750 | 1,800 | 100 ⑧ | 0.020 | 44° | 750 | N14Y | 0.035 | 2.5 | 14.2:1 | W/CAS, ECS ② |
| 6/1 bbl | 198 | A | 750 | 1,800 | 100 ⑧ | 0.020 | 44° | 750 | N14Y | 0.035 | TDC | 14.2:1 | W/CAS, ECS |
| 6/1 bbl | 225 | M | 700 | 1,600 | 100 ⑧ | 0.020 | 44° | 700 | N14Y | 0.035 | TDC | 14.2:1 | W/CAS, ECS |
| 6/1 bbl | 225 | A | 650 | 1,800 | 100 ⑧ | 0.020 | 44° | 650 | N14Y | 0.035 | TDC | 14.2:1 | W/CAS, ECS |
| V8/2 bbl | 318 | M | 750 | 1,600 | 100 ⑧ | 0.017 | 32° | 750 | N14Y | 0.035 | TDC | 14.2:1 | W/CAS, ECS |
| V8/2 bbl | 318 | A | 700 | 2,000 | 100 ⑧ | 0.017 | 32° | 700 | N14Y | 0.035 | TDC | 14.2:1 | W/CAS, ECS |
| V8/4 bbl | 340 | M | 950 | 2,000 | 110 ⑨ | 0.017 | 30°③; 40°④ | 950 | N9Y | 0.035 | 5 | 14.2:1 | W/CAS, ECS |
| V8/4 bbl | 340 | A | 900 | 2,000 | 110 ⑨ | 0.017 | 30°③; 40°④ | 900 | N9Y | 0.035 | 5 | 14.2:1 | W/CAS, ECS |
| V8/2 bbl | 383 | M | 750 | 1,700 | 100 ⑨ | 0.018 | 30.5° | 750 | J14Y | 0.035 | TDC | 14.2:1 | W/CAS, ECS |
| V8/2 bbl | 383 | A | 650 | 1,700 | 110 ⑨ | 0.018 | 30.5° | 650 | J14Y | 0.035 | 2.5 | 14.2:1 | W/CAS, ECS |
| V8/4 bbl ⑥ | 383 | M | 900 | 2,000 | 110 ⑨ | 0.018 | 30.5° | 900 | J11Y | 0.035 | TDC | 14.2:1 | W/CAS, ECS |
| V8/4 bbl ⑦ | 383 | A | 750 | 2,000 | 110 ⑨ | 0.018 | 30.5° | 750 | J11Y | 0.035 | TDC | 14.2:1 | W/CAS |
| V8/4 bbl | 383 | M | 700 | 1,700 | 110 ⑨ | 0.018 | 30.5° | 700 | J11Y | 0.035 | 2.5 | 14.2:1 | W/CAS, ECS |
| V8/4 bbl ⑦ | 440 | A | 650 | 1,600 | 110 ⑨ | 0.018 | 30.5° | 650 | J13Y | 0.035 | 5 | 14.2:1 | W/CAS, ECS |
| V8/4 bbl ⑥ | 440 | M | 900 | 2,000 | 110 ⑨ | 0.018 | 30.5° | 900 | J11Y | 0.035 | TDC | 14.2:1 | W/ECS |
| V8/4 bbl ⑥ | 440 | A | 800 | 1,800 | 110 ⑨ | 0.018 | 30.5° | 800 | J11Y | 0.035 | 2.5 | 14.2:1 | W/CAS, ECS |
| V8/3-2 bbl | 440 | M | 900 | 2,200 | 110 ⑨ | 0.017 | 30°③; 40°④ | 900 | J11Y | 0.035 | 5 | 14.2:1 | W/CAS, ECS |
| V8/3-2 bbl | 440 | A | 900 | 1,800 | 110 ⑨ | 0.017 | 30°③; 40°④ | 900 | J11Y | 0.035 | 5 | 14.2:1 | W/CAS, ECS |
| V8/2-4 bbl | 426 | M | 900F, R | 2,000R | 110 ⑨ | 0.017 | 30°③; 40°④ | 900 | N10Y | 0.035 | TDC | 14.2:1 | W/CAS, ECS |
| V8/2-4 bbl | 426 | A | 900F, R | 2,000R | 110 ⑨ | 0.017 | 30°③; 40°④ | 900 | N10Y | 0.035 | 5 | 14.2:1 | W/CAS, ECS |

① = ± 0.003 in.
② = CAS—Cleaner Air System; ECS—Evaporative Control System.
③ = One set of points.
④ = Both sets of points.
⑤ = ± 2 degrees.
⑥ = Carter carburetor.
⑦ = Holley carburetor.
⑧ = Should not vary more than 25 psi between cylinders.
⑨ = Should not vary more than 40 psi between cylinders.

# IGNITION TUNE-UP

## Table 1 TUNE-UP SPECIFICATIONS (continued)
### 1971 MODELS

| Engine Cyl./Carb. | CID | Trans-mission | Idle Speed Curb | Idle Speed Fast | Min. Comp. (psi) | Points Setting ① | Distributor Dwell Angle ④ | RPM | Spark Plugs (Champion) Type | Spark Plugs Gap | Timing (°BTC) ⑧ | Air-Fuel Ratio |
|---|---|---|---|---|---|---|---|---|---|---|---|---|
| 6/1 bbl | 198 | M | 800 | 1,900 | 100 ④ | 0.020 | 44° | 800 | N14Y | 0.035 | 2.5 | 14.2:1 |
| 6/1 bbl | 198 | A | 800 | 1,800 | 100 ④ | 0.020 | 44° | 800 | N14Y | 0.035 | 2.5 | 14.2:1 |
| 6/1 bbl | 225 | M | 750 | 1,600 | 100 ④ | 0.020 | 44° | 750 | N14Y | 0.035 | TDC | 14.2:1 |
| 6/1 bbl | 225 | A | 750 | 1,900 | 100 ④ | 0.020 | 44° | 750 | N14Y | 0.035 | TDC | 14.2:1 |
| 6/1 bbl ⑨ | 225 | M | 750 | 1,600 | 100 ④ | 0.020 | 44° | 750 | N14Y | 0.035 | 2.5 | 14.2:1 |
| 6/1 bbl ⑨ | 225 | A | 750 | 1,900 | 100 ④ | 0.020 | 44° | 750 | N14Y | 0.035 | 2.5 | 14.2:1 |
| 6/1 bbl ⑩ | 225 | M | 750 | 1,600 | 100 ⑤ | 0.017 | 32° | 750 | N14Y | 0.035 | TDC | 14.2:1 |
| 6/1 bbl ⑩ | 225 | A | 700 | 1,900 | 100 ⑤ | 0.017 | 32° | 700 | N14Y | 0.035 | TDC | 14.2:1 |
| V8/2 bbl | 318 | M | 900 | 1,800 | 110 ⑤ | 0.017 | 30°②; 40°③ | 900 | N9Y | 0.035 | 5 | 14.2:1 |
| V8/2 bbl | 318 | A | 900 | 1,800 | 110 ⑤ | 0.017 | 30°②; 40°③ | 900 | N9Y | 0.035 | 5 | 14.2:1 |
| V8/4 bbl | 340 | M | 950 | 2,600 | 110 ⑤ | 0.017 | 30°②; 40°③ | 950 | N9Y | 0.035 | 2.5 | 14.2:1 |
| V8/4 bbl | 340 | A | 1,000 | 2,800 | 100 ⑤ | 0.017 | 30°②; 40°③ | 1,000 | N9Y | 0.035 | 2.5 | 14.2:1 |
| V8/2-3 bbl | 340 | M | 750 | 1,800 | 100 ⑤ | 0.017 | 32° | 750 | N13Y | 0.035 | 2.5 | 14.2:1 |
| V8/2-3 bbl | 340 | A | 700 | 1,800 | 100 ⑤ | 0.017 | 32° | 700 | N13Y | 0.035 | 2.5 | 14.2:1 |
| V8/2 bbl | 360 | M | 750 | 1,900 | 100 ⑤ | 0.018 | 30.5° | 750 | J14Y | 0.035 | TDC | 14.2:1 |
| V8/2 bbl | 360 | A | 700 | 1,700 | 110 ⑤ | 0.018 | 30.5° | 700 | J14Y | 0.035 | TDC | 14.2:1 |
| V8/2 bbl | 383 | M | 900 | 1,800 | 110 ⑤ | 0.018 | 30.5° | 900 | J11Y | 0.035 | 2.5 | 14.2:1 |
| V8/2 bbl | 383 | A | 800 | 1,700 | 110 ⑤ | 0.018 | 30.5° | 800 | J11Y | 0.035 | 2.5 | 14.2:1 |
| V8/4 bbl | 383 | M | 750 | 1,800 | 110 ⑤ | 0.018 | 30.5° | 750 | J13Y | 0.035 | 5 | 14.2:1 |
| V8/4 bbl | 383 | A | 900 | 2,100 | 110 ⑤ | 0.018 | 30.5° | 900 | J11Y | 0.035 | TDC | 14.2:1 |
| V8/4 bbl | 440 | M | 900 | 1,800 | 110 ⑤ | 0.018 | 30.5° | 900 | J11Y | 0.035 | 2.5 | 14.2:1 |
| V8/4 bbl | 440 ⑦ | A | 900 | 1,800 | 110 ⑤ | 0.017 | 30°②; 40°③ | 900 | J11Y | 0.035 | 5 | 14.2:1 |
| V8/4 bbl | 440 ⑦ | M | 900 | 1,800 | 110 ⑤ | 0.017 | 30°②; 40°③ | 900 | J11Y | 0.035 | 5 | 14.2:1 |
| V8/3-2 bbl | 440 | A | 900 | 1,800 | 110 ⑤ | 0.017 | 30°②; 40°③ | 900 | J11Y | 0.035 | TDC | 14.2:1 |
| V8/2-4 bbl | 426 | M | 950F, R | 2,300R | 110 ⑤ | 0.017 | 30°②; 40°③ | 950 | N10Y | 0.035 | TDC | 14.2:1 |
| V8/2-4 bbl | 426 | A | 950F, R | 2,300R | 110 ⑤ | 0.017 | 30°②; 40°③ | 950 | N10Y | 0.035 | 2.5 | 14.2:1 |

① = ± 0.003 in.
② = One set of points.
③ = Both sets of points.
④ = Should not vary more than 25 psi between cylinders.
⑤ = Should not vary more than 40 psi between cylinders.
⑥ = ± 2 degrees.
⑦ = Special cam.
⑧ = ± 2.5 degrees.
⑨ = Except California (49-state cars).
⑩ = California only.

## Table 1 TUNE-UP SPECIFICATIONS (continued)

### 1972 MODELS

| Engine Cyl./Carb. | CID | Trans-mission | Idle Speed Curb | Idle Speed Fast | Min. Comp. (psi) | Points Setting ① | Distributor ② Dwell Angle ⑤ | RPM | Spark Plugs (Champion) Type | Gap | Timing (°BTC) ⑥ | Air-Fuel Ratio | Remarks |
|---|---|---|---|---|---|---|---|---|---|---|---|---|---|
| 6/1 bbl | 198 | M | 800 | 2,000 | 100 ③ | 0.020 | 44° | 800 | N14Y | 0.035 | 2.5 | 14.2:1 | Federal |
| 6/1 bbl | 198 | A | 800 | 1,900 | 100 ③ | 0.020 | 44° | 800 | N14Y | 0.035 | 2.5 | 14.2:1 | Federal |
| 6/1 bbl | 198 | M | 800 | 2,000 | 100 ③ | 0.020 | 44° | 800 | N14Y | 0.035 | 2.5 | 14.2:1 | Calif. |
| 6/1 bbl | 198 | A | 800 | 2,000 | 100 ③ | 0.020 | 44° | 800 | N14Y | 0.035 | 2.5 | 14.2:1 | Calif. |
| 6/1 bbl | 225 | M | 750 | 2,000 | 100 ③ | 0.020 | 44° | 750 | N14Y | 0.035 | TDC | 14.2:1 | Federal |
| 6/1 bbl | 225 | A | 750 | 2,000 | 100 ③ | 0.020 | 44° | 750 | N14Y | 0.035 | TDC | 14.2:1 | Federal |
| 6/1 bbl | 225 | M | 700 | 2,000 | 100 ③ | 0.020 | 44° | 700 | N14Y | 0.035 | TDC | 14.2:1 | Calif. |
| 6/1 bbl | 225 | A | 750 | 2,000 | 100 ③ | 0.020 | 44° | 750 | N14Y | 0.035 | TDC | 14.2:1 | Calif. |
| V8/2 bbl | 318 | M | 750 | 1,900 | 100 ④ | 0.017 | 32° | 750 | N13Y | 0.035 | TDC | 14.2:1 | Federal |
| V8/2 bbl | 318 | A | 750 | 1,700 | 100 ④ | 0.017 | 32° | 750 | N13Y | 0.035 | TDC | 14.2:1 | Federal |
| V8/2 bbl | 318 | M | 700 | 2,000 | 100 ④ | 0.017 | 32° | 700 | N13Y | 0.035 | TDC | 14.2:1 | Calif. |
| V8/2 bbl | 318 | A | 750 | 1,800 | 100 ④ | 0.017 | 32° | 750 | N13Y | 0.035 | TDC | 14.2:1 | Calif. |
| V8/4 bbl | 340 | M | 900 | 1,900 | 100 ④ | | | | N9Y | 0.035 | 2.5 | 14.2:1 | Federal |
| V8/4 bbl | 340 | A | 750 | 1,900 | 100 ④ | | | | N9Y | 0.035 | 2.5 | 14.2:1 | Federal |
| V8/4 bbl | 340 | M | 900 | 1,900 | 100 ④ | | | | N9Y | 0.035 | | 14.2:1 | Calif. |
| V8/4 bbl | 340 | A | 750 | 1,900 | 100 ④ | | | | N9Y | 0.035 | 2.5 | 14.2:1 | Calif. |

(continued)

# IGNITION TUNE-UP

## Table 1  TUNE-UP SPECIFICATIONS (continued)
### 1972 MODELS

| Engine Cyl./Carb. | CID | Trans-mission | Idle Speed Curb | Idle Speed Fast | Min. Comp. (psi) | Points Setting ① | Distributor Dwell Angle ⑤ | RPM | Spark Plugs (Champion) Type | Spark Plugs (Champion) Gap | Timing (°BTC) ⑥ | Air-Fuel Ratio | Remarks |
|---|---|---|---|---|---|---|---|---|---|---|---|---|---|
| V8/2 bbl | 360 | A | 700 | 1,900 | 100 ④ | 0.017 | 32° | 700 | N13Y | 0.035 | TDC | 14.2:1 | Federal |
| V8/2 bbl | 360 | A | 700 | 2,000 | 100 ④ | 0.017 | 32° | 700 | N13Y | 0.035 | TDC | 14.2:1 | Calif. |
| V8/2 bbl | 400 | A | 700 | 1,900 | 100 | 0.018 | 30.5° | 700 | J13Y | 0.035 | 5 | 14.2:1 | Federal |
| V8/2 bbl | 400 | A | 700 | 2,000 | 100 | 0.018 | 30.5° | 700 | J13Y | 0.035 | 5 | 14.2:1 | Calif. |
| V8/2 bbl | 400 | M | 900 | 1,900 | 100 | | | | J11Y | 0.035 | TDC | 14.2:1 | Federal |
| V8/4 bbl | 400 | A | 750 | 1,900 | 100 | | | | J11Y | 0.035 | 10 | 14.2:1 | Federal |
| V8/4 bbl | 400 | M | 800 | 2,000 | 100 | | | | J11Y | 0.035 | 2.5 | 14.2:1 | Calif. |
| V8/4 bbl | 400 | A | 750 | 2,000 | 100 | | | | J11Y | 0.035 | 5 | 14.2:1 | Calif. |
| V8/4 bbl | 440 | A | 750 | 1,600 | 100 | 0.017 | 32° | 750 | J11Y | 0.035 | 10 | 14.2:1 | Federal |
| V8/4 bbl | 440 | A | 700 | 1,500 | 100 | 0.019 | 30.5° | 700 | J11Y | 0.035 | 5 | 14.2:1 | Federal |
| V8/4 bbl | 440 | M | 900 | 1,800 | 110 | | | | J11Y | 0.035 | 2.5 | 14.2:1 | Federal |
| V8/4 bbl | 440 | A | 900 | 1,600 | 110 | | | | J11Y | 0.035 | 10 | 14.2:1 | Federal |
| V8/4 bbl | 440 | M | 800 | 2,000 | 110 | | | | J11Y | 0.035 | 2.5 | 14.2:1 | Calif. |
| V8/4 bbl | 440 | A | 900 | 1,800 | 110 | | | | J11Y | 0.035 | 5 | 14.2:1 | Calif. |
| V8/3-2 bbl | 440 | M | 900 | 1,800 | 110 | | | | J11Y | 0.035 | 2.5 | 14.2:1 | Federal |
| V8/3-2 bbl | 440 | A | 900 | 1,800 | 110 | | | | J11Y | 0.035 | 2.5 | 14.2:1 | Federal |

① = ± 0.003 in.
② = Point and dwell settings not required on cars equipped with electronic ignition.
③ = Should not vary more than 25 psi between cylinders.
④ = Should not vary more than 40 psi between cylinders.
⑤ = ± 2 degrees.
⑥ = ± 2.5 degrees.

## Table 1  TUNE-UP SPECIFICATIONS (continued)

### 1973 MODELS

| Engine | | Trans-mission | Idle Speed | | Min. Comp. (psi) | Spark Plugs (Champion) | | Timing (°BTC) ③ | Air-Fuel Ratio | Remarks |
| --- | --- | --- | --- | --- | --- | --- | --- | --- | --- | --- |
| Cyl./Carb. | CID | | Curb | Fast | | Type | Gap | | | |
| 6/1 bbl | 198 | M | 800 | 2,000 | 100 ① | N14Y | 0.035 | TDC | 14.2:1 | All models |
| 6/1 bbl | 198 | A | 750 | 1,700 | 100 ① | N14Y | 0.035 | TDC | 14.2:1 | All models |
| 6/1 bbl | 225 | M | 750 | 2,000 | 100 ① | N14Y | 0.035 | 2.5 | 14.2:1 | Federal |
| 6/1 bbl | 225 | A | 750 | 1,700 | 100 ① | N14Y | 0.035 | TDC | 14.2:1 | Federal |
| 6/1 bbl | 225 | M | 750 | 2,000 | 100 ① | N14Y | 0.035 | 2.5 | 14.2:1 | Calif. |
| 6/1 bbl | 225 | A | 750 | 1,700 | 100 ① | N14Y | 0.035 | TDC | 14.2:1 | Calif. |
| V8/2 bbl | 318 | M | 750 | 1,700 | 100 ② | N13Y | 0.035 | TDC | 14.2:1 | All models |
| V8/2 bbl | 318 | A | 750 | 1,700 | 100 ② | N13Y | 0.035 | TDC | 14.2:1 | All models |
| V8/4 bbl | 340 | M | 900 | 1,300 | 100 ② | N12Y | 0.035 | 5 | 14.2:1 | All models |
| V8/4 bbl | 340 | A | 750 | 1,800 | 100 ② | N12Y | 0.035 | 2.5 | 14.2:1 | All models |
| V8/2 bbl | 360 | M | 750 | 1,900 | 100 ② | N13Y | 0.035 | TDC | 14.2:1 | All models |
| V8/2 bbl | 360 | A | 750 | 1,900 | 100 ② | N13Y | 0.035 | TDC | 14.2:1 | All models |
| V8/2 bbl | 400 | M | 700 | 1,800 | 100 ② | J13Y | 0.035 | 10 | 14.2:1 | All models |
| V8/2 bbl | 400 | A | 700 | 1,800 | 100 ② | J13Y | 0.035 | 10 | 14.2:1 | All models |
| V8/4 bbl | 400 | M | 800 | 1,700 | 100 ② | J11Y | 0.035 | 2.5 | 14.2:1 | Federal |
| V8/4 bbl | 400 | A | 750 | 1,800 | 100 ② | J11Y | 0.035 | 7.5 | 14.2:1 | Federal |
| V8/4 bbl | 400 | M | 900 | 1,700 | 100 ② | J11Y | 0.035 | 2.5 | 14.2:1 | Calif. |
| V8/4 bbl | 400 | A | 750 | 1,800 | 100 ② | J11Y | 0.035 | 7.5 | 14.2:1 | Calif. |
| V8/4 bbl | 440 | A | 700 | 1,700 | 100 ② | J11Y | 0.035 | 10 | 14.2:1 | All models |
| V8/4 bbl | 440 HP | A | 800 | 1,700 | 100 ② | J11Y | 0.035 | 10 | 14.2:1 | All models |

① = Should not vary more than 25 psi between cylinders.
② = Should not vary more than 40 psi between cylinders.
③ = ± 2.5 degrees

# IGNITION TUNE-UP

## Table 1  TUNE-UP SPECIFICATIONS (continued)

### 1974 MODELS

| Engine | | Trans-mission | Idle Speed | | Min. Comp. (psi) | Spark Plugs (Champion) | | Timing (° BTC) ④ | Air-Fuel Ratio | Remarks |
| --- | --- | --- | --- | --- | --- | --- | --- | --- | --- | --- |
| Cyl./Carb. | CID | | Curb | Fast | | Type | Gap | | | |
| 6/1 bbl | 198 | M | 800 | 1,600 | 100 ① | N14Y | 0.035 | 2.5 | 14.2:1 | Federal |
| 6/1 bbl | 198 | A | 750 | 1,800 | 100 ① | N14Y | 0.035 | 2.5 | 14.2:1 | Federal |
| 6/1 bbl | 225 | M | 800 | 1,600 | 100 ① | N14Y | 0.035 | TDC | 14.2:1 | All models |
| 6/1 bbl | 225 | A | 750 | 1,800 | 100 ① | N14Y | 0.035 | TDC | 14.2:1 | All models |
| V8/2 bbl | 318 | M | 750 | 1,700 | 100 ② | N13Y | 0.035 | TDC | 14.2:1 | All models |
| V8/2 bbl | 318 | A | 750 | 1,500 | 100 ② | N13Y | 0.035 | TDC | 14.2:1 | All models |
| V8/2 bbl | 360 | A | 750 | 1,800 | 100 ② | N12Y | 0.035 | 5 | 14.2:1 | Federal |
| V8/4 bbl | 360 | A | 850 | 1,800 | 100 ② | N12Y | 0.035 | 5 | 14.2:1 | California |
| V8/4 bbl | 360 HP | M | 850 | 1,900 | 100 ② | N12Y | 0.035 | 5 | 14.2:1 | All models |
| V8/4 bbl | 360 HP | A | 850 | 1,900 | 100 ② | N12Y | 0.035 | 5 | 14.2:1 | All models |
| V8/2 bbl | 400 | A | 750 | 1,600 | 100 ② | J13Y | 0.035 | 7.5 ③ | 14.2:1 | Federal |
| V8/4 bbl | 400 | A | 750 | 2,000 | 100 ② | J13Y | 0.035 | 5 | 14.2:1 | All models |
| V8/4 bbl | 400 HP | A | 850 | 1,800 | 100 ② | J11Y | 0.035 | 5 | 14.2:1 | Federal |
| V8/4 bbl | 400 HP | A | 850 | 1,800 | 100 ② | J11Y | 0.035 | 2.5 | 14.2:1 | California |
| V8/4 bbl | 440 HP | A | 800 | 1,700 | 100 ② | J11Y | 0.035 | 5 | 14.2:1 | Federal |
| V8/4 bbl | 440 | A | 750 | 1,700 | 100 ② | J11Y | 0.035 | 10 | 14.2:1 | All models |
| V8/4 bbl | 440 HP | A | 800 | 1,700 | 100 ② | J11Y | 0.035 | 10 | 14.2:1 | All models |

① = Should not vary more than 25 psi between cylinders.
② = Should not vary more than 40 psi between cylinders.
③ = All except station wagons, which are timed at 5° BTC.
④ = ± 2 degrees.

## Table 1  TUNE-UP SPECIFICATIONS (continued)

### 1975 MODELS

| Engine | | Trans- mission | Idle Speed | | Min. Comp. (psi) | Spark Plugs (Champion) | | Timing (°BTC) ⑤ | Idle CO (%) | Remarks |
| --- | --- | --- | --- | --- | --- | --- | --- | --- | --- | --- |
| Cyl./ Carb. | CID | | Curb | Fast | | Type | Gap | | | |
| 6/1 bbl | 225 | M | 800 | 1,600 | 100 ① | BL13Y | 0.035 | TDC | 0.3 | All models |
| 6/1 bbl | 225 | A | 750 | 1,700 | 100 ① | BL13Y | 0.035 | TDC | 0.3 | Federal |
| 6/1 bbl | 225 | A | 750 | 1,700 | 100 ① | BL13Y | 0.035 | TDC | 1.5 | California |
| V8/2 bbl | 318 | M | 750 | 1,580 | 100 ② | N13Y | 0.035 | 2 | 0.3 | Federal |
| V8/2 bbl | 318 | A | 750 | 1,500 | 100 ② | N13Y | 0.035 | 2 ③ | 0.3 | Federal |
| V8/2 bbl | 318 | A | 750 | 1,500 | 100 ② | N13Y | 0.035 | TDC | 0.5 | California |
| V8/2 bbl | 318 | A | 900 | 1,500 | 100 ② | N13Y | 0.035 | 2° ATC ④ | 0.5 | Federal |
| V8/2 bbl | 360 | A | 750 | 1,600 | 100 ② | N12Y | 0.035 | 6 | 0.3 | Federal |
| V8/4 bbl | 360 HP | A | 850 | 1,600 | 100 ② | N12Y | 0.035 | 2 | 0.5 | Federal |
| V8/4 bbl | 360 | A | 750 | 1,600 | 100 ② | N12Y | 0.035 | 6 | 0.5 | California |
| V8/2 bbl | 400 | A | 750 | 1,600 | 100 ② | J13Y | 0.035 | 10 | 0.3 | Federal |
| V8/4 bbl | 400 | A | 750 | 1,800 | 100 ② | J13Y | 0.035 | 8 | 0.3 | Federal |
| V8/4 bbl | 400 | A | 750 | 1,800 | 100 ② | J13Y | 0.035 | 8 | 0.5 | California |
| V8/4 bbl | 400 HP | A | 750 | 1,800 | 100 ② | RJ87P | 0.035 | 6 | 0.5 | Federal |
| V8/4 bbl | 400 | A | 750 | 1,600 | 100 ② | RJ87P | 0.035 | 6 | 0.5 | All models |
| V8/4 bbl | 440 HP | A | 750 | 1,600 | 100 ② | J11Y | 0.035 | 10 | 0.3 | Federal |
| V8/4 bbl | 440 HP | A | 750 | 1,800 | 100 ② | J11Y | 0.035 | 10 | 0.5 | California |

① = Should not vary more than 25 psi between cylinders.
② = Should not vary more than 40 psi between cylinders.
③ = With catalytic converter.
④ = Without catalytic converter.
⑤ = ± 2 degrees.

# IGNITION TUNE-UP

**Table 1  TUNE-UP SPECIFICATIONS** (continued)

## 1976 MODELS

| Engine Cyl./Carb. | CID | Trans-mission | Idle Speed Curb | Idle Speed Fast | Min. Comp. (psi) | Spark Plugs (Champion) Type | Spark Plugs (Champion) Gap | Timing (° BTC) | Idle CO (%) | Remarks |
|---|---|---|---|---|---|---|---|---|---|---|
| 6/2 bbl | 225 | M | 750 | 1,600 | 100 ① | RBL13Y | 0.035 | 6 | 0.3 | Federal |
| 6/2 bbl | 225 | M | 800 | 1,600 | 100 ① | RBL13Y | 0.035 | 4 | 1.0 | California |
| 6/2 bbl | 225 | A | 750 | 1,700 | 100 ① | RBL13Y | 0.035 | 2 | 0.3 | Federal |
| 6/2 bbl | 225 | A | 750 | 1,700 | 100 ① | RBL13Y | 0.035 | 2 | 1.0 | California |
| V8/2 bbl | 318 | M | 750 | 1,500 | 100 ② | RN12Y | 0.035 | 2 | 0.3 | Federal |
| V8/2 bbl | 318 | A | 750 | 1,500 | 100 ② | RN12Y | 0.035 | 2 ③ | 0.3 | Federal |
| V8/2 bbl | 318 | A | 750 | 1,500 | 100 ② | RN12Y | 0.035 | TDC | 1.0 | California |
| V8/2 bbl | 360 | A | 900 | 1,500 | 100 ② | RN12Y | 0.035 | 2° ATC ④ | 0.5 | Federal |
| V8/2 bbl | 360 | A | 700 | 1,600 | 100 ② | RN12Y | 0.035 | 6 | 0.3 | Federal |
| V8/4 bbl | 360 HP | A | 750 | 1,600 | 100 ② | RN12Y | 0.035 | 6 | 2.0 | California |
| V8/4 bbl | 400 | A | 850 | 1,600 | 100 ② | RJ13Y | 0.035 | 2 | 0.5 | Federal |
| V8/2 bbl | 400 | A | 700 | 1,600 | 100 ② | RJ13Y | 0.035 | 10 | 0.3 | Federal |
| V8/4 bbl | 400 | A | 850 | 1,800 | 100 ② | RJ13Y | 0.035 | 6 | 0.5 | Federal |
| V8/4 bbl | 400 HP | A | 750 | 1,800 | 100 ② | RJ13Y | 0.035 | 8 | 0.5 | California |
| V8/4 bbl | 440 | A | 850 | 1,800 | 100 ② | RJ87P | 0.035 | 6 | 0.5 | Federal |
| V8/4 bbl | 440 | A | 750 | 1,600 | 100 ② | RJ13Y | 0.035 | 8 | 0.3 | All models |
| V8/4 bbl | 440 HP | A | 750 | 1,600 | 100 ② | RJ11Y | 0.035 | 10 | 0.3 | Federal |
| V8/4 bbl | 440 HP | A | 750 | 1,800 | 100 ② | RJ11Y | 0.035 | 8 | 0.5 | California |

① = Should not vary more than 25 psi between cylinders.
② = Should not vary more than 40 psi between cylinders.
③ = With catalytic converter.
④ = Without catalytic converter.

# CHAPTER SIX

# CARBURETOR AND FUEL PUMP

The only carburetor service required in normal tune-up work is the adjustment of idle speed. Curb idle speed is set by adjusting the air/fuel mixture to the proper ratio and then adjusting the idle speed adjusting screw to obtain the specified revolutions per minute (rpm). On 1975-1976 models, the air/fuel ratio is adjusted by observing (on an exhaust analyzer) the amount of hydrocarbons (HC) and carbon monoxide (CO) in the exhaust gas. On earlier models, a different type of exhaust analyzer is used to set the air/fuel ratio to the specification. Procedures for using both types of analyzers are given in this chapter. Even though the home mechanic is unlikely to have an accurate analyzer (and it would not be economical to purchase one), they sometimes can be obtained from equipment rental dealers for a small fee. A procedure is also given for adjusting the air/fuel ratio without an analyzer. This procedure should be used only in emergencies on 1975-1976 models equipped with catalytic converters. If the emergency procedure is used, have the air/fuel ratio set by your dealer or a competent, analyzer-equipped shop, as soon as possible, to prevent overheating of the catalytic converter.

Since 1970, Chrysler Corporation has equipped carburetor idle mixture screws with plastic caps which limit the amount of adjustment. These caps should not be removed to make adjustments.

## CURB IDLE ADJUSTMENT
## (1974 AND EARLIER)

This procedure requires the use of an accurate ignition tachometer and a Sun Electric Combustion-Vacuum Unit, Model 80, Exhaust Condenser, Model EC, and Hose 669-14, or equivalent.

1. Operate engine until normal operating temperature is reached. Verify that ignition timing meets specifications. See Vehicle Emission Control Information sticker on Table 1, Chapter Five. Do not remove air cleaner.
2. Place automatic transmission (if so equipped) in NEUTRAL position—not PARK.
3. Turn on air conditioning, if so equipped.
4. Connect tachometer to engine, using the manufacturer's instructions.
5. Insert analyzer probe into tailpipe as far as possible (at least 2 ft.). Use left tailpipe on dual exhaust cars.

NOTE: *Probe and connecting tube must be free of leaks to obtain correct readings.*

# CARBURETOR AND FUEL PUMP

6. Connect analyzer, allow it to warm up, and calibrate it, using manufacturer's instructions.

7. Set idle speed to the specified value (Table 1, Chapter Five) as follows:

> NOTE: *The analyzer is very sensitive. To obtain true reading, make adjustments to idle mixture screws in steps of no more than 1/16 turn.*

a. Turn each idle mixture screw (**Figures 1 through 6**) 1/16 turn counterclockwise. Wait at least 10 seconds and note analyzer reading.

b. Repeat Step A until meter indicates a definitely lower (richer) reading.

c. Adjust carburetor to give a 14.2 air/fuel ratio reading on the analyzer. Turn idle mixture screws counterclockwise to lower and clockwise to increase meter reading.

> NOTE: *Do not remove limiter caps from idle mixture screws.*

d. When the air/fuel ratio has been set, use the curb idle adjustment screw to obtain the specified engine idle speed.

## CURB IDLE ADJUSTMENT (1975-1976)

A Chrysler Huntsville Exhaust Emission Analyzer, or equivalent analyzer, reading out in hydrocarbons (HC) and carbon monoxide (CO) is required for this procedure. The analyzer should be hooked up according to the manufacturer's instructions.

Check the Vehicle Emission Control Information (VECI) sticker, located in the engine compartment of your car, to determine whether the analyzer probe should be inserted in front of the catalytic converter or in the tailpipe.

> NOTE: *If your car has dual exhaust pipes, use the left pipe if the sample is to be taken from the tailpipe.*

1. Warm up engine to normal operating temperature. Choke must be fully open and the throttle must be at curb idle speed. Transmission may be in PARK or NEUTRAL.

2. Connect exhaust analyzer and allow to warm up.

3. Verify that ignition timing is within ±2% of specifications given on VECI sticker, or Table 1, Chapter Five.

4. If the vehicle is equipped with an air pump, disconnect the air outlet hose and plug the air injection tube to the exhaust manifold.

5. If the VECI sticker requires sampling at the tailpipe, insert probe into tailpipe as far as possible (use left tailpipe on dual exhaust). Adjust CO to the VECI sticker specification ±0.3% by turning the idle mixture screw. Balance 2- and 4-barrel carburetors for lowest HC reading possible.

6. If the VECI sticker requires sampling in front of the catalytic converter, remove access hole plug and insert adapter (**Figure 7**). Adjust idle CO to sticker specification —0.1% to +0.2%. Balance 2- and 4-barrel carburetors for lowest possible HC content.

7. If required, readjust idle speed to specification, using the idle speed adjustment screw (not the idle mixture screw).

8. Remove probe and replace catalytic converter access plug (if removed).

> NOTE: *If access plug is damaged during removal, install a new plug, using anti-sieze compound (FEL-PRO-C100 or equivalent) on threads. Torque to 100-140 in.-lb. (115-162 cmkg).*

## CURB IDLE ADJUSTMENT (EMERGENCY)

> CAUTION
> *Use this procedure only in an emergency. If the idle mixture setting is altered on 1975-1976 vehicles equipped with catalytic converters, have the setting adjusted by your dealer as soon as possible to avoid damage and overheating.*

1. Warm up engine to normal operating temperature. Do not remove air cleaner. Turn air conditioner (if so equipped) on.

2. Connect a tachometer to the engine, using the manufacturer's instructions.

3. Disconnect vacuum hose from the distributor and plug hose.

# CHAPTER SIX

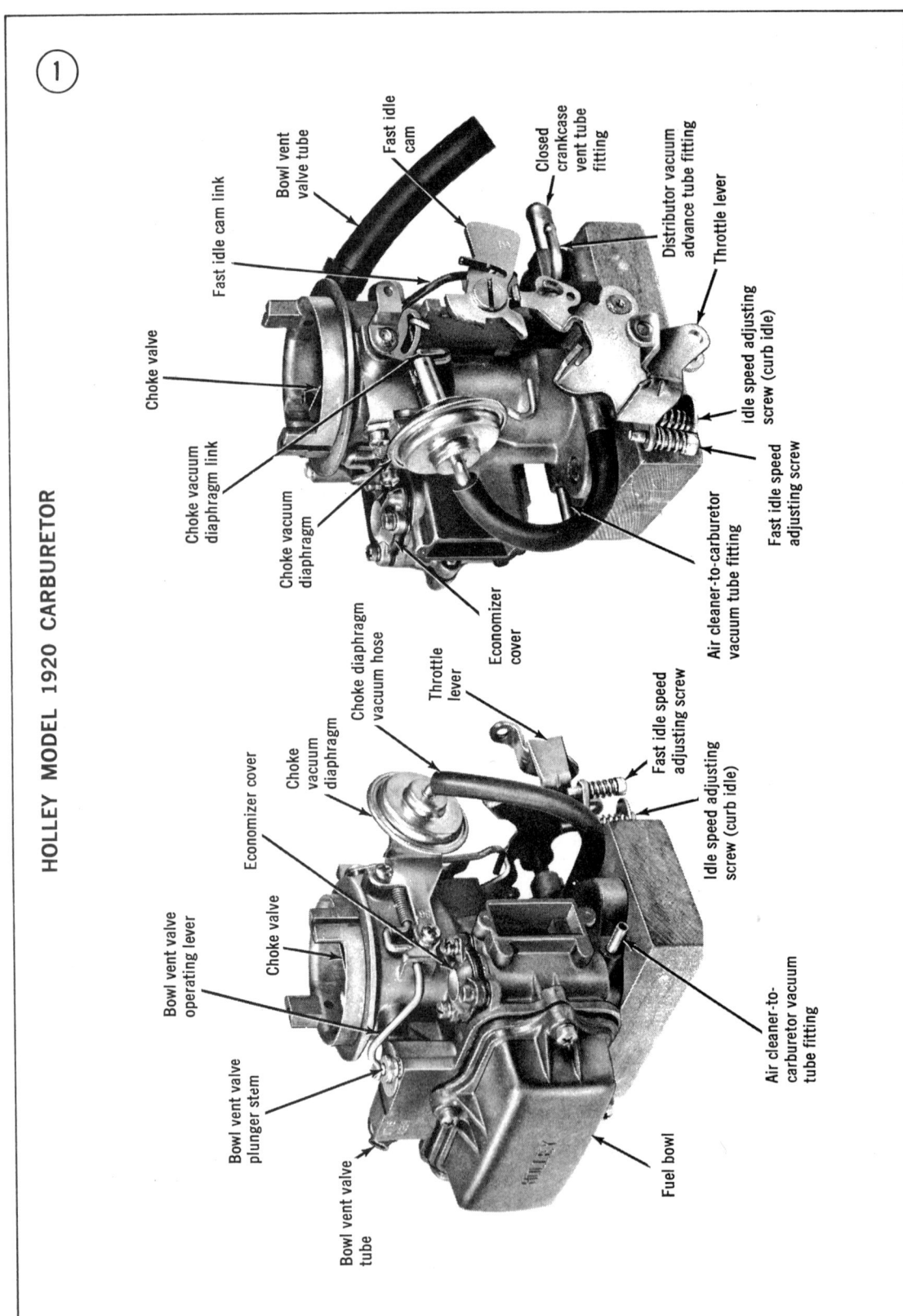

① HOLLEY MODEL 1920 CARBURETOR

# PERIODIC MAINTENANCE

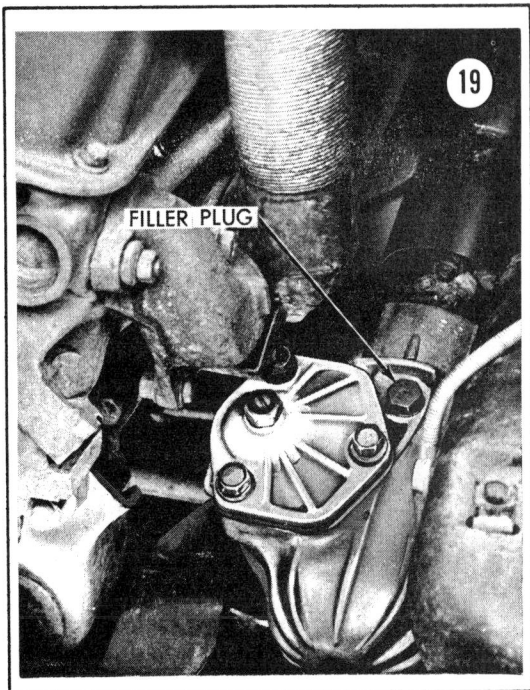

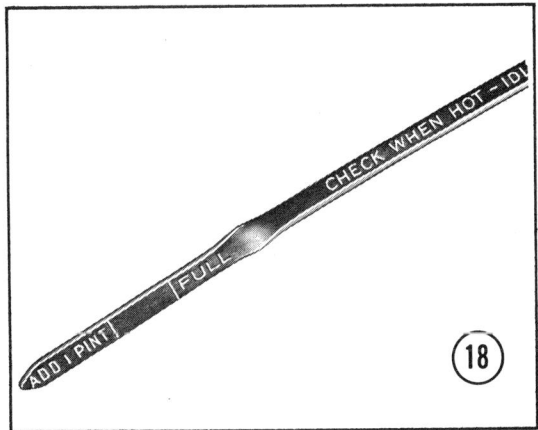

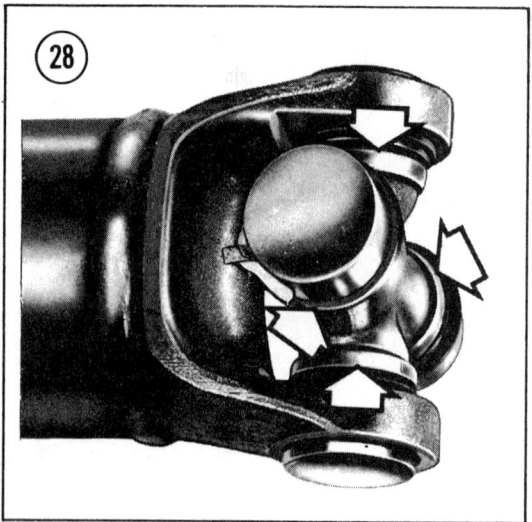

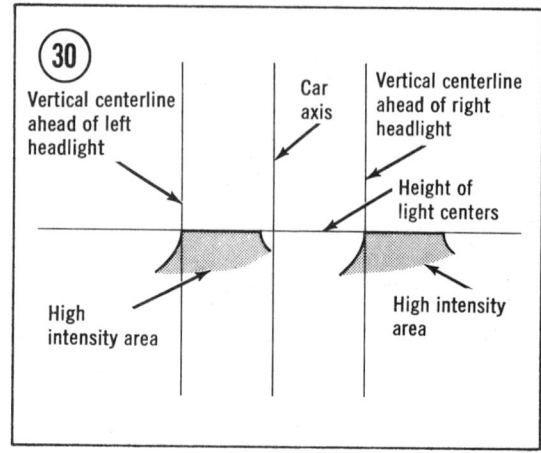

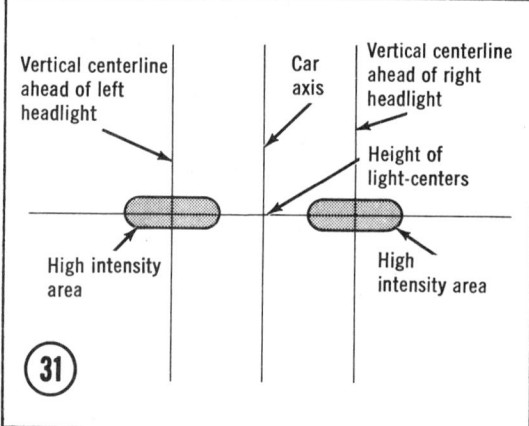

(**Figure 29**). With disc brakes, fluid level will drop as brake pads wear down. If car is equipped entirely with drum brakes, no noticeable drop in level should occur. In the latter case, if fluid is low, check for leak in hydraulic system. Use only brake fluid conforming to DOT 3.

18. *Brake hoses*—Check every 6 months for severe cracking, pulling, scuffing, or worn spots. Also check for twisting and interference with the wheel, tire, or chassis. All damaged tubing should be replaced. See Chapter Eight for procedure.

| 5th Digit of I.D. Number | 1968 | 1969 | 1970 | 1971 | 1972 | 1973 | 1974 | 1975 | 1976 |
|---|---|---|---|---|---|---|---|---|---|
| A | 170 | 170 | | | | | | | |
| B | 225 | 225 | 198 | 198 | 198 | 198 | 198 | | |
| C | ② | ② | 225 | 225 | 225 | 225 | 225 | 225 | 225 |
| D | 273 | 273 | | | | | | | |
| E | | | ② | ② | ② | ② | | | |
| F | 318 | 318 | | | | | | | |
| G | 383 | 383 | 318 | 318 | 318 | 318 | 318 | 318 | 318 |
| H | 383 ① | 383 ① | 340 | 340 | 340 | 340 | | | |
| J | 426 | 426 | | | | | 360 4 bbl | 360 4 bbl | 360 4 bbl |
| K | 440 | 440 | | 360 | 360 | 360 | 360 2 bbl | 360 2 bbl | 360 2 bbl |
| L | 440 ① | 440 ① | 383 | 383 | | | 360 4 bbl ① | 360 4 bbl ① | |
| M | ③ | ③ | | | 400 2 bbl | 400 2 bbl | 400 2 bbl | 400 2 bbl | 400 2 bbl |
| N | 340 | 340 | 383 ① | 383 ① | | | 400 4 bbl | 400 4 bbl | 400 4 bbl |
| P | 340 ① | | | | 400 4 bbl | 400 4 bbl | 400 4 bbl ① | | |
| R | | | 426 | 426 | | | | | |
| T | | | 440 | 440 | 440 | 440 | 440 | 440 | 440 |
| U | | | 440 ① | 440 ① | 440 ① | 440 ① | 440 ① | 440 ① | 440 ① |
| V | | | 440 3-2 bbl | 440 3-2 bbl | 440 3-2 bbl | | | | |
| Z | | | ③ | ③ | ③ | | | | |

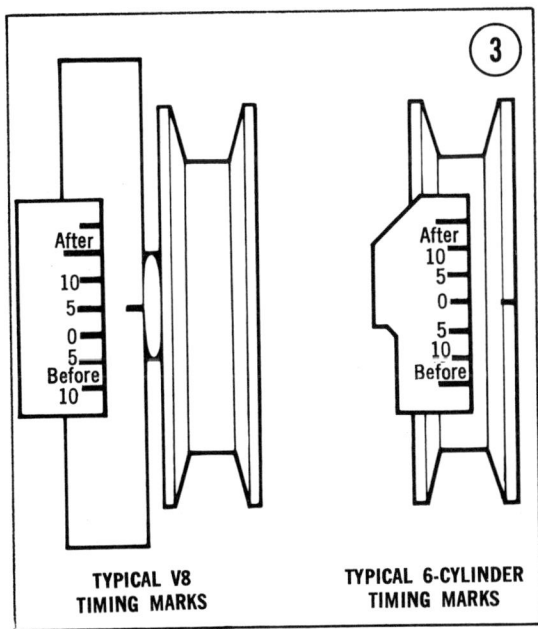

TYPICAL V8 TIMING MARKS

TYPICAL 6-CYLINDER TIMING MARKS

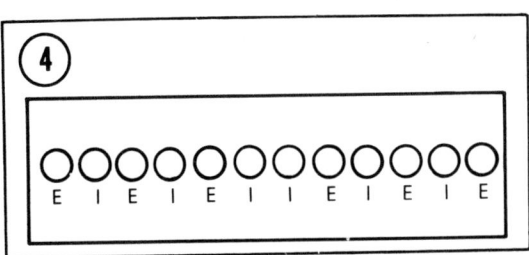

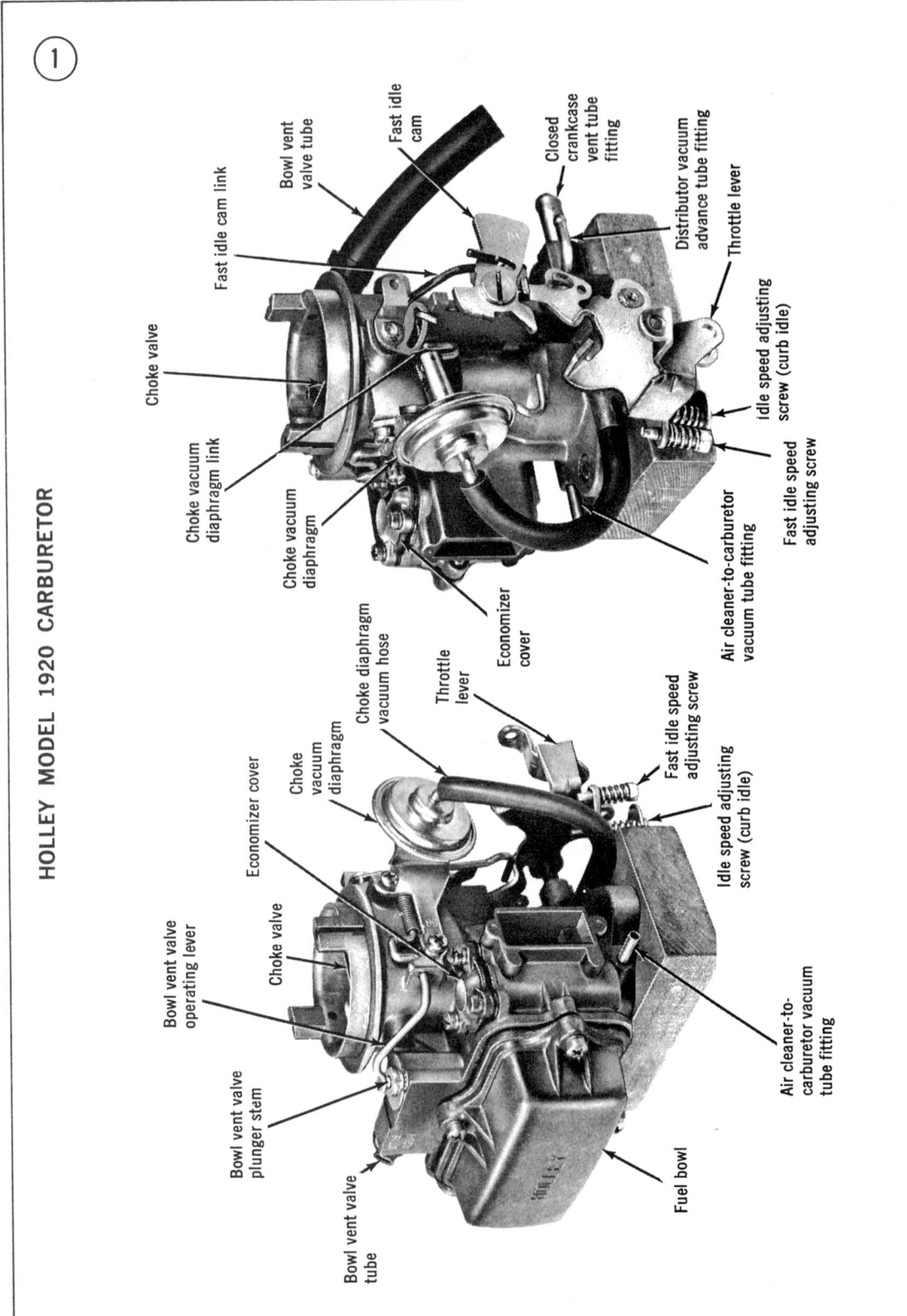

1. HOLLEY MODEL 1920 CARBURETOR

# BRAKES AND FRONT WHEEL BEARINGS

5. While holding adjusting lever out of the way, back off star wheel just enough to assure free wheel rotation with no brake shoe drag.

6. Repeat the procedure for all wheels, making sure adjustment is equal for all wheels. Reinstall adjustment hole covers. With parking brake released, take up parking brake cable slack until a slight drag is felt on both rear wheels, then loosen until wheels rotate freely. Back off adjustment nut 2 additional turns. Apply brake several times, then verify that wheels still rotate freely.

## HYDRAULIC SYSTEM BLEEDING

NOTE: *Chrysler Corporation recommends against the manual bleeding of the brake system. Instead, it recommends the use of a one-man bleeder tank which keeps the master cylinder full at all times. If care is taken to make sure the master cylinder is filled with recommended fluid (see Chapter Four), the following procedure can be used in an emergency.*

1. Tighten brakes on each wheel until brakes are locked.

2. Starting with right rear wheel, clean bleeder valve and attach bleeder hose. Insert other end of hose in half filled clear jar of brake fluid.

3. Open bleeder valve and have an assistant operate the brake pedal until no further air bubbles are being expelled from the system.

4. Close valve. Repeat the operation for the remaining wheels, starting with the left rear and ending with the right front.

5. Repeat the entire operation if air remains in the system (soft or low pedal).

6. Readjust brakes, using the procedure given above.

## DISC BRAKES

Several different types of disc brakes were used. In most instances, complete caliper overhaul requires special tools and skills. Therefore, the procedures given here are limited to removal and replacement of brake pads.

### Dart (1968-1972)

1. Raise vehicle on jackstands.
2. Remove wheel and tire assembly.
3. Remove pad hold-down clips (**Figure 19**).

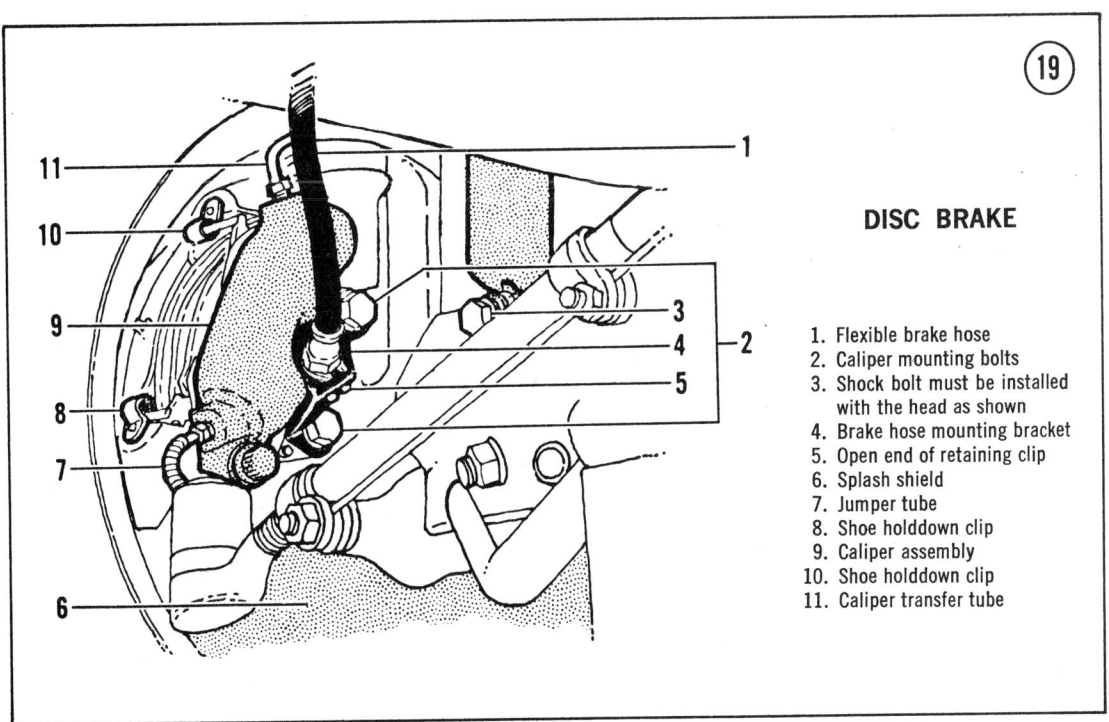

**DISC BRAKE**

1. Flexible brake hose
2. Caliper mounting bolts
3. Shock bolt must be installed with the head as shown
4. Brake hose mounting bracket
5. Open end of retaining clip
6. Splash shield
7. Jumper tube
8. Shoe holddown clip
9. Caliper assembly
10. Shoe holddown clip
11. Caliper transfer tube

4. Remove pads by grasping each pad by the tabs on the outer edges, using 2 pairs of pliers (**Figure 20**), and pulling outward.

> NOTE: *If a ridge of rust has formed on the rotor surface (outside the shoe contact area), force the pistons back into their bores slightly with water pump pliers as shown in the inset of Figure 20.*

5. Check the caliper for evidence of fluid leakage and damage to piston boots. Wipe cavity clean. If excessive fluid is present, or dust boots are damaged, the caliper should be rebuilt by your dealer or a competent, well-equipped brake shop.

6. Push pistons back in their bores as far as they will go, using a flat metal bar or tool.

> NOTE: *This operation will force fluid back into the master cylinder. Therefore, before starting the operation, remove a quantity of fluid from the cylinder reservoir.*

7. Insert new pads and linings into caliper, making sure linings face rotor and are firmly seated.

8. Install retaining clips and tighten bolts to 7-9 ft.-lb. (1.0-1.2 mkg).

9. Pump brake pedal several times until firm pedal is obtained and linings are properly seated.

10. Install wheel and tire assembly and wheel cover. Lower vehicle.

> NOTE: *Torque wheel stud to 55 ft.lb. (7.6 mkg).*

11. Fill master cylinder reservoir, if required, and road test vehicle.

## Dart (1973-1976), Polara (1974), and Monaco (1974-1976)

1. Raise vehicle on jackstands and remove front wheel covers and wheel and tire assemblies.

2. Remove caliper retaining clips and anti-rattle springs. See **Figure 21**.

3. Slide caliper out and away from disc.

4. Remove outboard pad first by prying between fingers on caliper and pad. See **Figure 22**.

5. Support caliper on front linkage.

6. Install new pads in caliper, making sure they are properly seated.

7. Hold pads in calipers and carefully reinstall calipers over discs.

8. Install clips and anti-rattle springs.

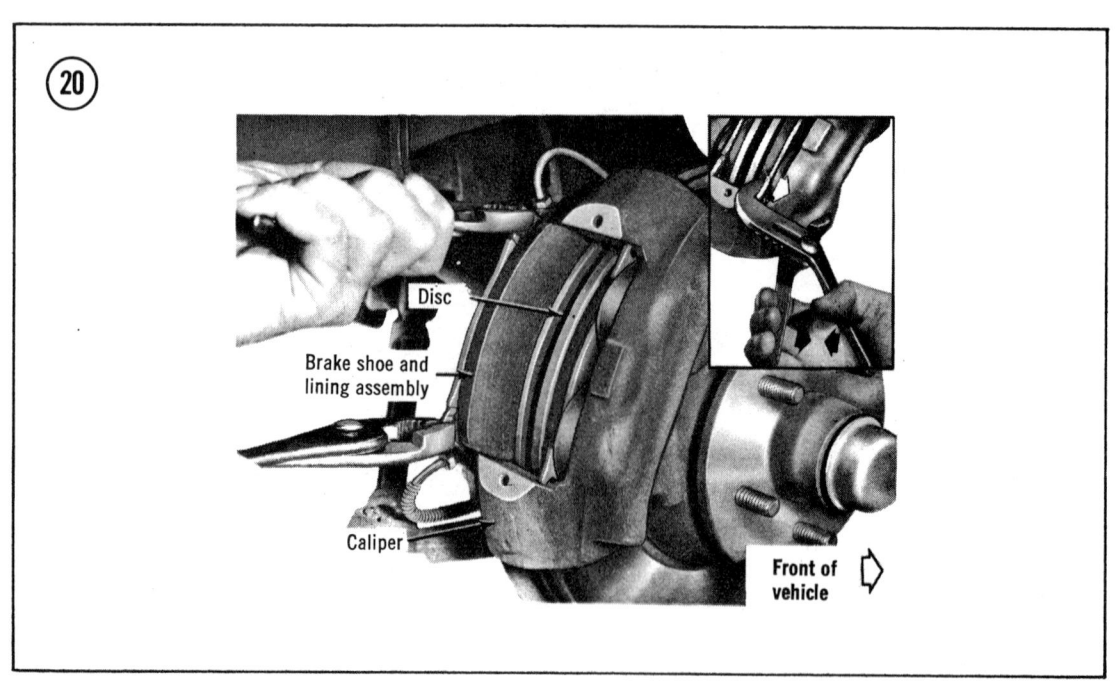

# BRAKES AND FRONT WHEEL BEARINGS

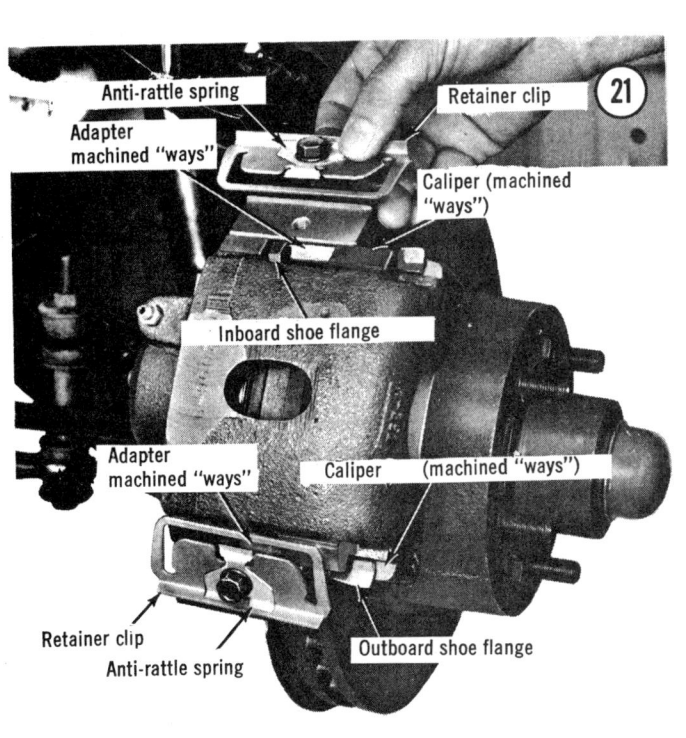

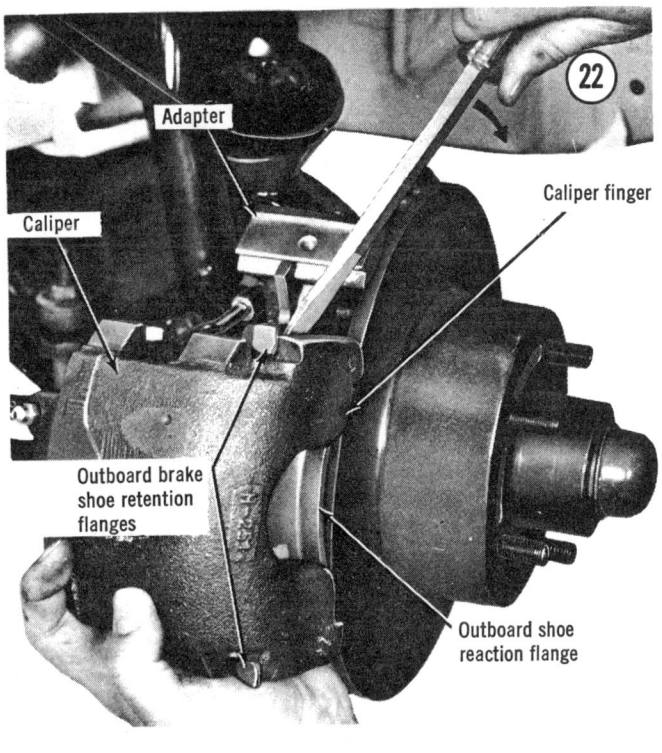

9. Pump brake several times to obtain a firm pedal.

10. Check master cylinder reservoir and add fluid if required.

> NOTE: *It should not be necessary to bleed system unless pistons were disturbed. However, if a firm pedal cannot be obtained, bleed the system.*

11. Install wheel and tire assemblies and wheel covers. Lower and road test vehicle.

## Coronet and Charger (1968-1969), Polara and Monaco (1968)

1. Raise vehicle on jackstands.
2. Remove wheel and tire assemblies (front).
3. Remove caliper mounting bolts (**Figure 23**).
4. Slide caliper assembly up and away from rotor. Rest assembly on steering linkage.
5. Remove brake pad and lining assemblies one at a time by sliding out of caliper assembly.
6. Slide new pad and lining assemblies into caliper, with curved side first and lining toward center. Spread with fingers until caliper pistons are seated in their bores.
7. Position caliper over disc and align mounting holes. Make sure linings slide easily over disc.
8. Install mounting bolts and torque to 105 ft.-lb. (14.52 mkg).

9. Verify that disc rotates freely with minimum drag.

10. Install wheel and tire assemblies and wheel covers. Pump foot pedal several times to obtain firm pedal. Lower vehicle.

11. Road test vehicle and make several stops to wear off foreign material.

## Coronet and Charger (1970-1976), Polara and Monaco (1969-1973), Challenger (1973-1974), Dart and Aspen (1976)

1. Raise vehicle on jackstands.
2. Remove wheel and tire assemblies.
3. Remove caliper guide pins, caliper-to-adapter positioners, and anti-rattle springs (**Figure 24**).
4. Lift caliper up and out of way, and support on steering linkage to avoid damage to brake hose.
5. Slide out brake pad and lining assemblies (**Figure 25**).
6. Remove and discard inner and outer bushings from caliper by pressing out with a suitable tool (**Figures 26 and 27**).
7. Install new inner and outer bushings in caliper by compressing flanges and working into holes.

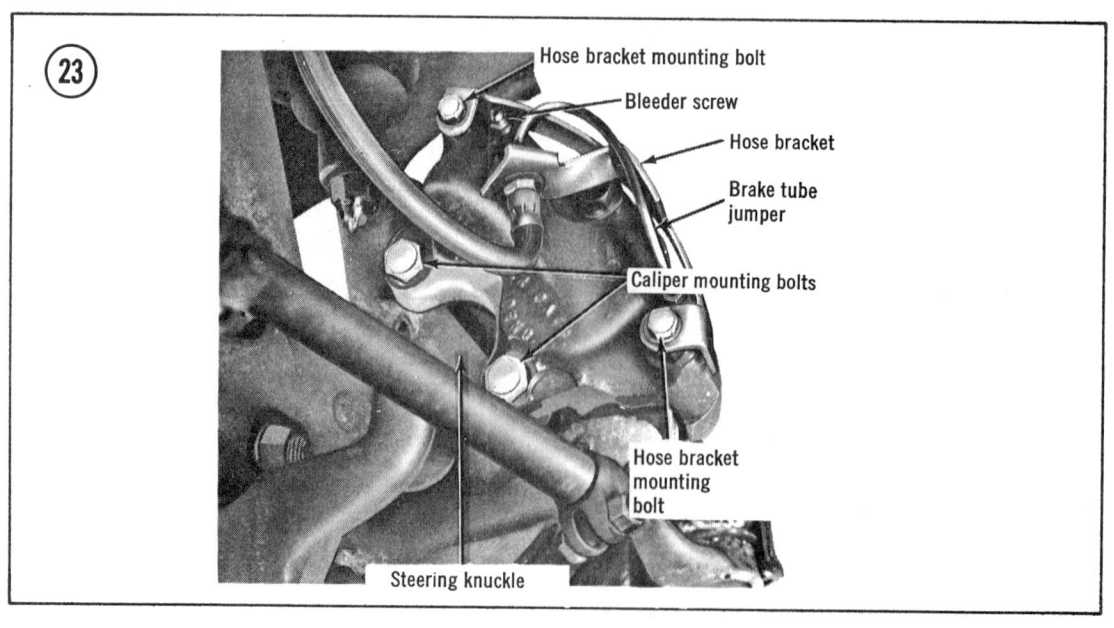

# BRAKES AND FRONT WHEEL BEARINGS

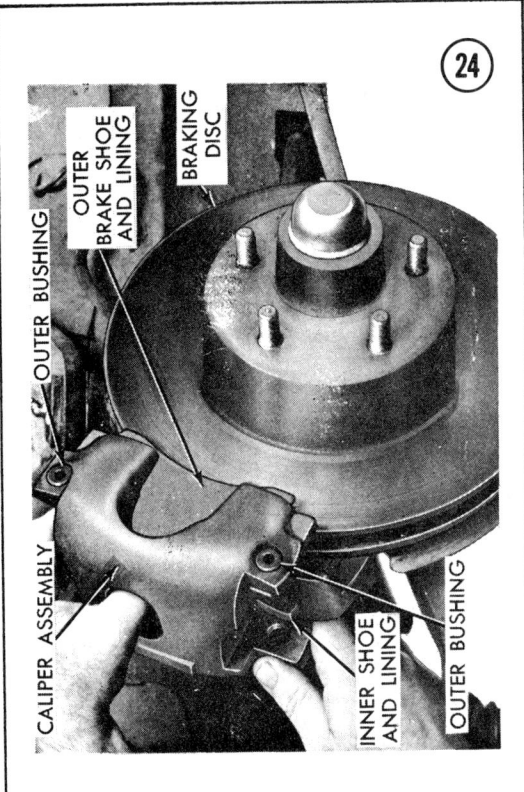

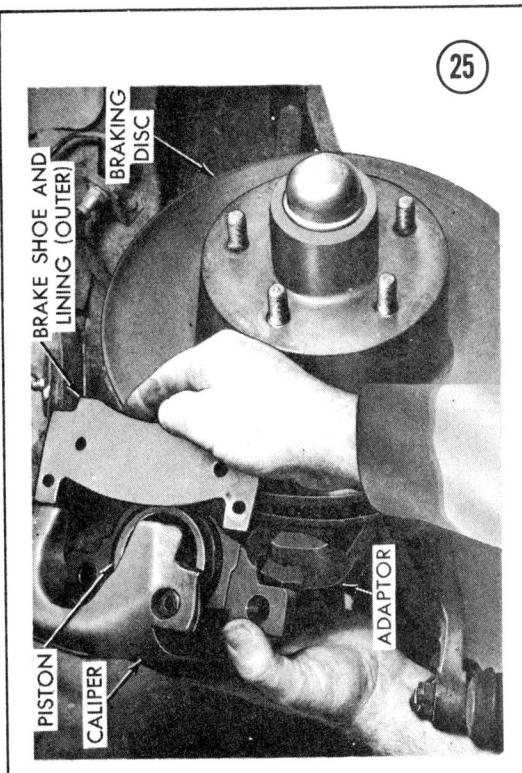

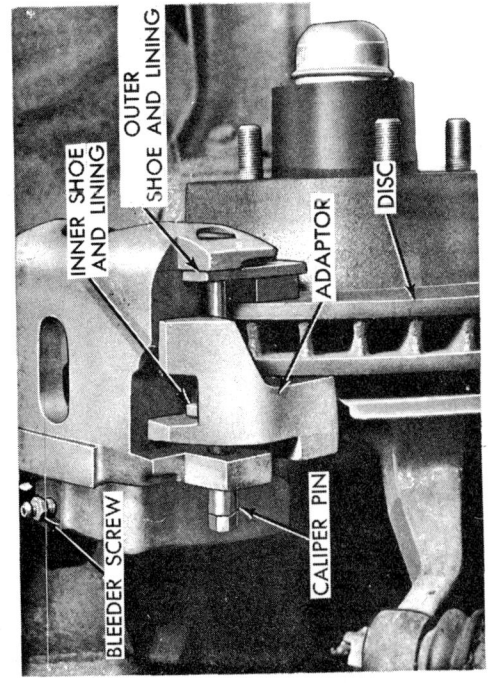

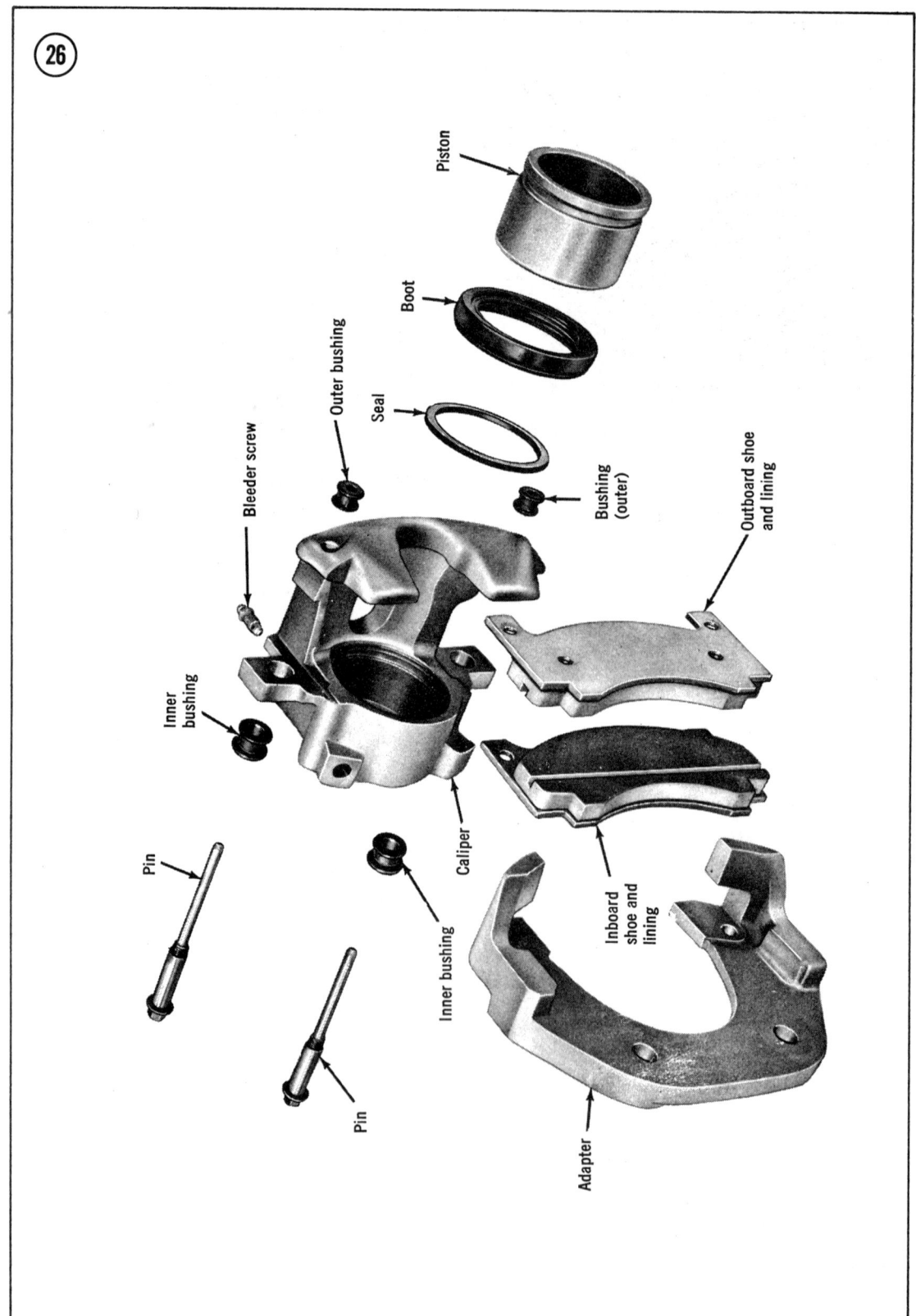

# BRAKES AND FRONT WHEEL BEARINGS

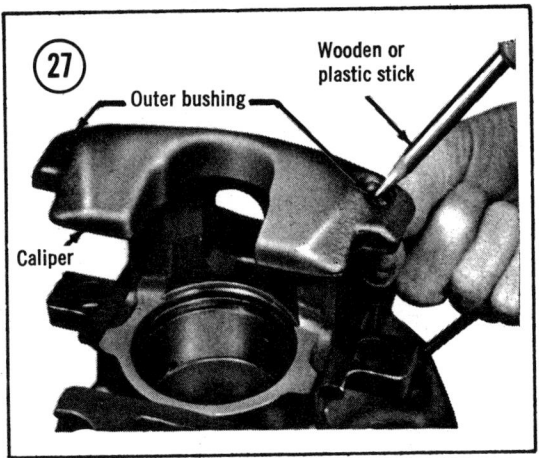

8. Carefully push pistons back into their bores, watching for master cylinder reservoir overflow.

9. Slide new linings into position in caliper and adapter (Figure 25). Make sure that metal portion of pad is fully seated in caliper recess, and that thinner pad (with adhesive on the back) is on the outboard side.

10. Carefully slide caliper into position while holding outboard shoe in position. Align guide pin holes in adapter and shoes.

11. Install guide pins (Figure 26) through bushings, caliper, adapter, both shoes, and outer bushings.

12. Press in on guide pins and thread pins into adapter. Care must be exercised to avoid cross threading. Torque to 25-35 ft.-lb. (3.46-4.84 mkg).

13. Pump brake pedal to obtain a firm pedal.

14. Install wheel and tire assemblies and wheel covers. Lower vehicle.

15. Fill master cylinder reservoir, if required, and road test vehicle.

**Polara and Monaco (1968)**

Polara and Monaco models equipped with Budd disc brakes (1968) should be taken to a dealer or brake shop for pad replacement, as special tools are required.

# CHAPTER NINE

# CLUTCH ADJUSTMENT

The only clutch adjustment is to restore the free play reduced by clutch wear.

### FREE PLAY ADJUSTMENT

1. Inspect the condition of the rubber pedal stop (see **Figures 1, 2, 3, or 4,** as appropriate). Replace stop if worn or damaged.
2. On 3-speed, 6-cylinder models, disconnect interlock clutch rod at transmission (see procedure below).
3. Adjust linkage by turning self-locking nut (see **Figure 5, 6, or 7,** as appropriate) to provide 5/32 in. free movement at outer end of fork. This should provide the specified 1-in. pedal free play.
4. On 3-speed, 6-cylinder models, reconnect the interlock clutch rod to transmission pawl.

### GEARSHIFT INTERLOCK ROD REMOVAL, REPLACEMENT, AND ADJUSTMENT

1. Remove interlock (clutch) rod from swivel by loosening screw (see **Figure 8**). Disconnect swivel from interlock pawl.
2. Adjust clutch pedal free play, using the procedure above.
3. Place FIRST-REVERSE transmission lever in neutral (middle) detent. In this position the interlock pawl will enter the slot in the FIRST-REVERSE lever.
4. Loosen clamp bolt and slide swivel on clutch rod to enter pawl. Make sure washers are in place as shown in Figure 8, then install clip. Hold pawl forward and tighten swivel clamp bolt to 125 in.-lb.

> NOTE: *Verify that clutch pedal is in the full returned position during this adjustment.*

> CAUTION
> *Do not pull clutch rod rearward to engage swivel in pawl.*

5. Check clutch action while shifting from neutral to first and neutral to reverse. Disengage clutch while shifting and engage clutch when in gear. Clutch action should be normal.
6. Disengage clutch and shift halfway into either first or reverse. Interlock should hold clutch pedal to within 1 or 2 inches from floor.

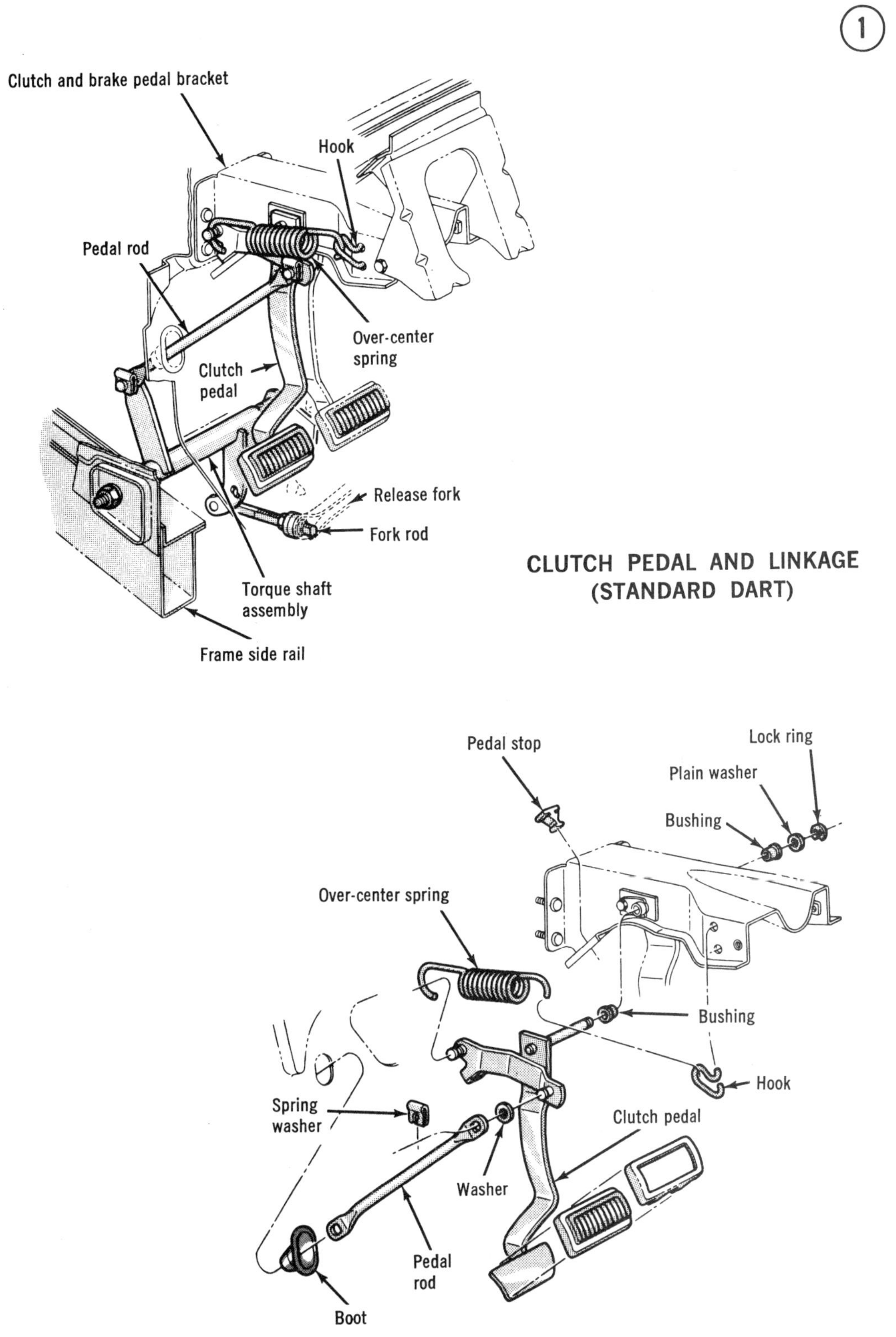

# CLUTCH ADJUSTMENT

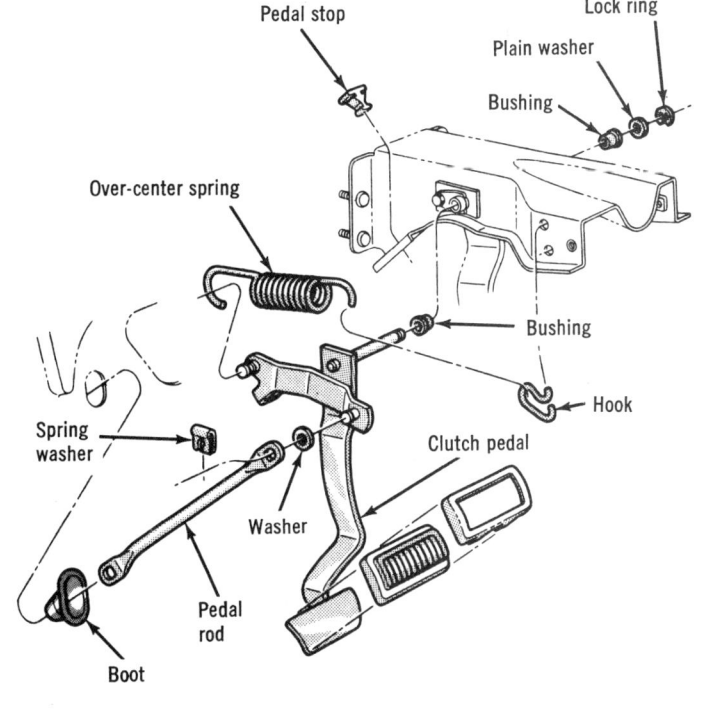

CLUTCH PEDAL AND LINKAGE (STANDARD DART)

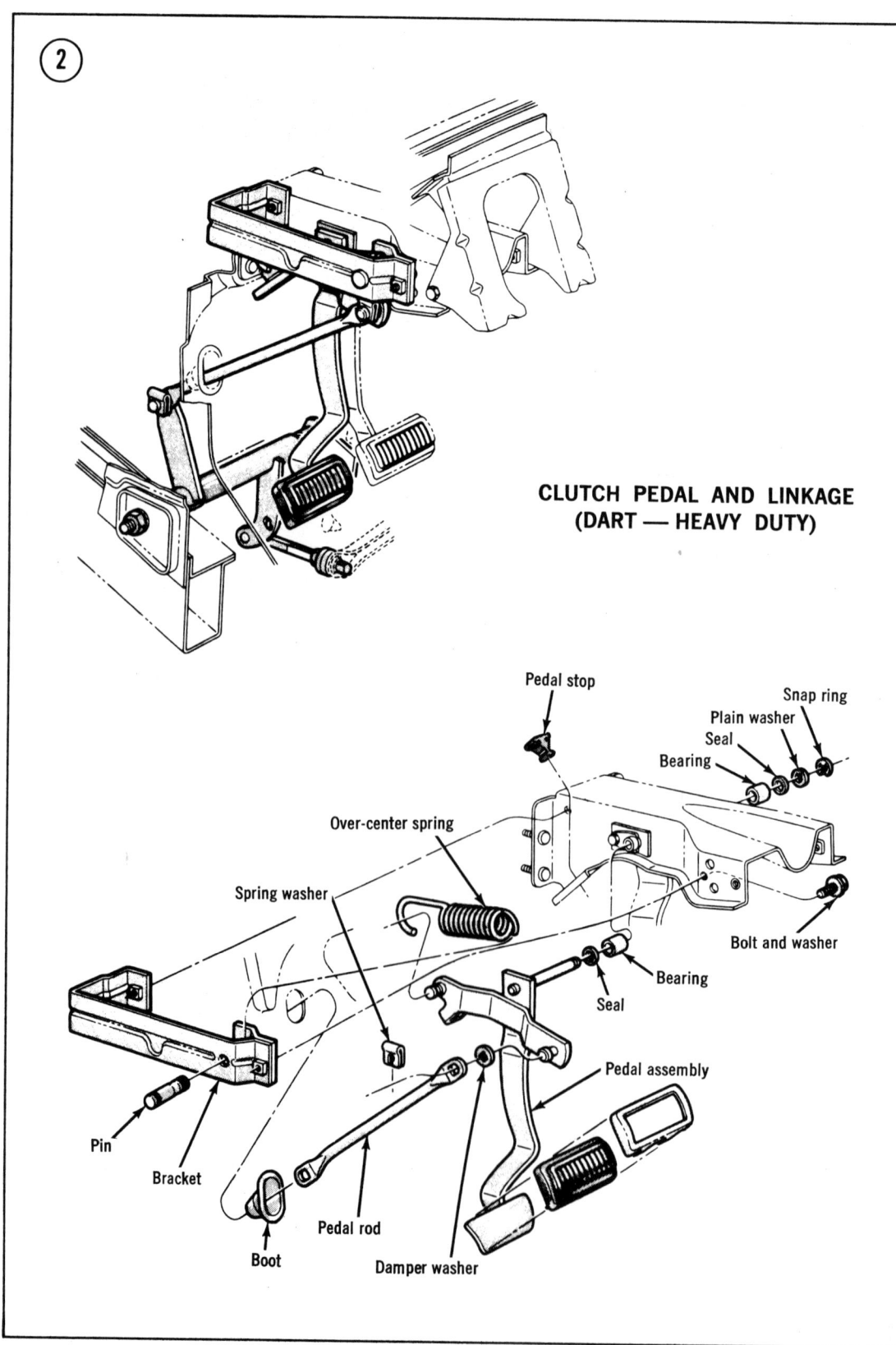

② CLUTCH PEDAL AND LINKAGE (DART — HEAVY DUTY)

# CLUTCH ADJUSTMENT

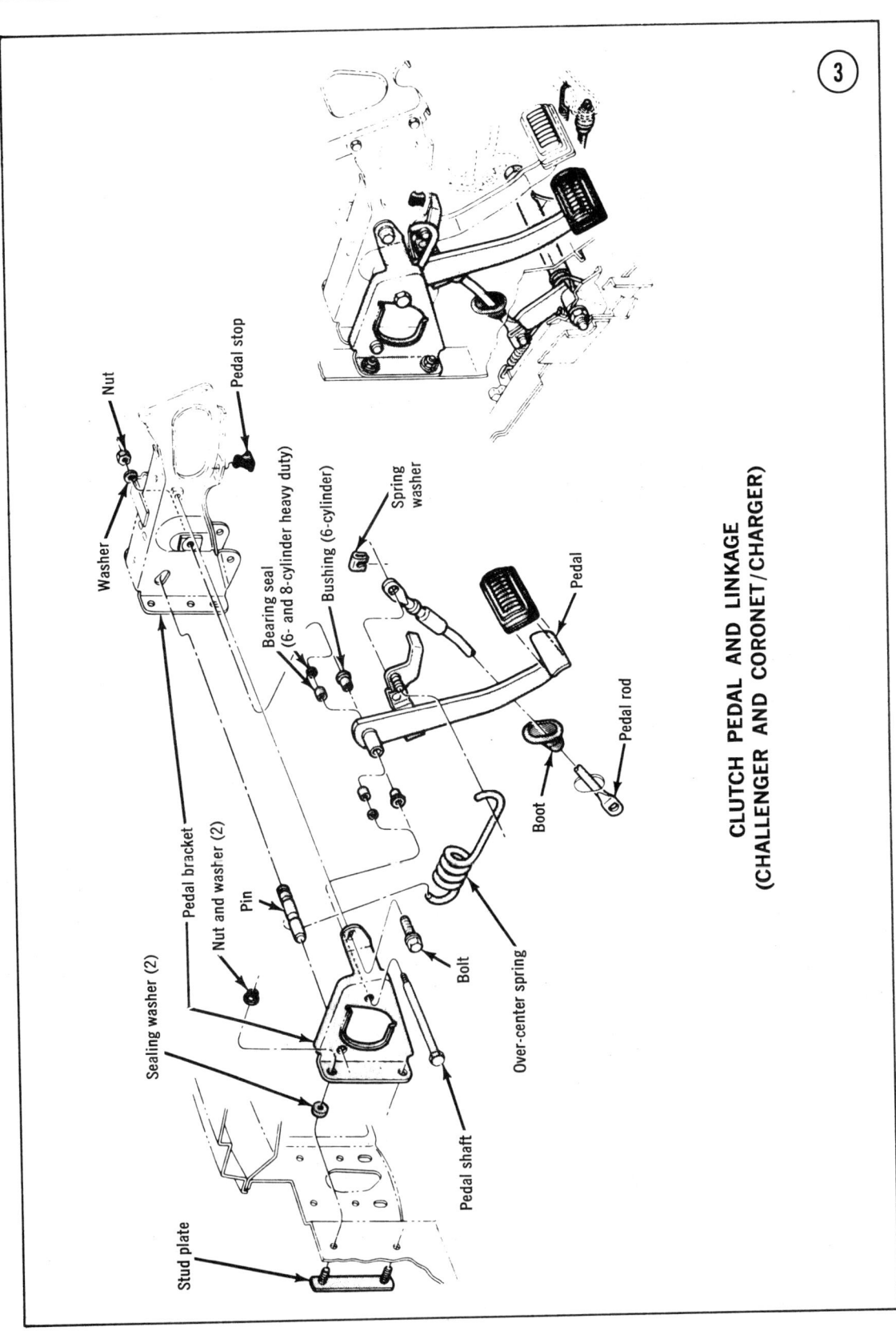

CLUTCH PEDAL AND LINKAGE
(CHALLENGER AND CORONET/CHARGER)

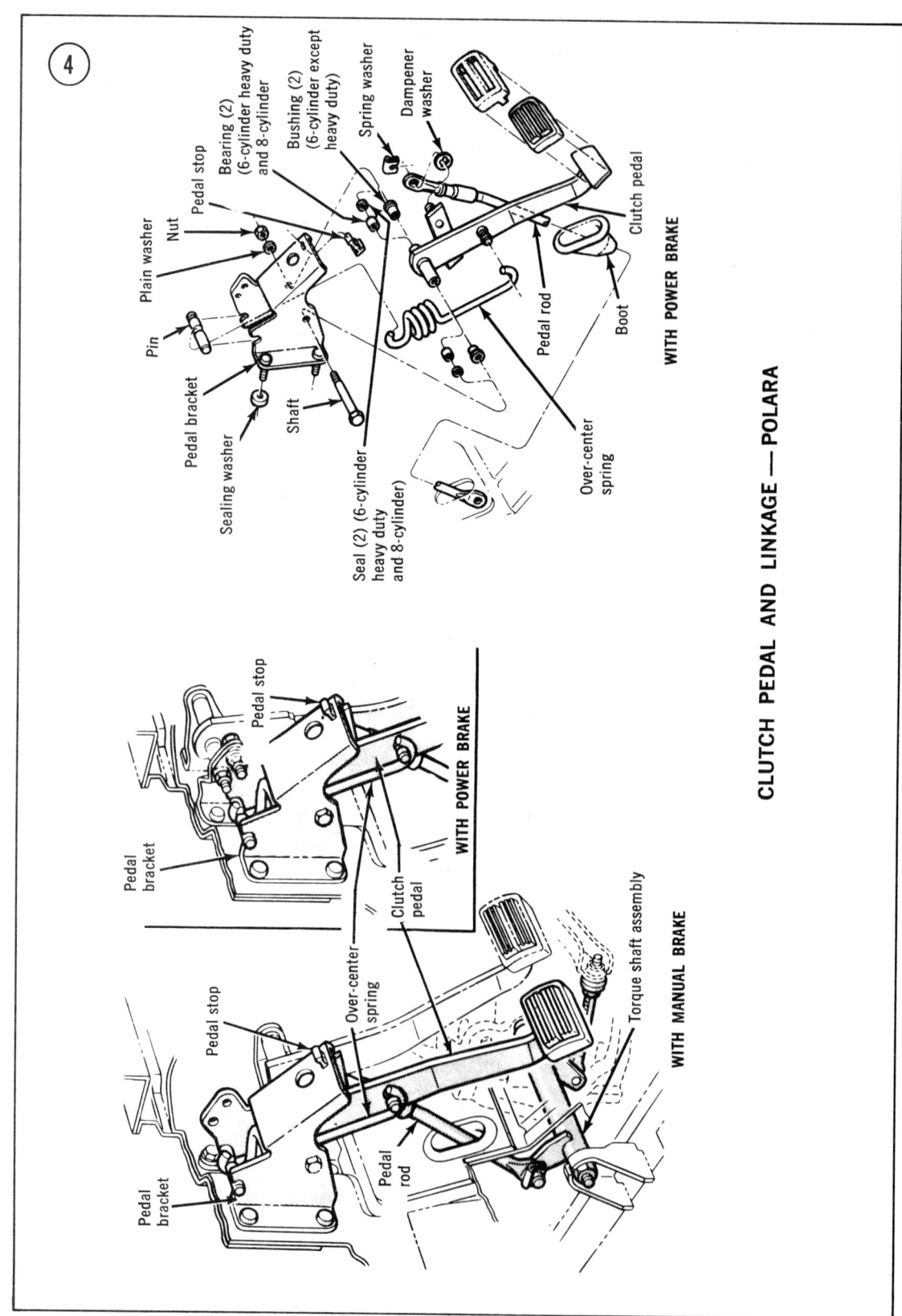

# CLUTCH ADJUSTMENT

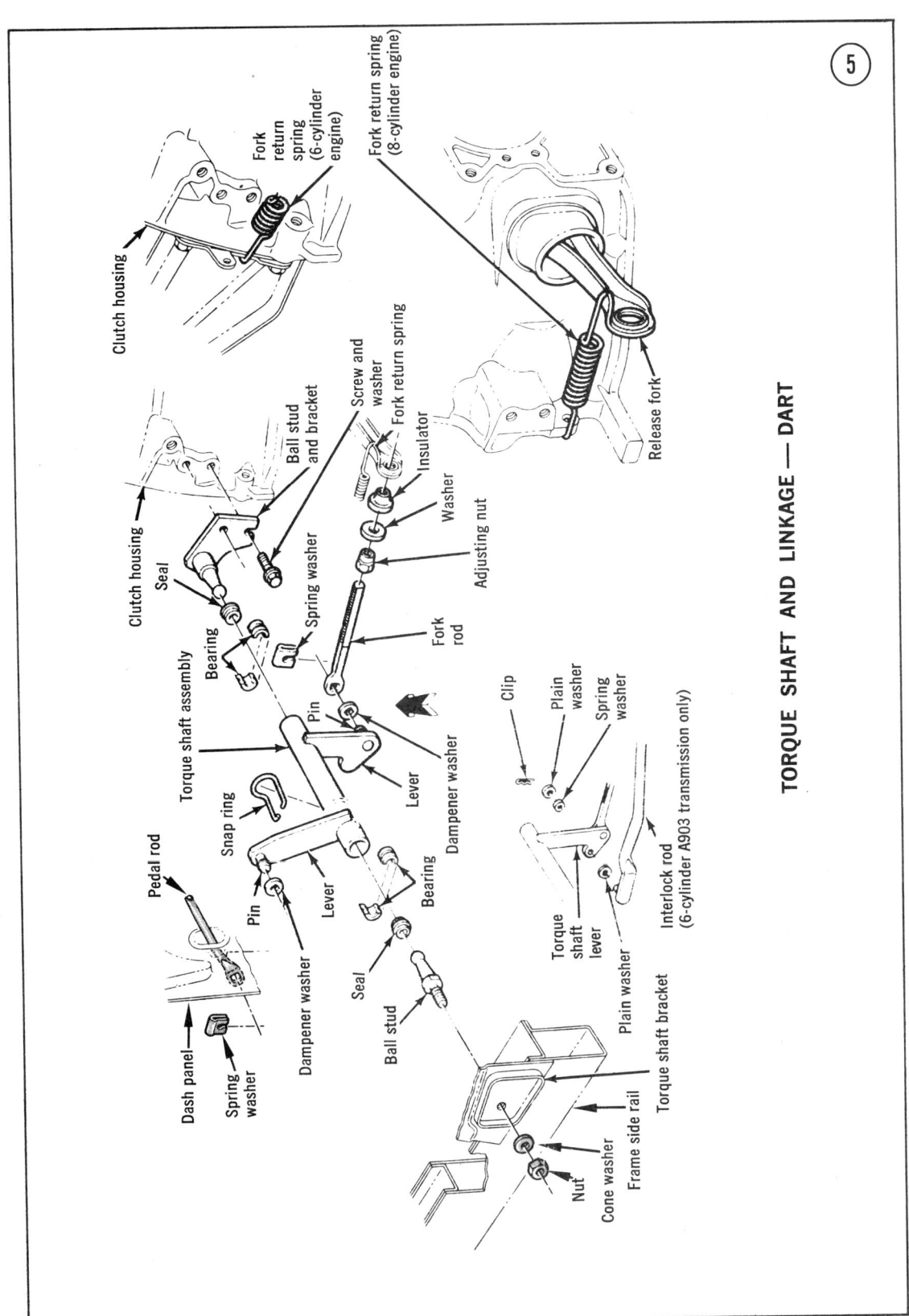

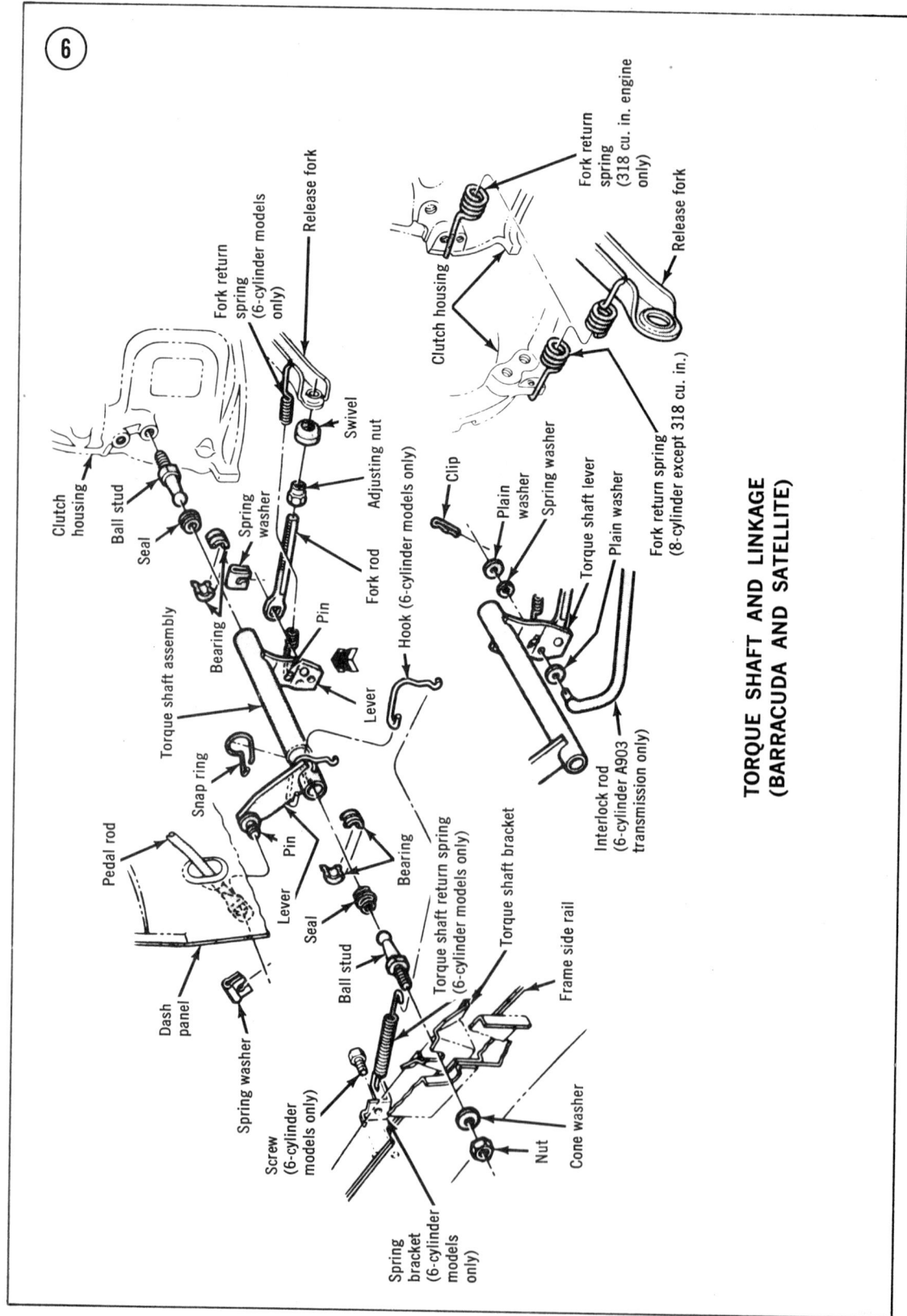

6. TORQUE SHAFT AND LINKAGE (BARRACUDA AND SATELLITE)

# CLUTCH ADJUSTMENT

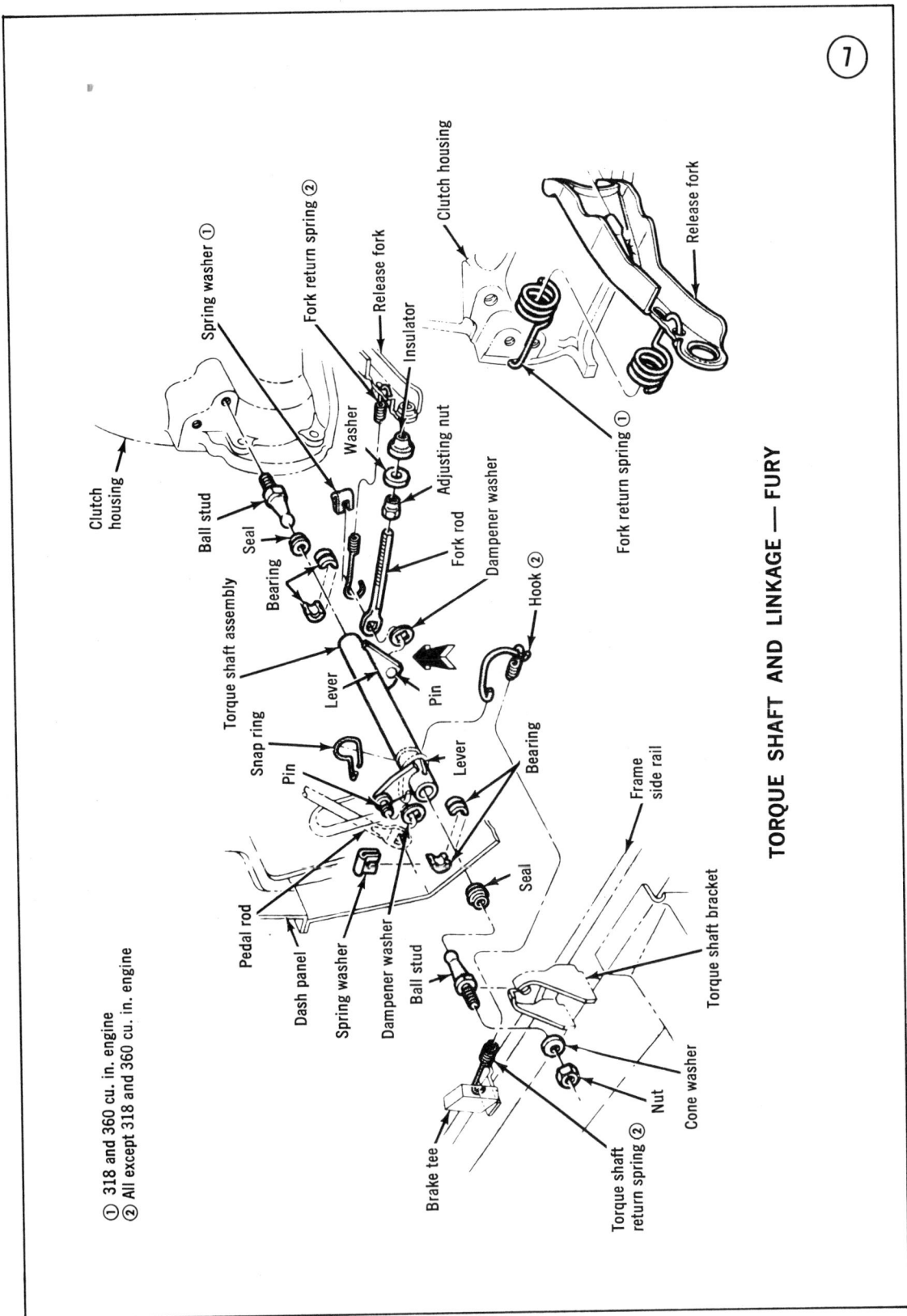

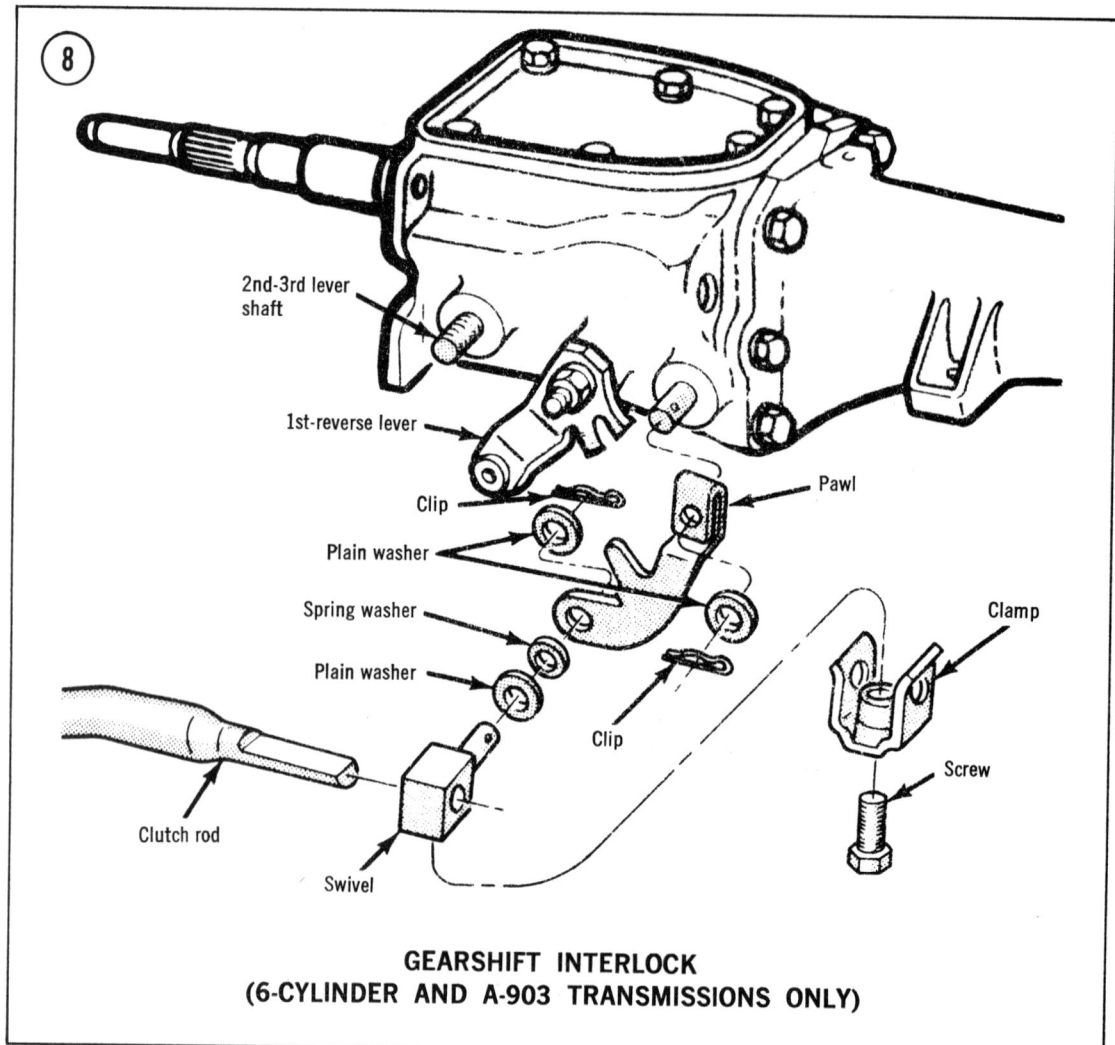

**GEARSHIFT INTERLOCK
(6-CYLINDER AND A-903 TRANSMISSIONS ONLY)**

# CHAPTER TEN

# SHOCK ABSORBERS

The shock absorbers used on all models are non-repairable and non-adjustable. Shock absorber service is limited to removal and installation. Although several types of shock absorbers are used on the various Dodge models, the removal and installation procedures are the same for all types.

## FRONT SHOCK ABSORBER REMOVAL

1. Remove nut and retainer or washer from upper end of shock absorber piston rod (**Figures 1, 2, 3, and 4**).
2. Raise vehicle and remove front wheels.
3. Remove nut from lower shock absorber attachment bolt.
4. Remove bolt from shock absorber eye and lower control arm mounting bracket.

> NOTE: *On late Polara and Monaco models (1972 and later), loosen and remove nut, retainer, and bushing from lower control arm.*

5. Compress shock absorber completely (by pushing upward). Remove from vehicle by pulling down and out of upper mounting bushing.

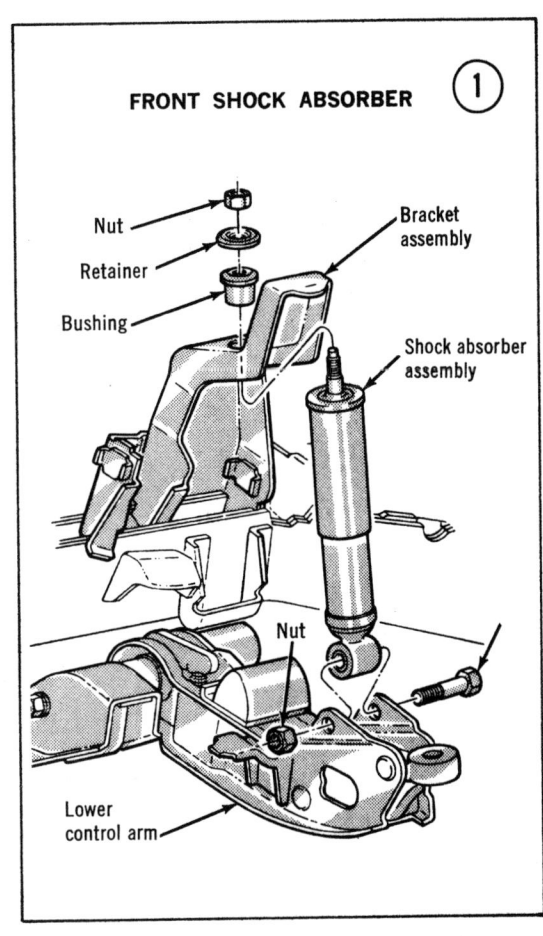

FRONT SHOCK ABSORBER

**106**  CHAPTER TEN

**FRONT SHOCK ABSORBER**

② Nut, Retainer, Bushing, Torsion bar, Bolt, Arm assembly, Retainer, Shock absorber, Nut

**FRONT SHOCK ABSORBER**

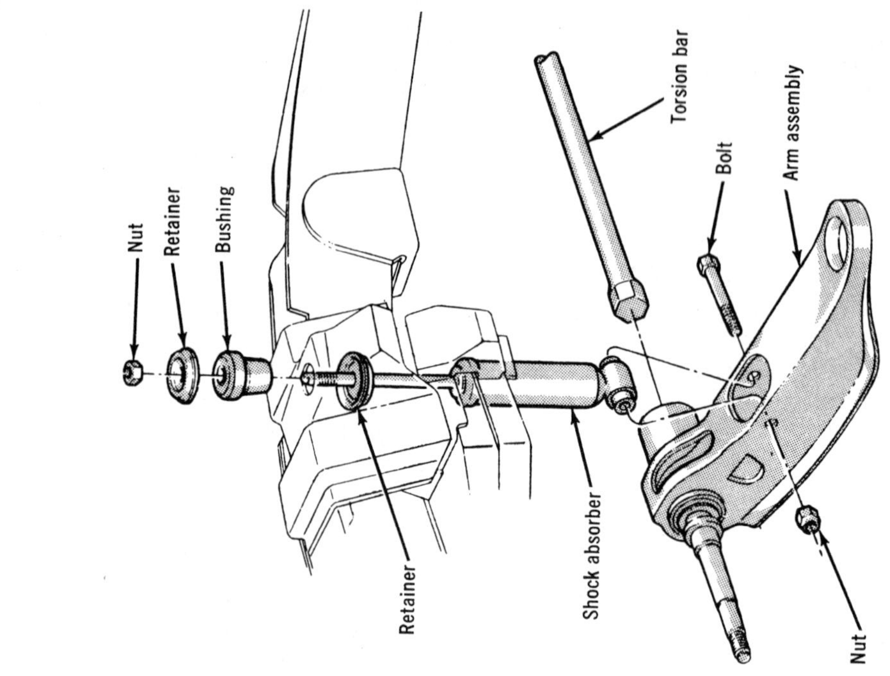

③ Nut, Bushing, Retainer, Frame assembly, Retainer, Shock absorber assembly, Bushing, Lower control arm, Retainer, Bushing, Nut

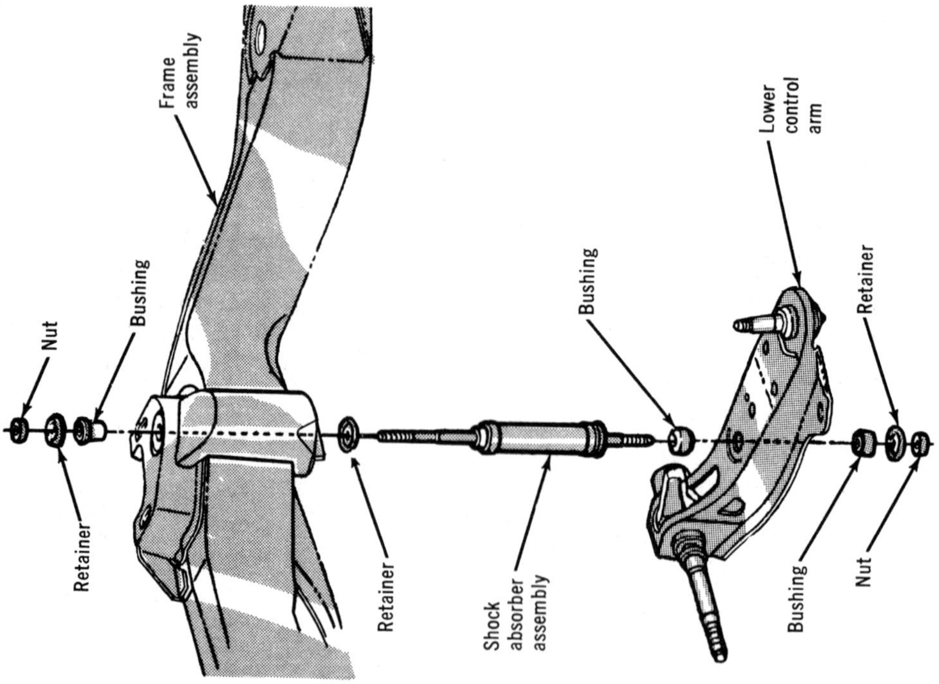

# SHOCK ABSORBERS

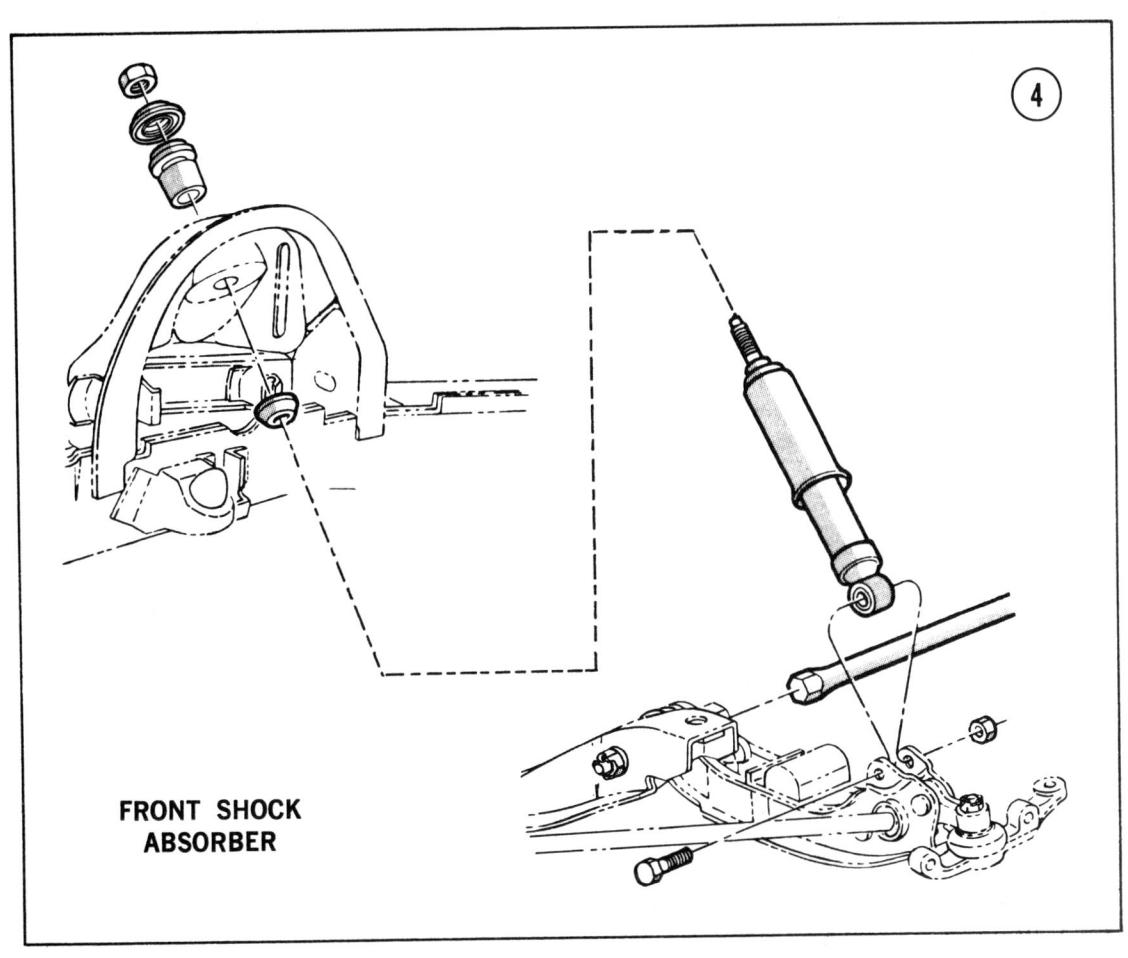

**FRONT SHOCK ABSORBER**

## REAR SHOCK ABSORBER REMOVAL

1. Raise vehicle and use floor stands under axle assembly to remove load from shock absorber. Refer to **Figures 5, 6, and 7**.

2. Remove nut and retainer holding shock absorber to spring plate mounting stud.

3. Remove shock absorber from stud. Disconnect air line, if so equipped.

4. Remove nut and bolt from upper mounting and remove shock absorber.

> NOTE: *Before installing any shock absorber, hold in vertical position and fully extend it. Invert unit and slowly compress it. Do not extend shock absorber while it is inverted. Repeat several times in order to expel all air trapped in the cylinder.*

## FRONT SHOCK ABSORBER INSTALLATION

1. Remove steel sleeve from upper rubber bushing and dip bushing in water (not oil). Start bushing into hole of upper mounting bracket, using a twisting motion. Tap bushing into position with a hammer and reinstall steel sleeve.

2. Expel air (see NOTE above) and compress shock absorber to its shortest length. Insert rod through upper bushing and install retainer and nut. Torque to 25 ft.-lb. (3.46 mkg).

> NOTE: *Concave side of retainer goes next to rubber bushing.*

3. Align lower eye with mounting bracket holes and install shock absorber and tighten nut. Lower vehicle and, with full weight on the wheels, torque nut to 50 ft.-lb. (6.9 mkg) and 35 ft.-lb. (4.84 mkg) on installation shown in Figure 3.

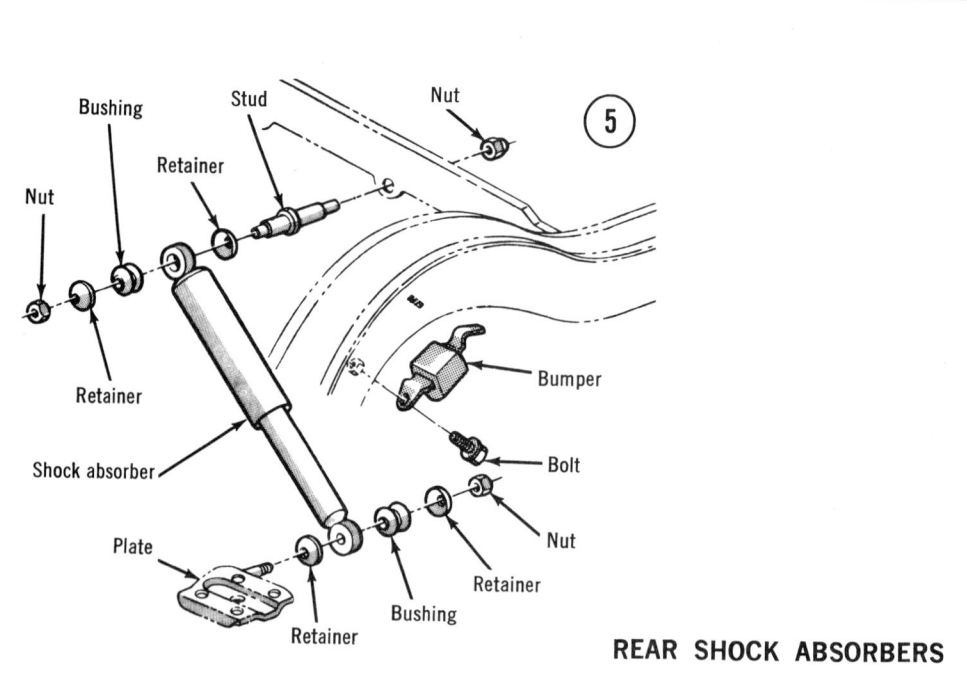

**REAR SHOCK ABSORBERS**

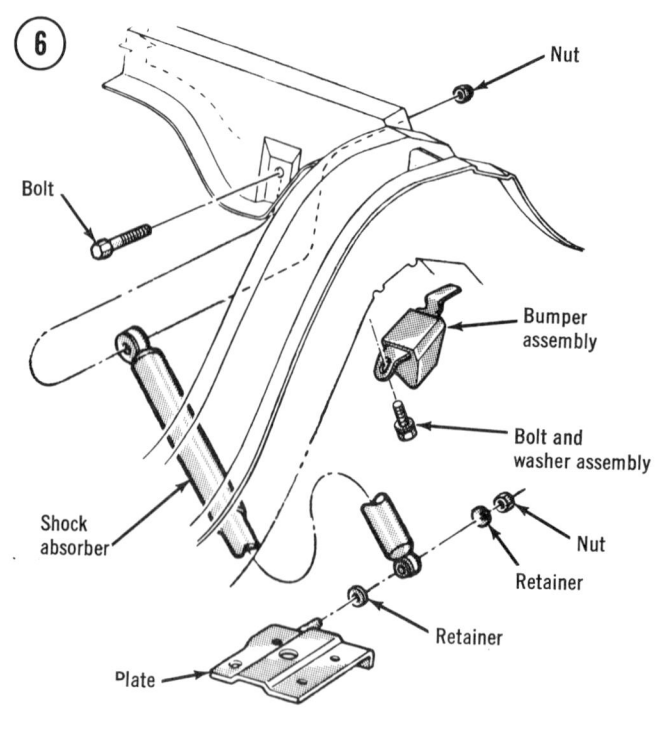

# SHOCK ABSORBERS

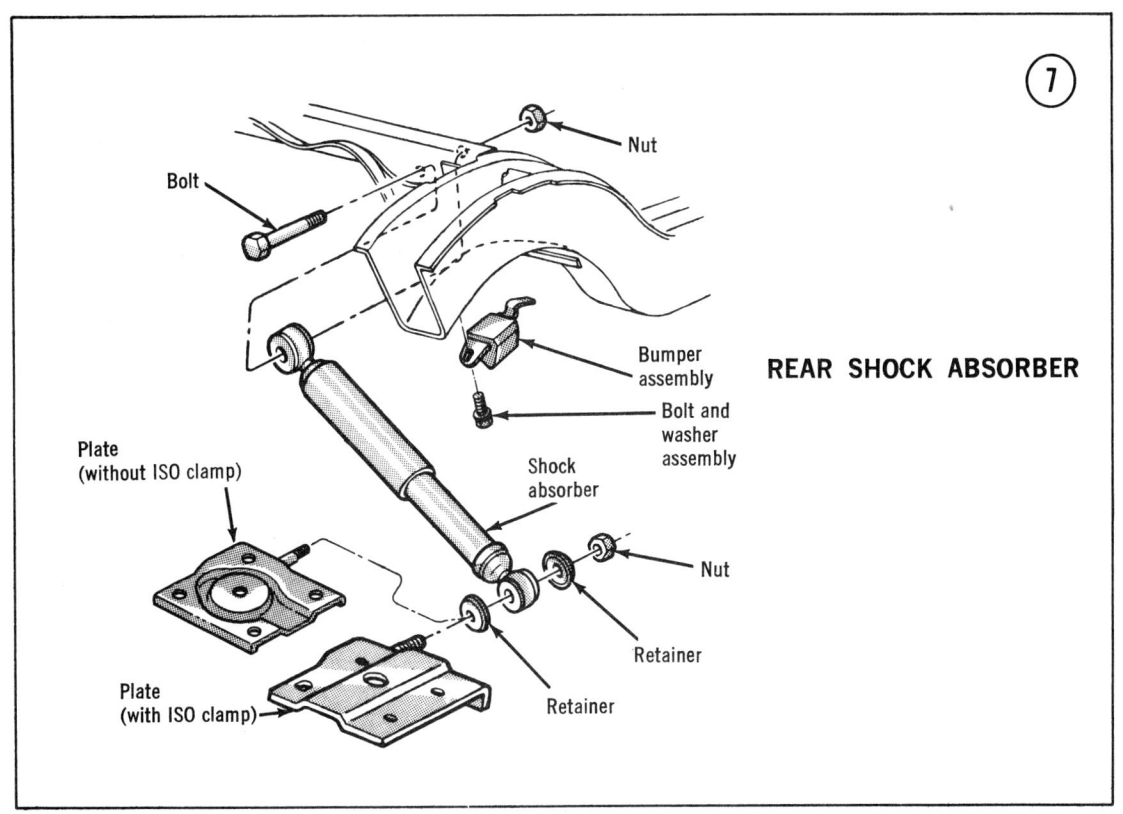

**REAR SHOCK ABSORBER**

## REAR SHOCK ABSORBER INSTALLATION

1. Align upper eye of shock absorber with mounting holes in crossmember and install bolt and nut. Do not fully tighten at this time. In installation shown in Figure 5, position washer on mounting stud and install shock absorber, then install cupped washer and nut.

2. Place washer on spring mounting plate stud and install shock absorber on stud. Install remaining cupped washer and nut. Do not fully tighten at this time. Reconnect air line if so equipped.

3. Lower vehicle so full weight is on wheels. Torque upper nut to 70 ft.-lb. (9.68 mkg) and to 50 ft.-lb. (6.9 mkg) on installation in Figure 5. Torque lower nut to 50 ft.-lb. (6.9 mkg).

# CHAPTER ELEVEN

# EMISSION CONTROL SYSTEMS

All models manufactured during the period covered by this book have some form of emission control. Before 1970, emission control was limited to positive crankcase ventilation systems. Starting in 1970, new systems have been added each year. A summary of the major systems is given in **Table 1**.

## SYSTEM DESCRIPTIONS AND SERVICE

### Positive Crankcase Ventilation System

This system (**Figure 1**) consists of a crankcase ventilation valve (PCV valve), mounted on a cylinder head cover, connected by a hose to the base of the carburetor. Another hose connects the carburetor air cleaner to the closed crankcase inlet filter (or filler cap in earlier models). The system is operated by manifold vacuum. Air is drawn into the crankcase via the carburetor air filter-to-crankcase inlet air cleaner hose. The air circulates through the cylinder head covers and crankcase and collects fumes. The fume-laden air exits through the PCV valve and the passage into the carburetor body and is mixed with the air/fuel mixture being drawn into the cylinders. Thus the fumes are burned and expelled through the exhaust system.

Service to the system consists of inspection and replacement of the PCV valve at the intervals given in Table 1, Chapter Three. Do not clean PCV valve; replace it.

### Manifold Heat Control Valve

This thermostatically controlled valve, located in the exhaust manifold system, channels exhaust gases through a "heat chamber" adjacent to the fuel intake system (carburetor or intake manifold) during engine warm-up. This heat helps in the vaporization of the fuel mixture when the engine is cold. As the engine becomes warm, the valve directs the exhaust gases directly into the exhaust pipe.

Service to the manifold heat control valve consists of cleaning and lubrication of the valve shaft bearings (**Figure 2**, typical) with a solvent (not oil) at the intervals given in Table 1, Chapter Three.

### Air Injection System (Air Pump)

This system injects a controlled amount of air into the exhaust system, causing the gases to oxidize. This reduces the amount of carbon monoxide in the exhaust. The system consists of an air pump, a diverter valve, a check valve, injection tubes, and connecting hoses (**Figure 3**).

# EMISSION CONTROL SYSTEMS

**Table 1  EMISSION CONTROL SYSTEMS**

| System | Through 1969 | 1970 | 1971 | 1972 | 1973 | 1974 | 1975 | 1976 |
|---|---|---|---|---|---|---|---|---|
| Positive crankcase ventilation | X | X | X | X | X | X | X | X |
| Manifold heat control valve | X | X | X | X | X | X | X | X |
| Air injection system (air pump) | | | | X | X | X | X | X |
| Vapor saver system | | X | X | X | X | X | X | X |
| Exhaust gas recirculation | | | | X | X | X | X | X |
| Electric assist choke | | | | | X | X | X | X |
| Orifice spark advance control | | | | | X | X | X | X |
| Coolant controlled idle enrichment | | | | | | | X | X |
| Catalytic converter | | | | | | | X | X |
| EGR maintenance reminder | | | | | | | X | X |

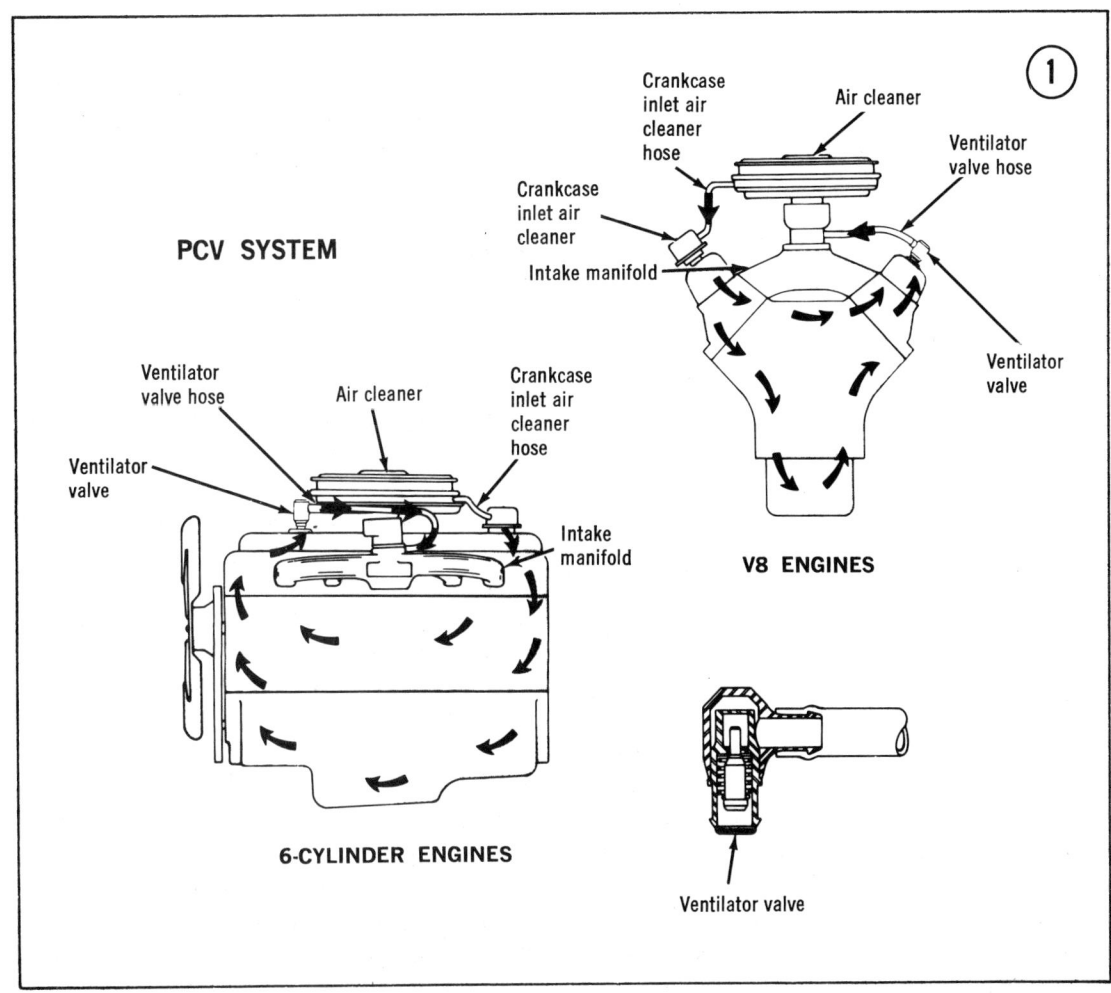

# CHAPTER ELEVEN

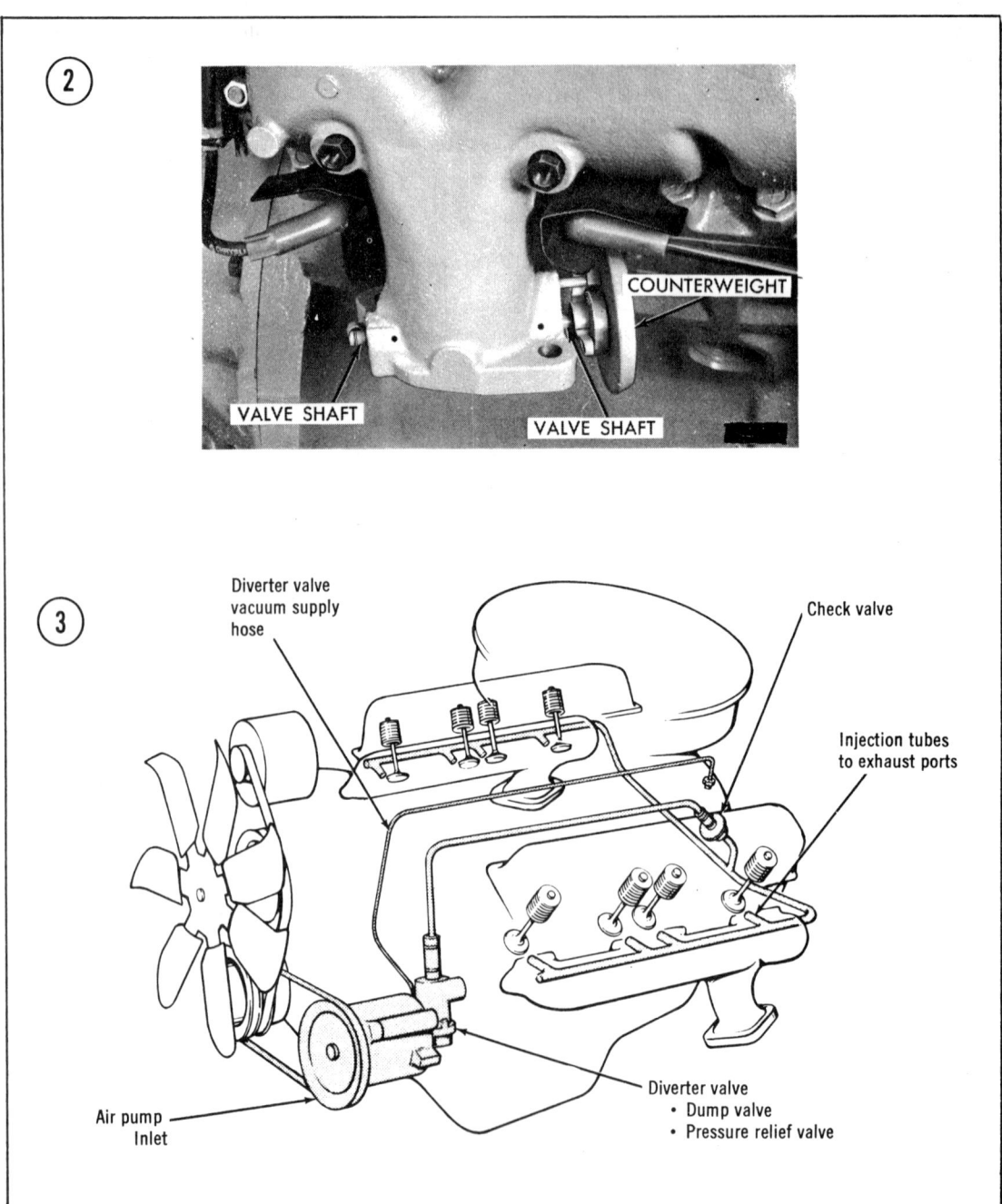

The diverter valve also serves as a pressure relief valve.

Service is limited to checking the drive belt annually for proper tension (see *Accessory Drive Belts,* Chapter Seven) and adjusting as required and replacing damaged centrifugal filter fans. The pump is non-repairable, and must be replaced if damaged.

*Air Pump Replacement*

1. Disconnect air and vacuum hoses from diverter valve.

2. Loosen attachment bolts and remove belt. Remove bolts.

3. Remove pump from vehicle and remove diverter valve, brackets, and pulley from pump.

# EMISSION CONTROL SYSTEMS

4. Reverse the above steps to install pump.

5. Adjust belt tension (refer to *Accessory Drive Belts,* Chapter Seven).

## Filter Fan Replacement

> NOTE: *It is almost impossible to remove a filter fan without destroying it. The fan should not be removed unless it requires replacement.*

1. Remove damaged fan by inserting needle nosed pliers between fins and breaking fan from hub. Do not pry off with screwdriver. Take care to prevent fragments from entering pump (**Figure 4**).

2. Place new fan on shaft, then use pulley and bolts as tool to press fan into place (**Figure 5**). Apply torque evenly and make certain outer edge of fan enters housing.

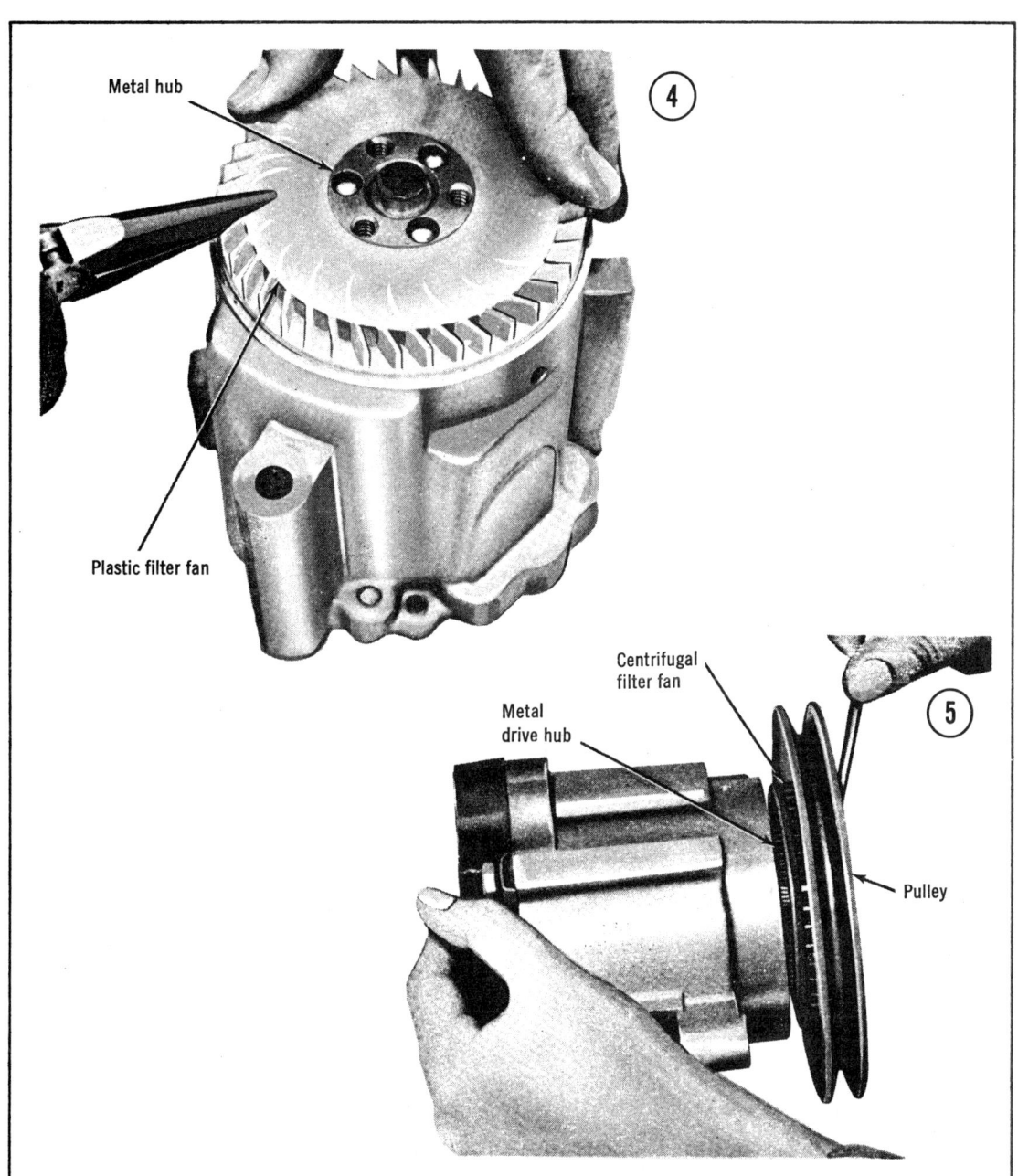

#### CAUTION
*Do not install fan by hammering or pressing on it, as damage will result.*

NOTE: *Slight interference between fan and pump housing bore is normal and some squealing may occur during the first 20-30 miles of operation.*

### Vapor Saver System

This system controls the emission of gasoline vapors from the carburetor and fuel tank into the atmosphere. It consists of a charcoal canister, a pressure/vacuum fuel tank cap, and connecting lines between the fuel tank, the carburetor, and the canister (**Figure 6**). When fuel evaporates in the carburetor float chamber or the fuel tank, the vapors are collected in the charcoal canister. Vapors are held until they can be drawn into the intake manifold when the engine is running.

The only service required for this system is annual replacement of the canister filter element (**Figure 7**).

### Exhaust Gas Recirculation (EGR) System

This system controls the amount of oxides of nitrogen (NOX) in engine exhaust gases by allowing a predetermined amount of hot exhaust gas to recirculate and dilute the incoming air/fuel mixture (**Figure 8**, typical).

Service consists of inspecting the system and replacing hardened or cracked hoses and faulty connectors, and checking the operation of the EGR valve, as follows.

1. Warm engine to normal operating temperature. Allow engine to idle with throttle closed, then accelerate abruptly to about 2,000 rpm (not over 3,000 rpm).

2. Observe EGR valve stem during acceleration or visible movement (change in relative position of groove on valve stem). See **Figure 9**.

3. Repeat test several times, if required, to confirm movement.

NOTE: *Valve stem movement indicates correct system functioning. If the valve stem does not move during repeated testing, have system checked to isolate problem area.*

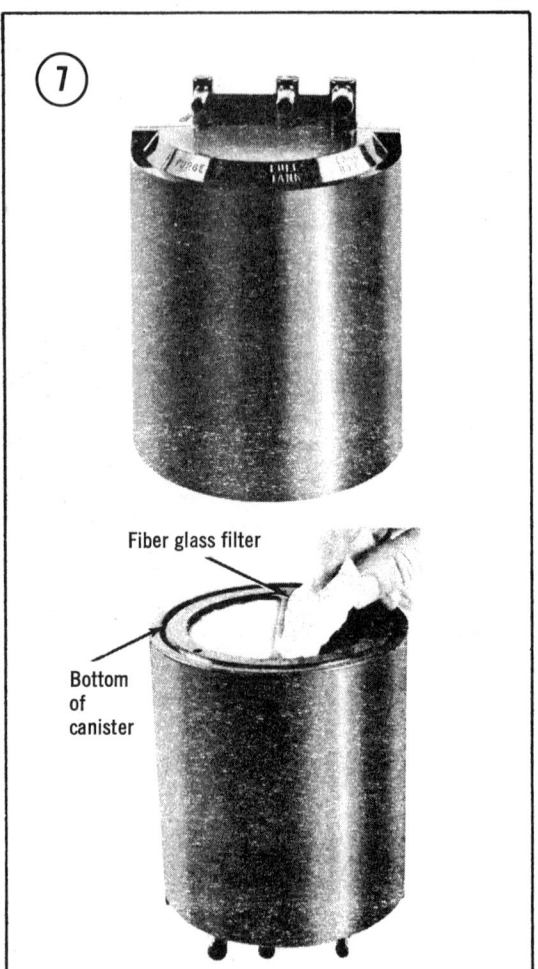

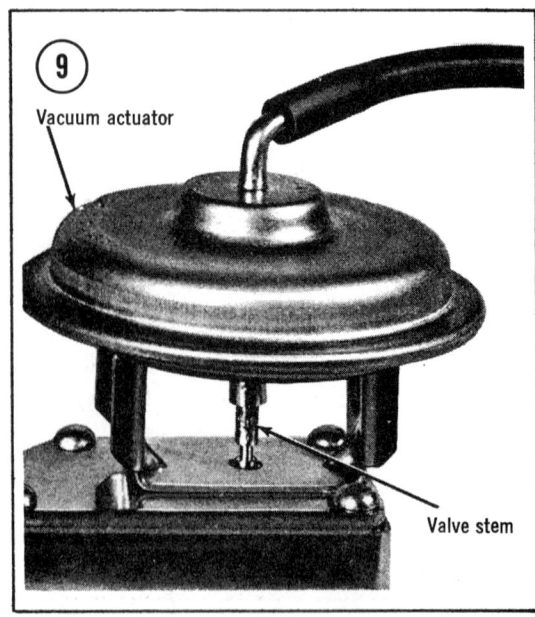

# EMISSION CONTROL SYSTEMS

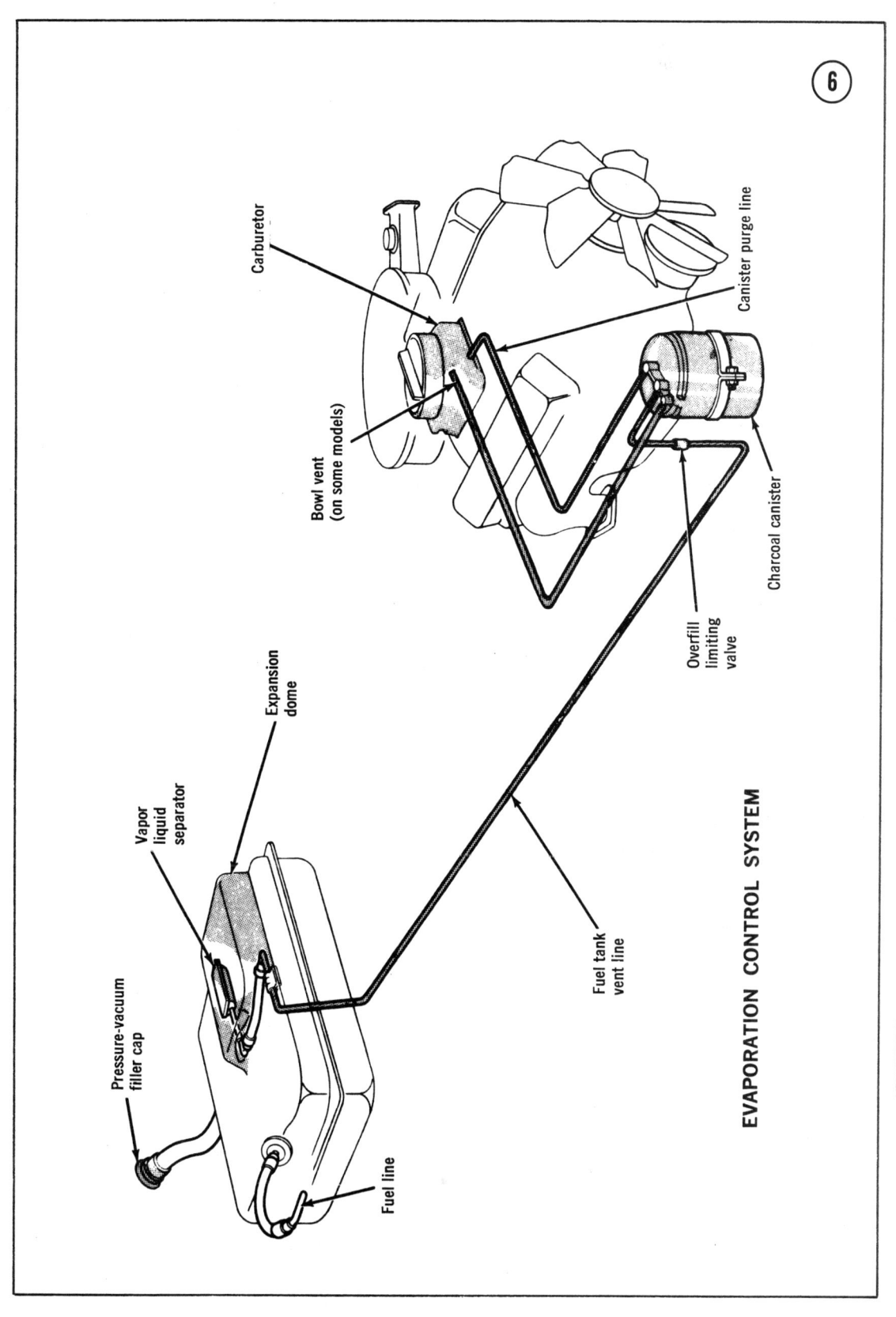

EVAPORATION CONTROL SYSTEM

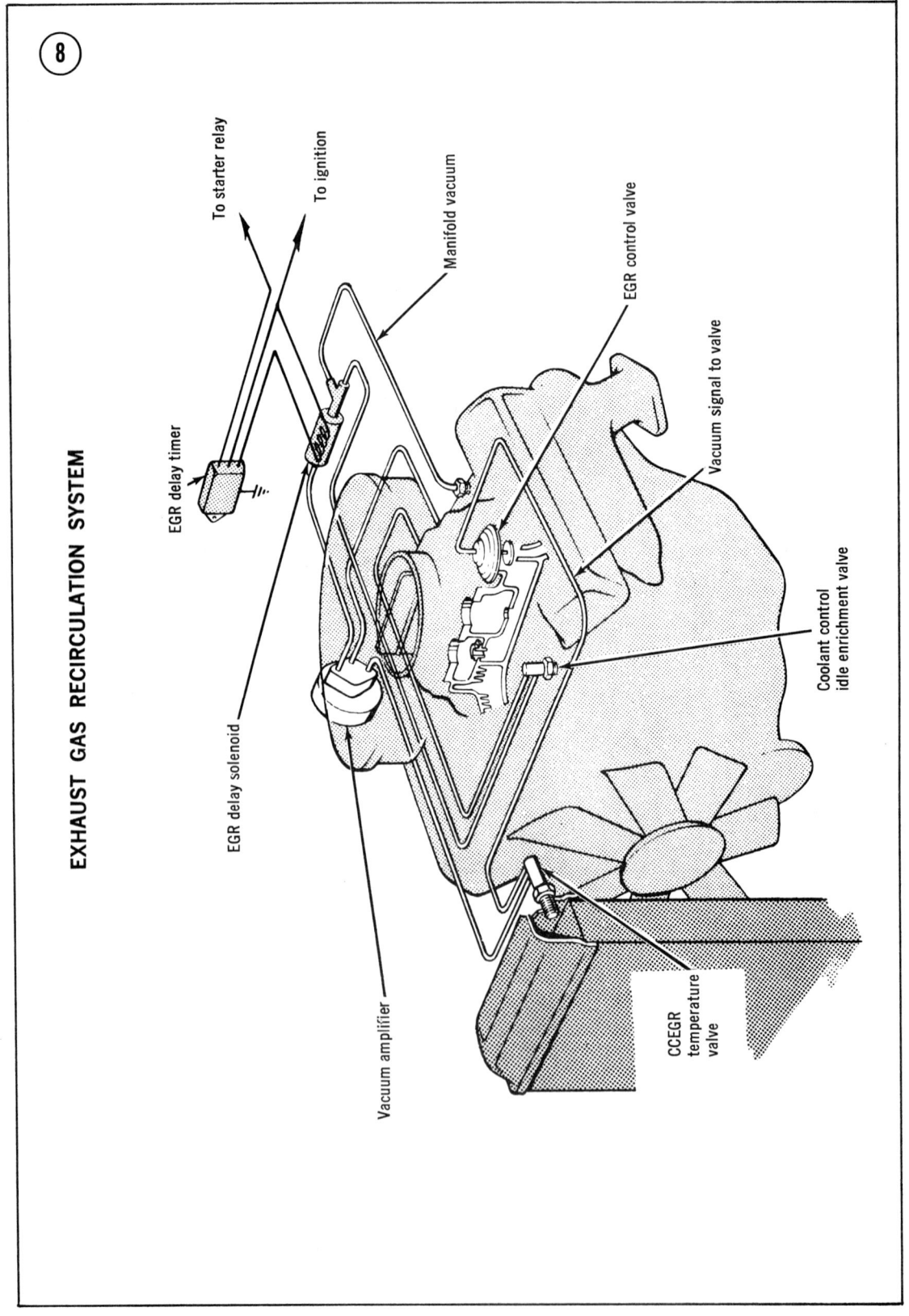

# EMISSION CONTROL SYSTEMS

## Electric Assist Choke System

This system consists essentially of an electric heating element which supplements engine heat during engine warming to reduce the duration of choke operation (**Figure 10**).

The electric assist choke system does not require periodic servicing or adjustment.

## Orifice Spark Advance Control System (OSAC)

An orifice in the OSAC valve (**Figures 11 and 12**) causes a delay in the ported vacuum to the distributor when accelerating from idle to port throttle when ambient temperature is above 60°F (15°C). During deceleration the valve allows instantaneous application of vacuum to the distributor. This control of spark advance aids in the control of oxides of nitrogen in the exhaust.

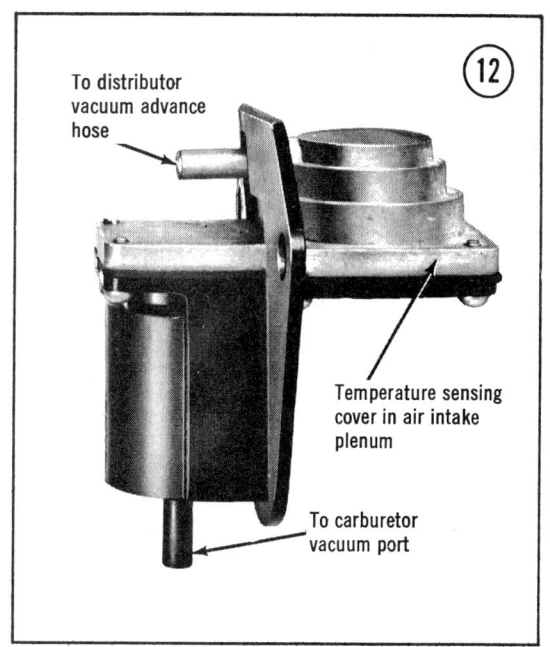

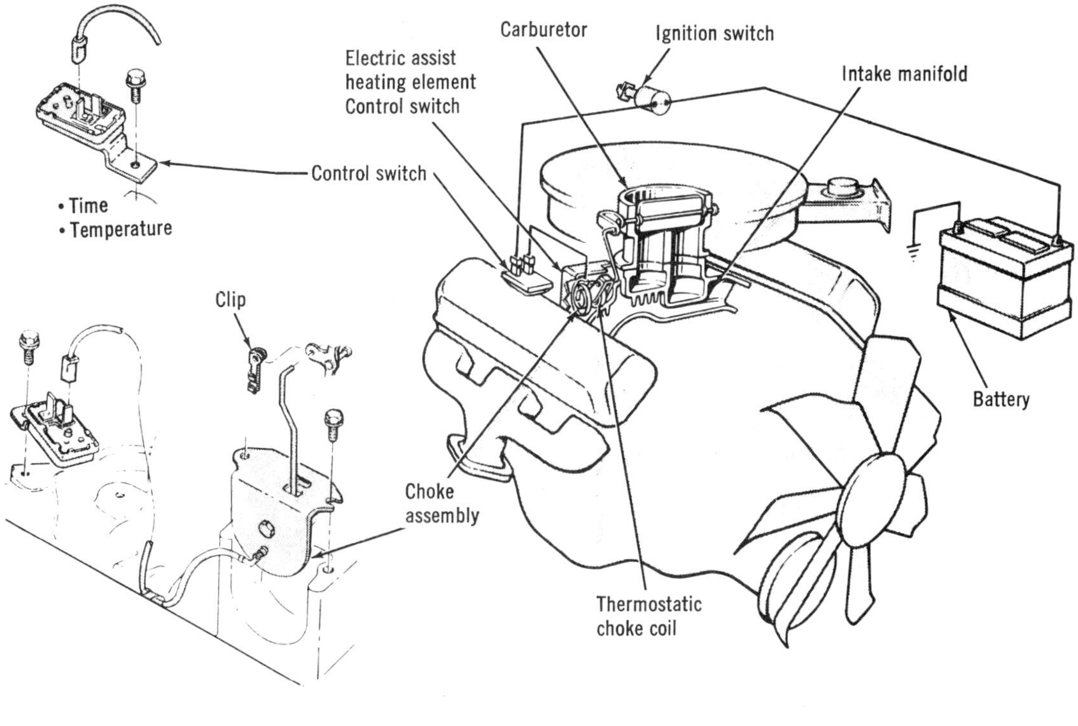

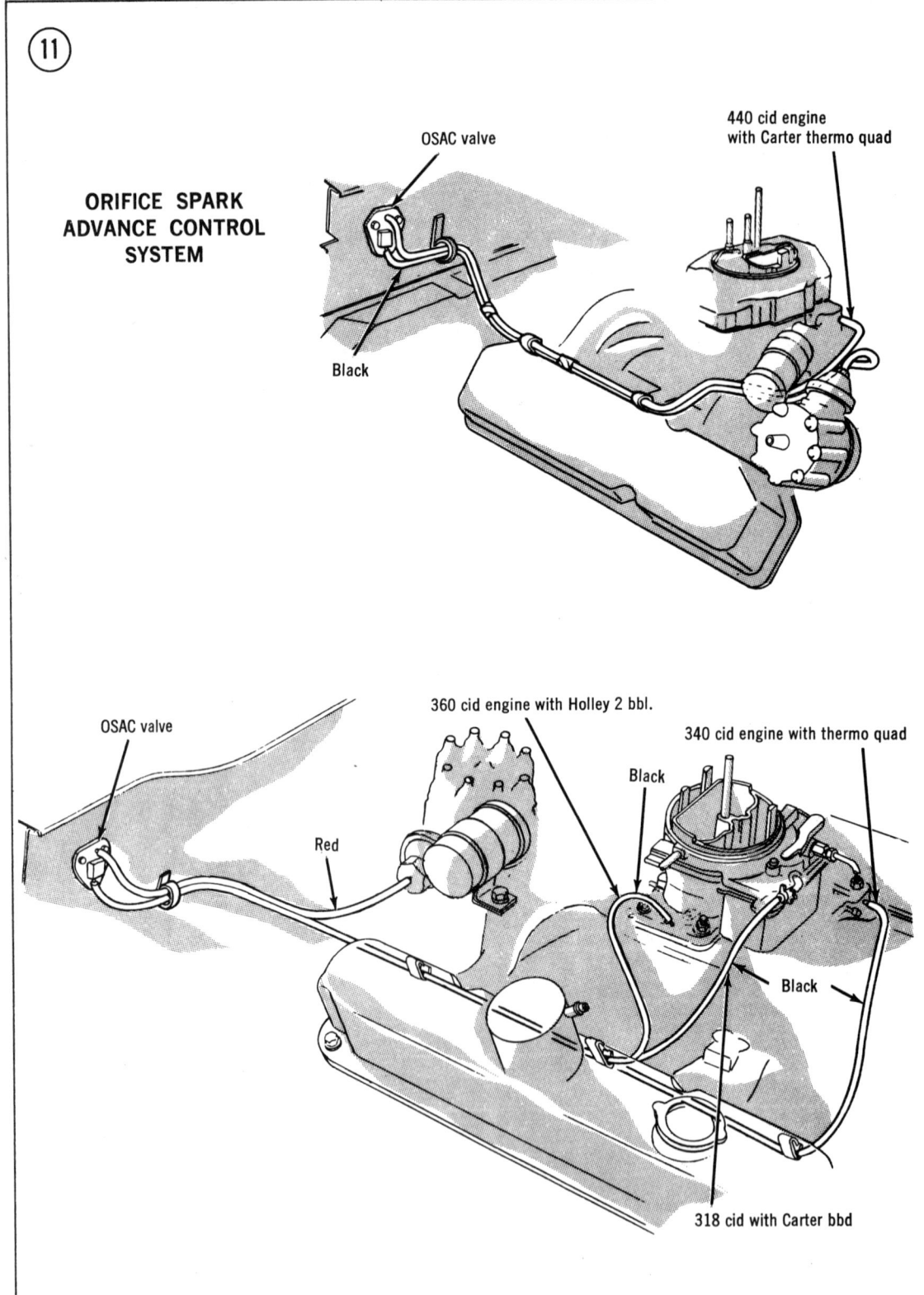

# EMISSION CONTROL SYSTEMS

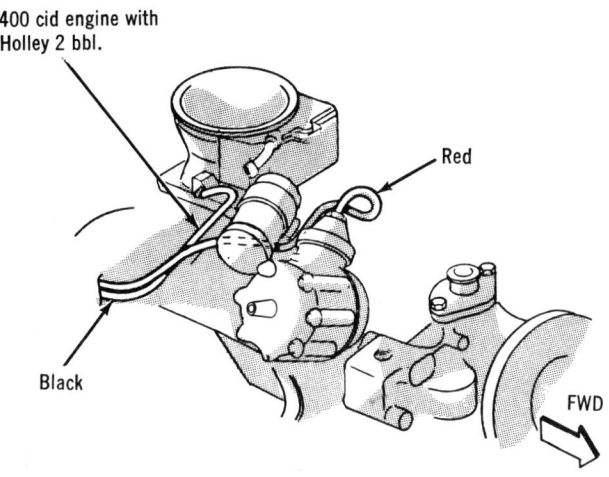

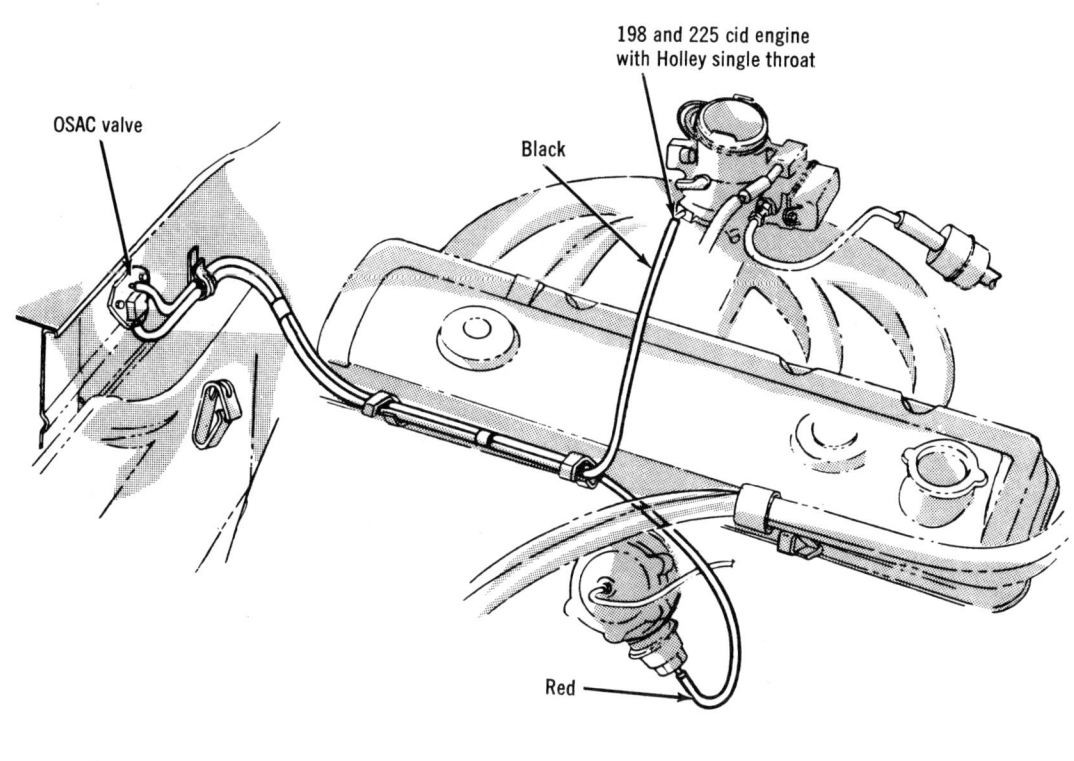

The OSAC valve does not require periodic service, and is non-repairable. To check valve operation, operate engine in NEUTRAL at 2,000 rpm and disconnect hose leading to distributor rom valve. Connect a vacuum gauge to valve fitting. If a very gradual increase in vacuum over a period of about 15 seconds is noted, the valve is operating properly (the time will vary with different engines). If vacuum pops up immediately, or no vacuum is observed, replace valve.

NOTE: *This test should be conducted when outside temperature is about 68°F (20C°).*

### Coolant Controlled Idle Enrichment System

This is a time delay mechanism in the EGR system (discussed above) which is dependent upon a thermostatic valve in the engine cooling system.

### Catalytic Converter

The catalytic converter is used to oxidize hydrocarbons and carbon monoxide in engine exhaust. The converter which is located in the exhaust system (**Figure 13**), consists of a stainless steel shell containing 2 ceramic mono-

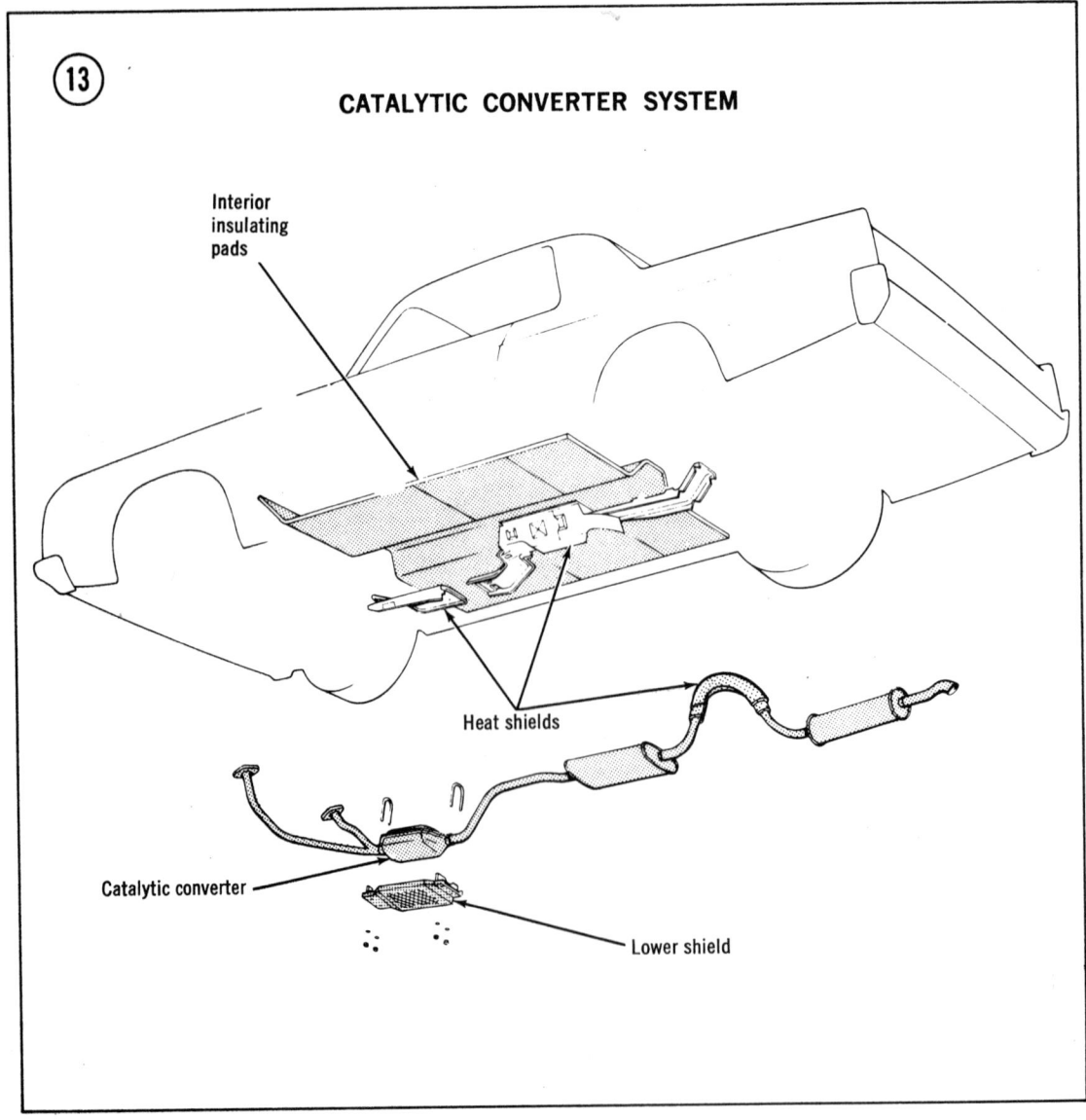

# EMISSION CONTROL SYSTEMS

lithic elements coated with a catalytic agent (palladium and platinum). See **Figure 14**. Combustion results when exhaust gases pass over the catalyst, resulting in temperatures up to 1,600°F (880°C). Special heat shields are used to prevent this heat from entering the passenger compartment (Figure 13). Cars equipped with catalytic converters must use lead-free gasoline, as lead destroys the effectiveness of the catalyst.

Cars equipped with the catalytic converter have a system to protect the catalyst from overheating (**Figure 15**). Check the throttle solenoid for operation, with engine not running, by disconnecting wire and holding throttle valve open (**Figure 16**). Apply 12 volts directly to solenoid wire. Solenoid stem should extend and remain extended. If not, replace the unit. Solenoid stem should retract when voltage is removed.

## EGR Maintenance Reminder

The EGR maintenance reminder consists of an inline switch in the speedometer cable system which actuates a warning light on the instrument panel after each 15,000 miles as a service reminder. The switch must be reset to turn off the warning light and to start a new 15,000-mile cycle. The switch is reset with a screwdriver.

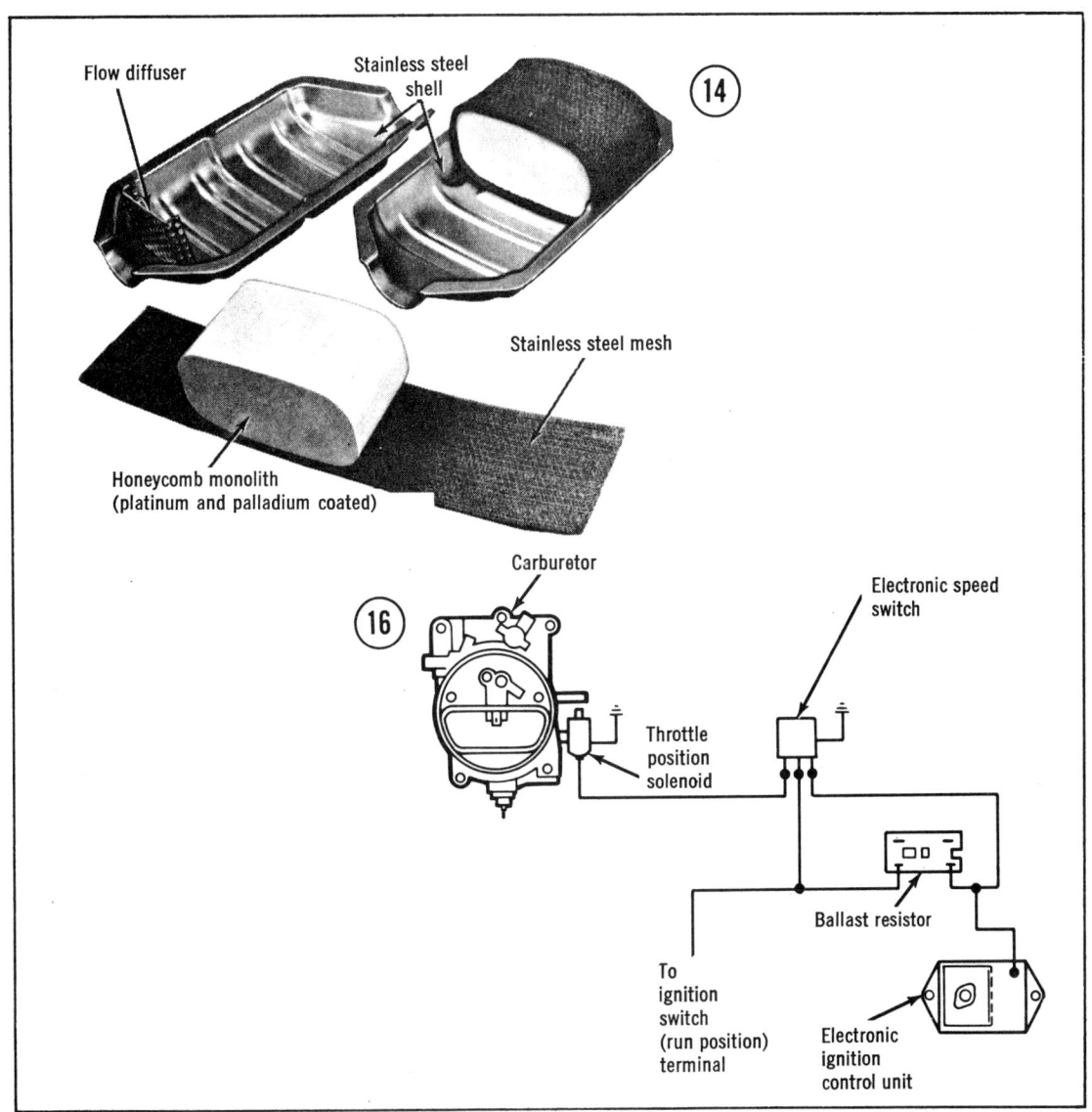

CHAPTER ELEVEN

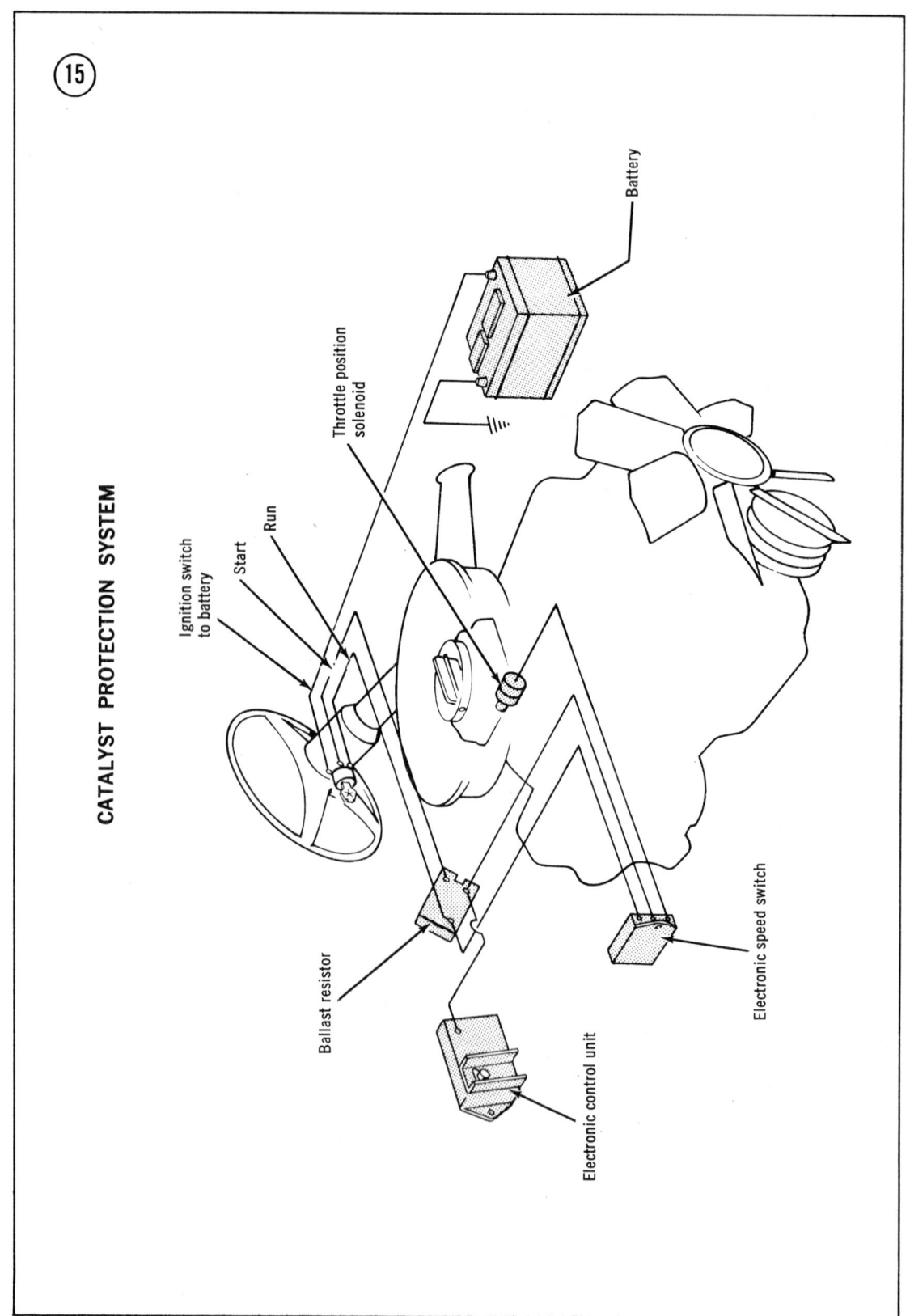

# CHAPTER TWELVE

# STARTER AND ALTERNATOR

Repairs to starters and alternators are beyond the scope of this book. Simple procedures are given, however, for determining if these components are functioning properly. Faulty components can be removed from the vehicle and taken to a dealer or automotive electrical shop for repairs.

## STARTER

NOTE: *Remove high tension wire from distributor cap center tower and ground wire to frame. Crank engine with remote starter. If voltage drop in the next 3 steps exceeds 0.1 volt, check circuit involved and clean all connections and replace defective cables.*

1. Connect a voltmeter between the car frame and the negative battery terminal (not the battery cable clamp). Crank the engine and note the voltage drop.
2. Connect voltmeter between the car frame and the starting motor housing. Crank engine and note the voltage drop.
3. Connect voltmeter between the battery positive terminal (not the cable clamp) and the starting motor terminal stud (or the solenoid terminal stud). Crank engine and note voltage drop.
4. Connect voltmeter positive lead to battery positive terminal and negative lead to negative terminal. Crank engine and note voltage reading. Reading should be at least 9.6 volts and cranking speed should be even.

NOTE: *Battery must be in good condition and have a hydrometer reading (specific gravity) of 1.220 or higher for each cell.*

5. If voltage reading while cranking is significantly below 9.6 volts, remove starter and/or have it checked.

## ALTERNATOR

1. With ignition system off, disconnect positive cable from battery and insert a test lamp between battery positive terminal and end of positive battery cable. If lamp lights, a short circuit exists which must be corrected before proceeding.
2. Reconnect cable and start engine. Verify that all electrical systems are off (lights, radio, etc.).
3. Place a current indicator (ammeter) over the positive battery cable. If a *charge* of about 5 amps is indicated, the alternator is working. If a *draw* of about 5 amps is indicated, a problem exists somewhere in the charging system. Remove and/or have the alternator checked.

# SUPPLEMENT

# 1977 AND LATER SERVICE INFORMATION

> Most of the information provided in the basic book for 1976 models also applies to 1977 and later models. This supplement explains the minor differences between models.
>
> The chapter headings in this supplement correspond to those in the main portion of this book. If a chapter is not included in the supplement, there are no changes affecting 1977 and later models.

# CHAPTER THREE

# PERIODIC MAINTENANCE

Periodic maintenance on 1977 and later models is similar to that for previous models, except that the maintenance tasks have been separated into two groupings: required and recommended services. See **Tables 1 through 3**. Required services are related to the emission control systems for the most part and are necessary for proper vehicle operation. They must be performed at the indicated intervals on new vehicles to protect your emission system's warranty. Recommended services should be performed at the indicated intervals to ensure proper vehicle operation and long vehicle life.

The maintenance services listed in **Tables 1 through 3** are described in Chapters Three, Four, and Five of the basic book, with the exception of automatic choke inspection and adjustment. This task requires special tools and skills, and should be referred to your Dodge dealer's service shop.

**Table 1    REQUIRED MAINTENANCE SERVICES (1977-1979 MODELS)**

**Every 7,500 miles or 6 months, whichever comes first**
- Apply solvent to carburetor choke shaft.
- Change engine oil.
- Apply solvent to fast idle cam and pivot pin.

**Every 15,000 miles**
- Check cooling system and service as required.
- Change engine oil filter (replace at 7,500 miles and every second oil change thereafter).
- Check idle speed and air-fuel mixture and adjust as required.
- Check positive crankcase ventilation valve and replace if necessary.
- Replace spark plugs if leaded fuel is used. Check ignition cables and replace as required.
- Adjust valve clearances (6-cylinder engines only).
- Inspect hoses in emission control systems and replace as required.

**Every 30,000 miles**
- Check automatic choke and adjust as required.
- Replace carburetor air filter.
- Clean crankcase inlet air cleaner.
- Replace fuel filter.
- Apply solvent to heat control valve.
- Replace positive crankcase ventilation valve.

Table 2   RECOMMENDED MAINTENANCE (1977-1979 MODELS)*

**Every oil change**
- Check power steering fluid level. Replenish if required.
- Check condition and tension of drive belts. Replace and/or adjust as required.
- Inspect upper and lower control arm bushings and replace if required.

**Every 6 months**
- Check exhaust system for leaks and missing or damaged parts. Repair or replace as required.
- Inspect brake master cylinder fluid level and replenish as required.
- Inspect transmission fluid level and replenish as required.
- Check condition of brake and power steering hoses and replace if leaking or in deteriorated condition.
- Check air conditioner belt condition, as well as tension and operation of controls. Check sight glass for flow of refrigerant.
- Inspect ball-joints, steering linkage, and universal joints, paying particular attention to condition of seals.
- Lubricate hood lock, release mechanism, and safety catch.

**Every 10,000 miles**
- Rotate tires and inspect them for wear. Replace if necessary.
- Tighten radiator hose clamps.

**At 30,000 miles or 24 months, then every 15,000 miles or 12 months**
- Drain, flush, and refill cooling system.

**Every 15,000 miles**
- Inspect brake linings. Replace if required.

**Every 22,500 miles**
- Inspect and relubricate front wheel bearings.

**Every 30,000 miles or 3 years**
- Lubricate ball-joints and tie rod ends.

*For vehicles subjected to severe usage, see **Table 3**.

# 1977 AND LATER SERVICE INFORMATION

Table 3  RECOMMENDED MAINTENANCE-SEVERE USAGE (1977-1979 MODELS)*

**Every oil change**
- Check power steering fluid level. Replenish if required.
- Check condition and tension of drive belts. Replace and/or adjust as required.
- Inspect upper and lower control arm bushings and replace if required.

**Every 3,000 miles or 3 months**
- Change engine oil.

**Every 6 months**
- Check exhaust system for leaks and missing or damaged parts. Repair or replace as required.
- Inspect brake master cylinder fluid level and replenish as required.
- Inspect transmission fluid level and replenish as required.
- Check condition of brake and power steering hoses and replace if leaking or in deteriorated condition.
- Check air conditioner belt condition, as well as tension and operation of controls. Check sight glass for flow of refrigerant.
- Inspect ball-joints, steering linkage, and universal joints, paying particular attention to condition of seals.
- Lubricate hood lock, release mechanism, and safety catch.

**Every 6,000 miles**
- Replace engine oil filter (replace at initial oil change, then at every second oil change).

**Every 9,000 miles**
- Relubricate wheel bearings.

**Every 10,000 miles**
- Rotate tires and inspect them for wear. Replace if necessary.
- Tighten radiator hose clamps.

**Every 15,000 miles**
- Inspect brake linings. Replace if required.
- Change automatic transmission fluid and filter, and adjust bands.
- Relubricate steering and suspension ball-joints.

**At 30,000 miles or 24 months, then every 15,000 miles or 12 months**
- Drain, flush, and refill cooling system.

**Every 30,000 miles**
- Change manual transmission fluid.

**Every 36,000 miles**
- Change rear axle (differential) lubricant.

*Taxi, trailer tow, limousine service, etc. Perform these services in addition to those in **Table 1**.

# CHAPTER FOUR

## LUBRICANTS AND FLUIDS

> The information contained in Chapter Four of the basic book also applies to 1977 and later models, except that the crankcase capacity for *all* Dodge engines used during this period is 4 quarts, plus 1 quart at filter change.

# CHAPTER FIVE

## IGNITION TUNE-UP

The *Tune-Up Sequence* described in Chapter Five of the basic book also applies generally to 1977 and later models, with minor exceptions. Tune-up specifications should be taken from the Vehicle Emission Control Information sticker located in the engine compartment of your car. If this sticker is missing or cannot be read, use the specifications given in **Tables 4 through 6** of this supplement. If you do not know the displacement of your engine, check the fifth digit of the vehicle identification number against information given in **Table 7**.

If you use the information given in **Table 4**, you also must know the vehicle weight class. This is the "wet" curb weight plus 300 lb., rounded off to the nearest 500 lb. ("Wet" means crankcase filled with the specified amount of engine oil and the fuel tank full.)

All 1977 and later models are equipped with either the electronic ignition system or the "Electronic Lean Burn" (ELB) ignition system. The ELB system is called "Electronic Spark Control" (ESC) system on 1979 models. Testing, adjusting, and repairing of these systems requires the use of special equipment, training, and experience. Service by the home mechanic should be limited to the procedures given in this book, and these should be attempted only if the necessary equipment (described in the procedures) is available. Adjustment of either system by experimentation is very risky, and could lead to poor performance and/or system failure.

### IGNITION TIMING

The procedure given in *Ignition Timing* in Chapter Five of the basic book may be used on all models, except that on cars with ELB or ESC ignition systems the terminals on the carburetor switch (see **Figure 1**) should be connected to a good ground on the engine with a jumper wire during the check and adjustment. Remove the jumper wire at the end of the test.

# 1977 AND LATER SERVICE INFORMATION

**Table 4    TUNE-UP SPECIFICATIONS**

**1977 MODELS**

| | Engine Cylinder/Carburetor | CID | Transmission | Gross Vehicle Weight (lbs.) | Basic Timing | Curb Idle (rpm) | Propane Enriched Idle (rpm) |
|---|---|---|---|---|---|---|---|
| **Electronic Ignition (Fed./Canada)** | 6/1 bbl | 225 | M | 3,500 | 12° BTDC | 700 | 835 |
| | 6/1 bbl | 225 | A | 3,500 | 12° BTDC | 700 | 790 |
| | 6/1 bbl | 225 | M | 4,000 | 6° BTDC | 700 | 805 |
| | 6/1 bbl | 225 | A | 4,000 | 12° BTDC | 700 | 830 |
| | 6/2 bbl | 225 | M | 4,000 | 12° BTDC | 750 | 930 |
| | 6/2 bbl | 225 | A | 4,000 | 12° BTDC | 750 | 900 |
| | 8/2 bbl | 318 | M | 4,500 | 8° BTDC | 700 | 810 |
| | 8/2 bbl | 318 | A | 4,500 | 8° BTDC | 700 | 780 |
| | 8/2 bbl | 360 | A | 5,000 | 10° BTDC | 700 | 810 |
| **Electronic Ignition (Calif.)** | 6/1 bbl | 225 | M/A | 4,000 | 8° BTDC | 750 | — |
| | 6/2 bbl | 225 | M/A | 4,000 | 4° BTDC | 850 | — |
| | 8/2 bbl | 318 | M | 4,500 | TDC | 850 | — |
| | 8/4 bbl | 360 | A | 5,000 | 6° BTDC | 750 | — |
| | 8/4 bbl | 440 | A | 5,000 | 8° BTDC | 750 | — |
| **Electronic Ignition (Fed. High Alt.)** | 6/1 bbl | 225 | A | 4,000 | 8° BTDC | 750 | 820 ① |
| | 8/2 bbl | 318 | A | 4,500 | TDC | 850 | 900 ② |
| | 8/4 bbl | 360 | A | 4,500/5,000 | 6° BTDC | 750 | 830 ③ |
| **Lean Burn Ignition (Fed./Canada)** | 8/4 bbl | 360 | A | 4,500 | 10° BTDC | 750 | 860 |
| | 8/4 bbl | 400 | A | 5,500 | 10° BTDC | 750 | 880 |
| | 8/4 bbl | 440 | A | 5,500 | 12° BTDC | 750 | 850 |
| **Lean Burn Ignition (Calif.)** | 8/4 bbl | 440 | A | 5,500 | 8° BTDC | 750 | — |
| **Lean Burn Ignition (Fed. High Alt.)** | 8/4 bbl | 440 | A | 5,500 | 8° BTDC | 750 | 850 ④ |

① Below 4,000 ft. Above 4,000 ft., adjust to 850 rpm.
② Below 4,000 ft. Above 4,000 ft., adjust to 930 rpm.
③ Below 4,000 ft. Above 4,000 ft., adjust to 850 rpm.
④ Below 4,000 ft. Above 4,000 ft., adjust to 870 rpm.

**Table 4  TUNE-UP SPECIFICATIONS** (continued)

**1978 MODELS**

| | Engine Cylinder/Carburetor | CID | Transmission | Gross Vehicle Weight (lbs.) | Basic Timing | Curb Idle (rpm) | Propane Enriched Idle (rpm) |
|---|---|---|---|---|---|---|---|
| **Electronic Ignition (Fed./Canada)** | 6/1 bbl | 225 | M | 3,500 | 12° BTDC | 700 | 835 |
| | 6/1 bbl (Federal only) | 225 | A | 3,500 | 12° BTDC | 700 | 790 |
| | 6/1 bbl (Canada only) | 225 | A | 3,500 | 2° ATDC | 750 | 880 |
| | 6/1 bbl | 225 | A/M | 4,000 | 12° BTDC | 700 | 790 |
| | 6/2 bbl | 225 | M | 3,500/4,000 | 12° BTDC | 750 | 930 |
| | 6/2 bbl | 225 | A | 3,500/4,000 | 12° BTDC | 750 | 900 |
| **Electronic Ignition (California)** | 6/1 bbl | 225 | A/M | 4,000 | 8° BTDC | 750 | 850 |
| | 6/1 bbl | 225 | A | 3,500/4,000 | 8° BTDC | 750 | 880 |
| | 6/1 bbl | 225 | A | 4,000 | 8° BTDC | 750 | 820 |
| | 8/4 bbl | 360 | A | 4,500/5,000 | 6° BTDC | 750 | 830 |
| | 8/4 bbl | 360 | A | 4,000/4,500 | 8° BTDC | 750 | 830 |
| | 8/4 bbl | 440 | A | 5,000 | 8° BTDC | 750 | 860 |
| **Electronic Ignition (Fed. High Alt.)** | 6/1 bbl | 225 | A | 4,000 | 8° BTDC | 750 | 880 ① |
| | 8/4 bbl | 360 | A | 4,500/5,000 | 6° BTDC | 750 | 830 ② |
| | 8/4 bbl | 360 | A | 4,000/4,500 | 8° BTDC | 750 | 830 ② |
| **Lean Burn Ignition (Fed./Canada)** | 8/2 bbl | 318 | M | 4,000/5,000 | 16° BTDC | 700 | 810 |
| | 8/2 bbl | 318 | A | 4,000/5,000 | 16° BTDC | 750 | 850 |
| | 8/4 bbl (Canada only) | 318 | A | 4,000/5,000 | 16° BTDC | 750 | 825 |
| | 8/2 bbl | 360 | A | 4,000/4,500/5,000 | 20° BTDC ③ | 750 | 890 |
| | 8/4 bbl | 360 | A | 4,000 | 16° BTDC | 750 | 900 |
| | 8/4 bbl | 400 | A | 4,500 | 24° BTDC ④ | 750 | 840 ④ |
| | 8/4 bbl | 400 | A | 4,500/5,000 | 20° BTDC | 750 | 840 |
| | 8/4 bbl | 440 | A | 5,000 | 16° BTDC | 750 | 825 |
| **Lean Burn Ignition (California)** | 8/4 bbl | 318 | A | 4,000/5,000 | 10° BTDC | 750 | 825 |
| **Lean Burn Ignition (Fed. High Alt.)** | 8/2 bbl | 318 | A | 4,500 | 16° BTDC | 750 | 830 ⑤ |

① Below 4,000 ft. Above 4,000 ft., adjust to 910 rpm.
② Below 4,000 ft. Above 4,000 ft., adjust to 850 rpm.
③ 12° BTDC on Canadian 4,000/4,500 GVWR cars.
④ On Canadian vehicles, 20° BTDC. Adjust propane-enriched idle speed to 825 rpm.
⑤ Below 4,000 ft. Above 4,000 ft., adjust to 880 rpm.

**Table 4  TUNE-UP SPECIFICATIONS** (continued)

**1979 MODELS**

| | Engine Cylinder/Carburetor | CID | Transmission | Gross Vehicle Weight (lbs.) | Basic Timing | Curb Idle (rpm) | Propane Enriched Idle (rpm) |
|---|---|---|---|---|---|---|---|
| Electronic Ignition (Fed./Canada) | 6/1 bbl | 225 | M | 3,500 | 12° BTDC | 675 | 835 |
| | 6/1 bbl | 225 | A | 3,500 | 12° BTDC | 675 | 790 |
| | 6/2 bbl | 225 | A | 3,500/4,000 | 12° BTDC | 725 | 900 |
| Electronic Ignition (California) | 6/1 bbl | 225 | A | 3,500/4,000 | 8° BTDC | 750 | 900 |
| | 6/1 bbl | 225 | A | 4,000 | 8° BTDC | 750 | 820 |
| Electronic Spark Control (Fed./Canada) | 8/2 bbl | 318 | A | All | 16° BTDC | 750 | 850 |
| | 8/4 bbl | 360 | A | All | 16° BTDC | 750 | 900 |
| | 8/4 bbl | 360 | A | All | 12° BTDC | 750 | 900 |
| Electronic Spark Control (California) | 8/2 bbl | 318 | A | All | 16° BTDC | 750 | 825 |
| | 8/4 bbl | 360 | A | All | 16° BTDC | 750 | 900 |

## Table 5  SPARK PLUGS

| Model | Champion Type |
|---|---|
| 1977 | |
| All 6 cyl. | RBL15Y |
| 318, 360 | RN12Y |
| 400, 440 | RJ13Y |
| 1978-1979 | |
| All 6 cyl. | RBL16Y |
| 318, 360 | RN12Y |
| 400, 440 | OJ13Y |

## Table 6  CO AT IDLE (California)

| | |
|---|---|
| 6 cylinder (1977-1979) | |
| 1 bbl. | 0.3% |
| 2 bbl. | 0.5% |
| 8 cylinder | |
| 318 | 0.5% |
| 360 | 0.5% |
| 440 (electronic ign.) | 1.0% |
| 440 (lean burn) | 0.3% |

## Table 7  ENGINE DISPLACEMENT CODE

| 5th Digit of I.D. Number | Engine Displacement in Cubic Inches | | |
|---|---|---|---|
| | 1977 | 1978 | 1979 |
| C | 225  1 bbl. | 225  1 bbl. | 225  1 bbl. |
| D | 225  2 bbl. | 225  2 bbl. | 225  2 bbl. |
| G | 318  2 bbl. | 318  2 bbl. | 318  2 bbl. |
| H | — | 318  4 bbl. | 318  4 bbl. |
| J | 360  4 bbl. | 360  4 bbl. | 360  4 bbl. |
| K | 360  2 bbl. | 360  2 bbl. | — |
| L | 360  4 bbl. | 360  4 bbl. | 360  4 bbl. |
| M | 400  4 bbl. | 400  4 bbl. | — |
| T | 440  4 bbl. | 440  4 bbl. | — |

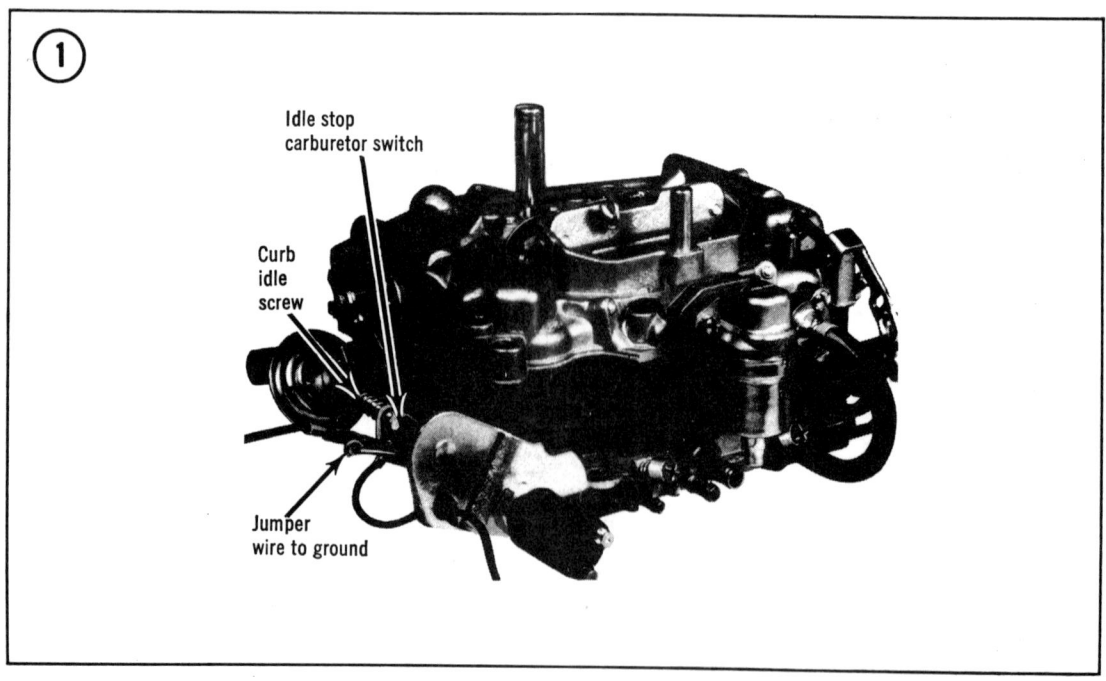

# CHAPTER SIX

# CARBURETOR AND FUEL PUMP

All 1977 and later models, except 1977 models produced for initial sale in California, require the use of a propane-assisted idle/speed/mixture adjustment procedure. This procedure requires the use of a propane metering tool (Chrysler tool C-4464 or equivalent) and a container of propane. See **Figure 2**. The 1977 California models require the use of a Chrysler Huntsville exhaust analyzer (or equivalent).

You may be able to obtain the propane tool through your Dodge dealer, or an equivalent tool may be available through an auto parts dealer. If you cannot find the tool locally, try Miller Special Tools, Division of Utica Tool Company, Inc., 32615 Park Lane, Garden City, Michigan 48135. In Canada, try C&D Riley Enterprises, Ltd., P.O. Box 2483, Walkerville, Ontario N8Y 4Y2. The United States address should be used when enquiring from other countries.

The propane tool should not be excessively expensive, and you should consider purchasing one if you plan to do all your own service work.

Exhaust analyzers of the type and quality required are fairly expensive. However, you may be able to rent one from an equipment rental company.

Carburetor adjustment is critical on late models, especially those equipped with the electronic lean burn (ELB) ignition system. In this system, signals from a number of sensors are fed into a computer to determine the exact instant of ignition of the air-fuel mixture produced by the carburetor under varying operating conditions. Correct adjustment also is necessary on all models to ensure proper operation of other emission control systems. For these reasons, adjustments of curb idle speed and air-fuel mixture by any method other than those described in this chapter are not recommended.

## PROPANE-ASSISTED IDLE SPEED ADJUSTMENT (1977-1979)

Make all adjustments with engine fully warmed up, headlights and air conditioner off, transmission in neutral, and the idle stop carburetor switch (ELB or ESC models) grounded with a jumper wire between the switch terminal and a good ground on the engine. See **Figure 1**. The vacuum hoses at the exhaust gas recircula-

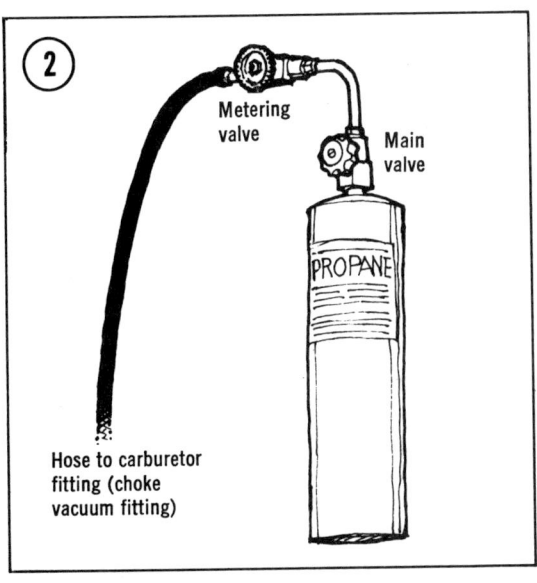

tion (EGR) valve, if so equipped, and the distributor or spark control unit must be disconnected and plugged.

1. With the transmission in neutral and parking brake set, start vehicle and allow it to warm up with the fast idle screw resting on the 2nd step of the fast idle cam (**Figure 3**, typical). Allow engine to reach normal operating temperature, then kick off the fast idle cam.

2. Connect a tachometer to the engine, using the manufacturer's instructions. Remove the air cleaner vacuum supply hose, if so equipped, or the choke vacuum diaphragm hose, from the nipple on the carburetor. Connect the propane tool supply hose to the nipple. See **Figure 4** (typical). Open the propane ON-OFF valve.

3. With the engine idling, slowly open the propane metering valve until maximum engine speed is reached (too much propane will reduce engine speed). Leave propane flowing at this rate, and do not touch metering valve until throttle is adjusted.

> NOTE: *Start test with an adequate supply of propane. If engine speed begins to drop off for no obvious reason, check the propane supply.*

4. With propane flowing, adjust curb idle screw until engine speed reaches the "Enriched RPM" shown on the Vehicle Emission Control Information label in the engine compartment. If this label is missing or defaced, use the "Propane Enriched Idle" speed given in **Table 3** of this supplement. If necessary, adjust the propane flow to obtain maximum engine speed.

> NOTE: *When the specified "enriched rpm" is obtained, do not readjust the curb idle speed.*

5. Turn off propane and adjust idle mixture screw (see **Figure 5**, typical) to obtain the smoothest idle within 100 rpm (plus or minus) of the specified curb idle speed.

> NOTE: *Idle mixture adjusting screws are equipped with limiter caps. If the specified curb idle speed and quality cannot be obtained within the range allowed by the limiter cap, verify the speed specification, check and adjust, if required, basic engine timing, and check*

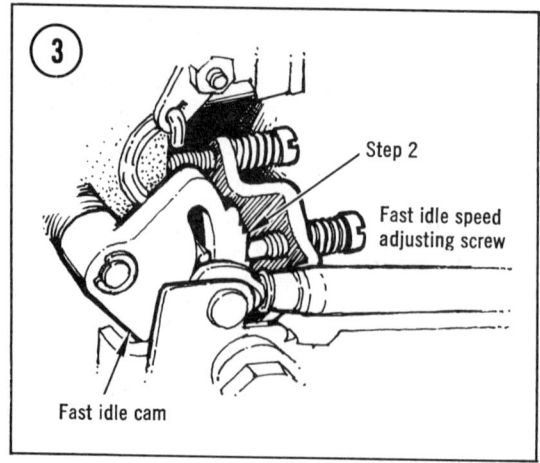

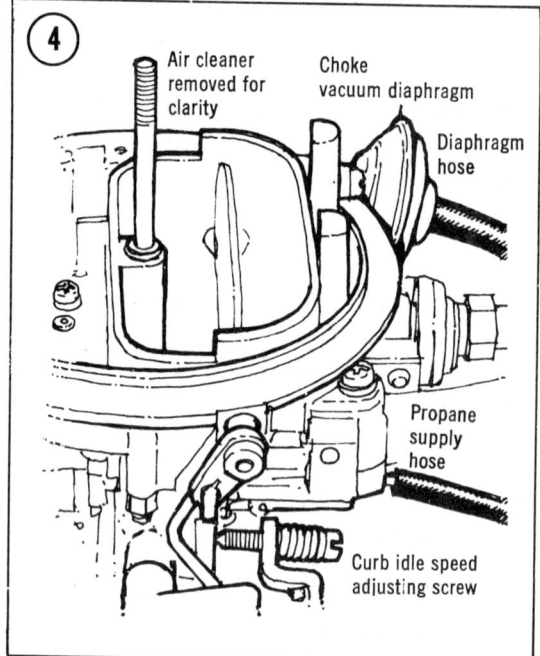

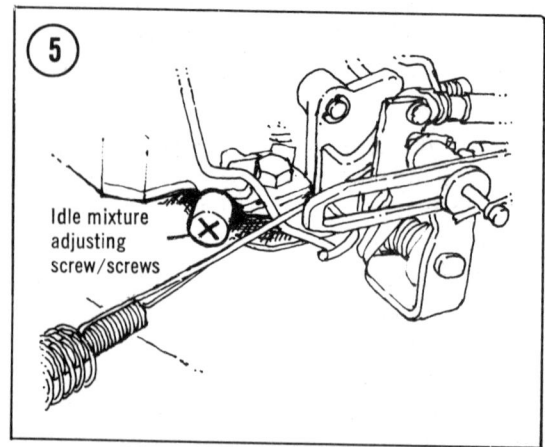

# 1977 AND LATER SERVICE INFORMATION

*for carburetor and manifold vacuum leaks before removing the limiter cap.*

*On 1977 318 cid engines with the high altitude package, adjust for the smoothest idle at 100 rpm below the specified curb idle speed.*

6. Turn on propane again and check maximum speed to make sure the idle setting was not disturbed. If the maximum speed varies more than 25 rpm from the specified enriched rpm, repeat Steps 4 through 6.

7. Turn off propane and remove the propane enrichment tool.

NOTE: *On 1977 318 cid engines with the high altitude package, reset curb idle speed to specification by adjusting the curb idle speed solenoid.*

8. Reinstall the vacuum hose that was removed in Step 2. Remove the jumper wire used to ground the idle stop carburetor switch.

## CURB IDLE ADJUSTMENT (1977 CALIFORNIA MODELS)

NOTE: *This procedure also may be used for 1978 California models.*

This procedure requires the use of a Chrysler Huntsville exhaust emission analyzer (or equivalent), which would be installed according to the manufacturer's instructions. Check the Vehicle Emission Control Information (VECI) label in the engine compartment to determine whether the analyzer probe should be installed in the tailpipe or ahead of the catalytic converter. Allow the engine to sit without running for at least an hour before starting this procedure.

1. Start the engine and allow it to warm up with the transmission in neutral and the fast idle speed adjustment screw on the 2nd step of the fast idle cam. Allow the engine to reach normal operating temperature (5-10 minutes).

2. Disconnect and plug distributor vacuum hose. If equipped with the electronic lean burn (ELB or ESC) ignition, disconnect and plug the vacuum hose to the vacuum transducer on the air cleaner.

3. Disconnect and plug the air supply hose from the air pump.

4. Use the idle mixture screw (see **Figure 5**) to adjust the air-fuel mixture to obtain the specified percentage of carbon monoxide (CO). Then use the idle speed adjusting screw to obtain the smoothest idle within 100 rpm (plus or minus) of the specified curb idle speed. See the VECI label for specifications. If this label is missing or defaced, refer to **Table 3** of this supplement.

NOTE: *Before making each idle speed or mixture adjustment, "blow out" the engine by accelerating to 2,000 rpm for at least 10 seconds and then returning to curb idle speed. Allow at least 30 seconds, but no longer than one minute, for the meters to stabilize before taking the reading. Take the reading with the engine operating at idle, with the transmission in neutral and air conditioner and headlights off.*

5. Recheck the CO content of the exhaust. Repeat Step 3 if necessary to bring the CO content and idle speed within specifications.

6. Disconnect and plug the exhaust gas recirculation (EGR) vacuum line at the EGR valve. Position the fast idle adjustment screw on the 2nd step of the fast idle cam (see **Figure 3**) and, if necessary, adjust the fast idle speed to the specified rpm (see VECI label).

7. Reconnect the distributor and EGR vacuum hoses. If equipped with ELB or ESC, reconnect hose to vacuum transducer. If exhaust sample was taken ahead of catalytic converter, remove probe and install plug. Torque plug to 100-140 in.-lb. If sample was taken from tailpipe, remove probe.

## FUEL PUMP CHECKS

The procedures given in Chapter Six of the basic book apply to 1977 and later models, except that the following fuel pump pressures are specified (all years):

| | |
|---|---|
| 225 cid engine | 3½-5 psi |
| 318 cid engine | 5-7 psi |
| 360 cid engine | 5-7 psi |
| 400 cid engine | 4-7 psi |
| 440 cid engine | 6-7½ psi |

# CHAPTER NINE

# CLUTCH ADJUSTMENT

### FREE PLAY ADJUSTMENT

Use the procedure *Free Play Adjustment (1967)* given in Chapter Nine of the basic book, except refer to **Figures 6 and 7** for Aspen and **Figures 8 and 9** for other models.

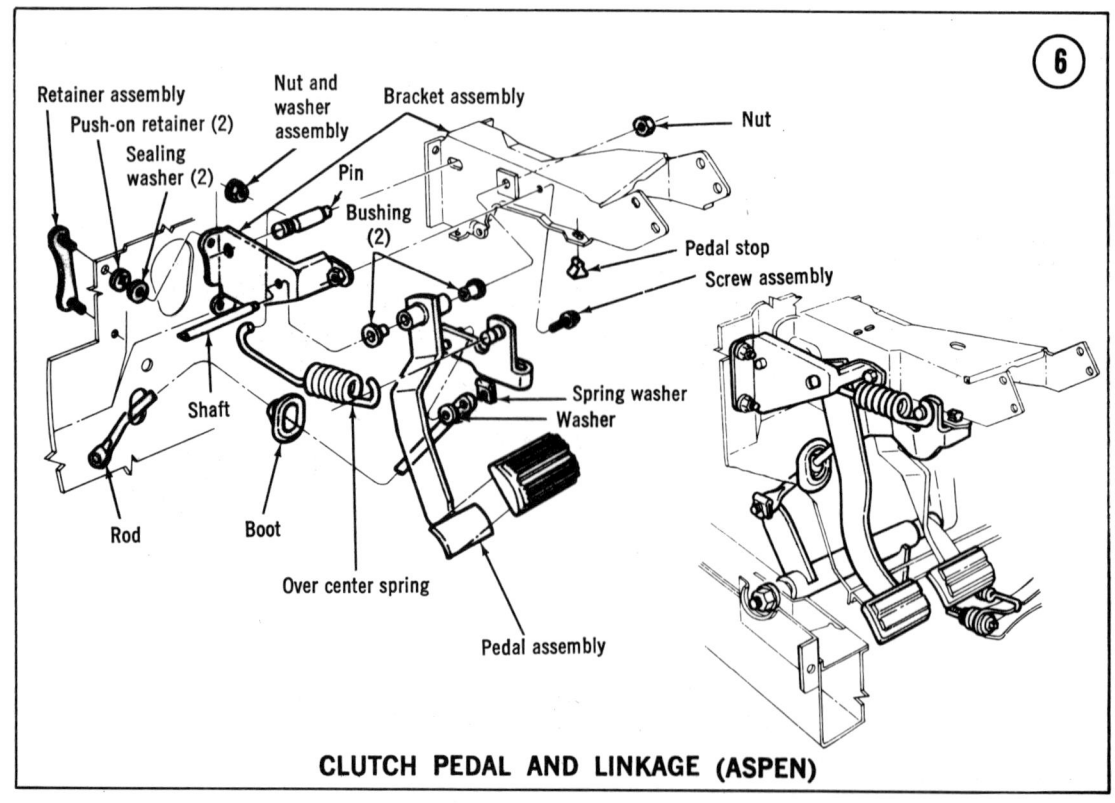

**CLUTCH PEDAL AND LINKAGE (ASPEN)**

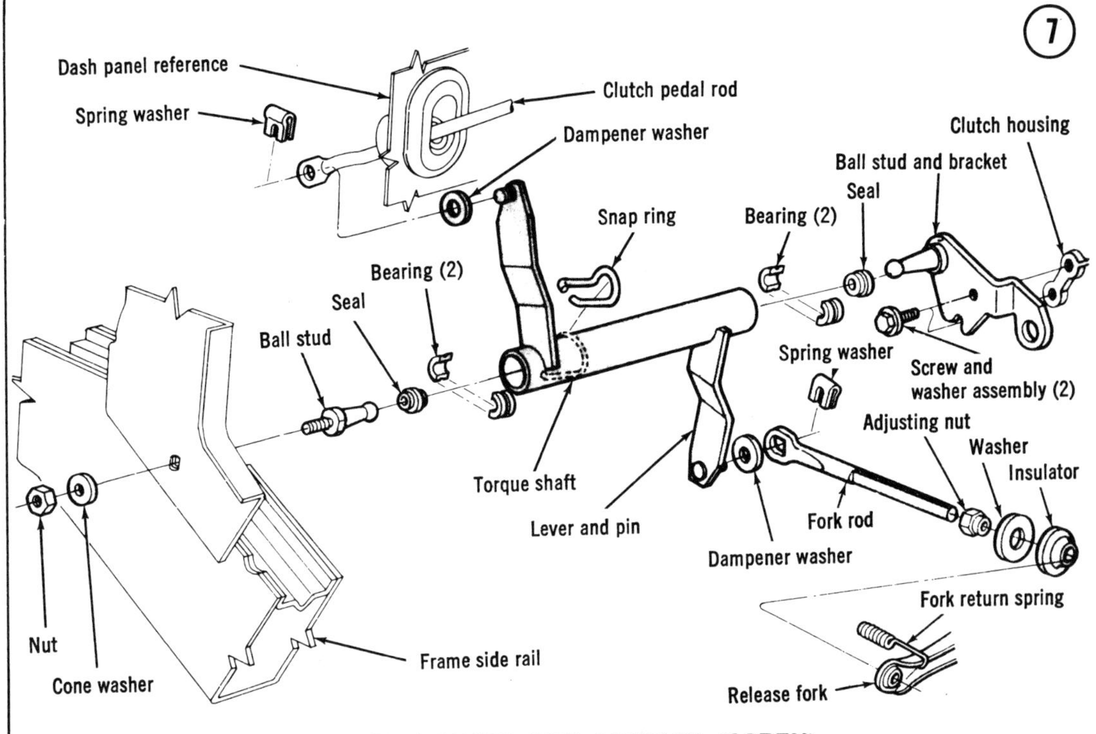

# 1977 AND LATER SERVICE INFORMATION

**TORQUE SHAFT AND LINKAGE (ASPEN)**

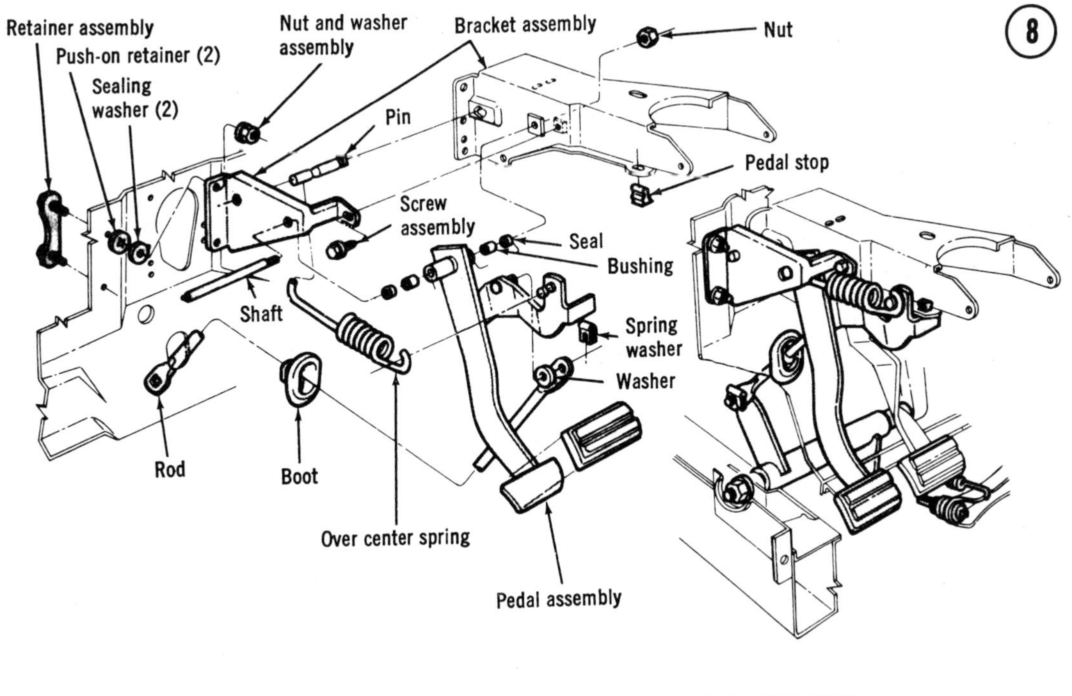

**CLUTCH PEDAL AND LINKAGE (ALL OTHERS)**

**138** SUPPLEMENT

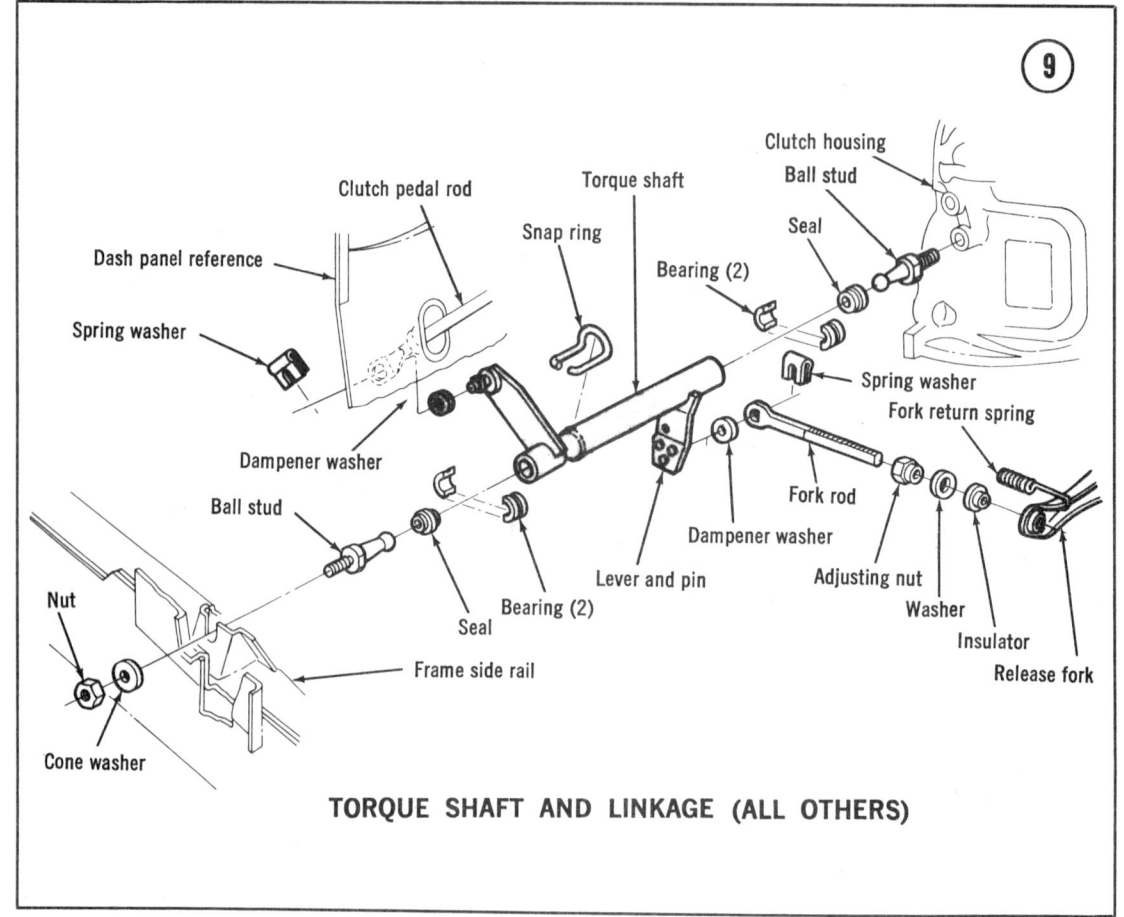

**TORQUE SHAFT AND LINKAGE (ALL OTHERS)**

# CHAPTER TEN

## SHOCK ABSORBERS

The removal and installation procedures given in Chapter Ten of the basic book may be used, except that **Figure 10** (Aspen) and **Figure 11** (other models) should be referred to when removing and installing rear shock absorbers.

# 1977 AND LATER SERVICE INFORMATION

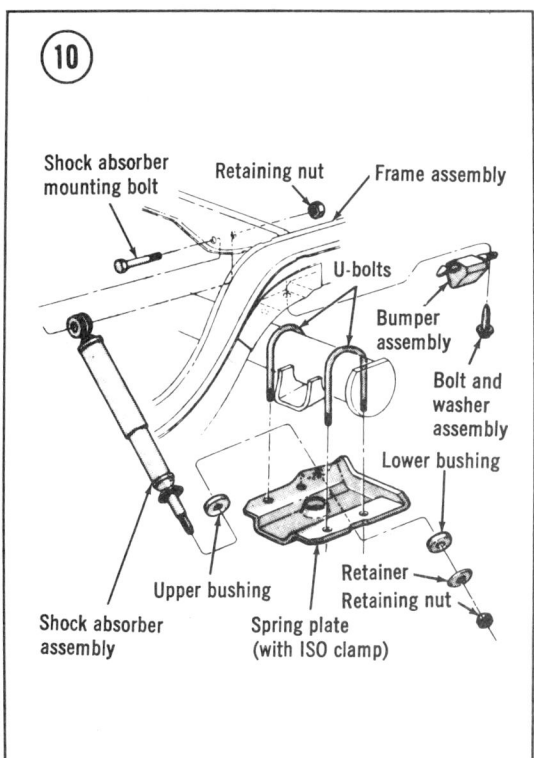

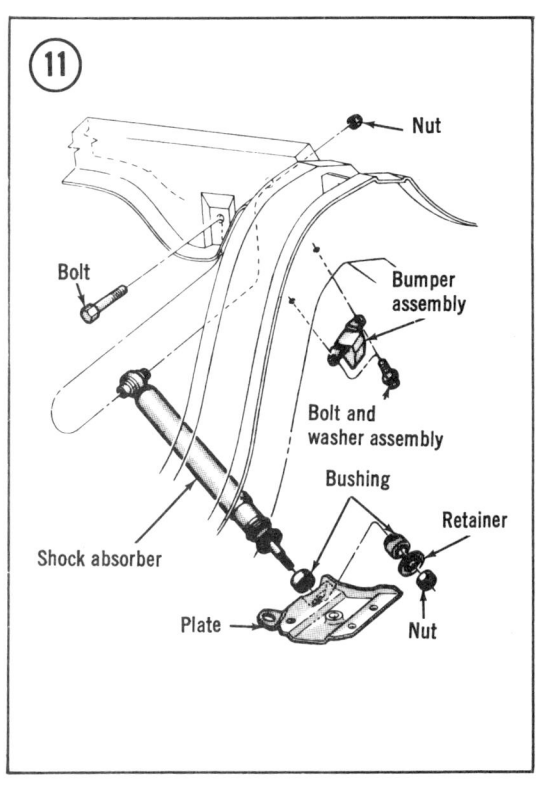

# INDEX

## A

Air injection system .................110-114
Alternator .........................8-9, 123
Axle, rear ..........................25, 37

## B

Battery service ......................15-19
Brakes
   Adjustment .......................88-89
   Bleeding ............................89
   Disc brake ........................89-95
   Drum brake ........................72-84
   Fluid type ..........................37
   Hose maintenance ....................28
   Maintenance .........................29
   Master cylinder ..................27-28
   Pedal linkage bushing ............30-31
   Troubleshooting .....................13
   Wheel bearing lubrication, front ....84
   Wheel cylinders ..................84-88
Breaker points ......................42-43

## C

Cable resistance check ..............41-42
Carburetor
   Air filter maintenance ..............20
   Carter TQ series ....................58
   Carter 1½ inch BBD ..................57
   Curb idle adjustment ......54-64, 133-135
   Holley 2210 series ..................59
   Holley model 1920 ...................56
   Holley model 2300 ................62-63
   Holley model 4160 ................60-61
Catalytic converter ................120-122
Catalytic overtemperature protection system   32
Charging system troubleshooting ......8-9
Chassis lubrication ..................36
Choke shaft maintenance ............20-23
Clutch
   Clutch pedal and linkage (Aspen) ....136
   Clutch pedal and linkage (Challenger
     and Coronet/Charger) ..............99
   Clutch pedal and linkage (Dart) .....97
   Clutch pedal and linkage (heavy-duty
     Dart) .............................98
   Clutch pedal and linkage (1977-1979
     models except Aspen) .............137
   Clutch pedal and linkage (Polara) ..100
   Free play adjustment .....96-103, 136-138
   Gearshift interlock rod .........96, 104
   Torque shaft and linkage (Aspen) ...137
   Torque shaft and linkage (Barracuda
     and Satellite) ...................102
   Torque shaft and linkage (Dart) ....101
   Torque shaft and linkage (Fury) ....103
   Torque shaft and linkage (1977-1979
     models except Aspen) .............138
   Torque shaft bushing maintenance ..30-32
   Troubleshooting .....................13
Compression test ....................40-41
Compression tester ....................4
Cooling system
   Cleaning ............................71
   Drive belt inspection ............66-70
   Fans ................................71
   Flushing .........................70-71
   Lubrication .........................36
   Maintenance .........................19
   Pressure cap ........................71
   Radiator hose .......................71
Crankcase air inlet ..................28
Crankcase ventilation system maintenance ...28
Curb idle adjustment ..........54-64, 133-135

## D

Disc brakes ........................89-95
Distributor maintenance .........30-31, 32
Drive belt maintenance .............66-70
Drum brakes ........................72-84
Dwell meter ..........................3

## E

Emission control systems
   Air injection system ............110-114
   Catalytic converter .............120-122
   Coolant controlled idle enrichment system  120
   Electric assist choke system .......117
   EGR maintenance indicator ..........121
   Exhaust gas recirculation system ..29, 114, 116
   Manifold heat control valve ........110
   Orifice spark advance control system ...117-120
   Positive crankcase ventilation system .....110
   Troubleshooting .................12-13
   Vapor saver system .............114, 115
Engine
   Displacement code ...............39, 132
   Idle speed, timing, and mixture .....32
   Lubrication ......................34-36
   Oil .............................15, 19
   Troubleshooting ..................9-10
Exhaust analyzer .....................6
EGR maintenance indicator ...........121
Exhaust gas recirculation system ....29, 114, 116

## F

| | |
|---|---|
| Fans | 71 |
| Fuel pressure gauge | 4 |
| Fuel system | |
|     Filter maintenance | 30 |
|     Pump checks | 64-65, 135 |
|     Pump specifications | 65 |
|     Troubleshooting | 12 |
| Fuel vapor canister maintenance | 30 |

## G

| | |
|---|---|
| Gearshift interlock rod | 96, 104 |
| Gearshift linkage maintenance | 32 |

## H

| | |
|---|---|
| Headlight alignment | 28 |
| Hood latch and safety catch | 28 |
| Hydraulic system bleeding | 89 |
| Hydrometer | 6 |

## I

| | |
|---|---|
| Identification numbers | 1-2 |
| Idle speed adjustment | 54-64, 133-135 |
| Ignition tune-up | |
|     Breaker points | 42-43 |
|     Cable resistance check | 41-42 |
|     Compression test | 40-41 |
|     Engine displacement code | 39, 132 |
|     Sequence | 38 |
|     Spark plugs | 30, 41, 132 |
|     Specifications | 44-53, 129-132 |
|     Timing | 43, 128 |
|     Troubleshooting | 10-12 |
|     Valve lash adjustment (6-cylinder) | 43 |

## L

| | |
|---|---|
| Lubricants and fluids | |
|     Axle, rear | 37 |
|     Brake fluid type | 37 |
|     Chassis | 36 |
|     Cooling system | 36 |
|     Engine | 15, 19, 34-36, 128 |
|     Manual steering gear | 36 |
|     Power steering | 36 |
|     Transmission | 36-37 |

## M

| | |
|---|---|
| Maintenance, periodic | |
|     Axle, rear | 25 |
|     Battery | 15, 19 |
|     Brake hoses | 28 |
|     Brake pedal linkage bushings | 30-31 |
|     Brakes | 29 |
|     Carburetor air filter | 20 |
|     Catalytic overtemperature protection system | 32 |
|     Choke shaft and fast idle cam | 20-23 |
|     Clutch torque shaft bearings | 30-32 |
|     Coolant level | 14-15 |
|     Cooling system | 19 |
|     Crankcase air inlet | 28 |
|     Crankcase ventilation system | 28 |
|     Distributor | 30-31 |
|     Distributor cap and ignition wiring | 32 |
|     Engine idle speed, timing, and mixture | 32 |
|     Engine oil level | 15, 19, 34-36, 128 |
|     Exhaust gas recirculation system | 29 |
|     Fuel filter | 30 |
|     Fuel vapor canister | 30 |
|     Gearshift linkage | 32-33 |
|     Headlight alignment | 28 |
|     Manifold heat control valve | 23-24, 110 |
|     Master cylinder, brake | 27, 28 |
|     Oil filter | 19 |
|     Orifice spark advance control | 32 |
|     Power steering | 20 |
|     Recommended (1977-1979 models) | 126-127 |
|     Required (1977-1979 models) | 125 |
|     Schedule of maintenance | 16-18 |
|     Spark plugs | 30 |
|     Steering gear, manual | 25 |
|     Steering linkage | 26 |
|     Suspension ball-joints | 26 |
|     Throttle linkage | 29 |
|     Tire rotation | 20-22 |
|     Transmission | 23-25 |
|     Universal joints | 26 |
|     Wheel bearings, front | 30 |
|     Windshield washer fluid | 15 |
| Manifold heat control valve | 23-24, 110 |
| Master cylinder, brake | 27-28 |

## O

| | |
|---|---|
| Oil, engine | 15, 19, 34-36, 128 |
| Oil filter | 19, 34-35 |
| Orifice spark advance control system | 32, 117-120 |

## P

| | |
|---|---|
| Parts replacement | 2 |
| Positive crankcase ventilation system | 110 |
| Power steering lubrication | 36 |
| Power steering maintenance | 20 |
| Propane-assisted idle speed adjustment (1977-1979) | 133-135 |

## R

| | |
|---|---|
| Radiator hose | 71 |
| Regulator troubleshooting | 8-9 |

# INDEX

## S

Service hints . . . . . . . . . . . . . . . . . . . . . . . . . . 2
Shock absorbers
    Installation, front . . . . . . . . . . . . . . . . . 107-109
    Installation, rear . . . . . . . . . . . . . . 109, 138-139
    Removal, front . . . . . . . . . . . . . . . . . . . 105-107
    Removal, rear . . . . . . . . . . . . . 107-108, 138-139
Spark plugs . . . . . . . . . . . . . . . . . . . . . 30, 41, 132
Specifications, fuel pump . . . . . . . . . . . . . . . . 65
Specifications, ignition . . . . . . . . . 44-53, 129-132
Starter . . . . . . . . . . . . . . . . . . . . . . . . . . . . 8, 123
Steering gear, manual . . . . . . . . . . . . . . . . 25, 36
Steering linkage maintenance . . . . . . . . . . . . 26
Suspension (see Shock absorbers)
Suspension ball-joint maintenance . . . . . . . . . 26

## T

Tachometer . . . . . . . . . . . . . . . . . . . . . . . . . . . 3
Throttle linkage maintenance . . . . . . . . . . . . 29
Timing light . . . . . . . . . . . . . . . . . . . . . . . . . . 3
Tire rotation . . . . . . . . . . . . . . . . . . . . . . . 20-22
Tools
    Compression tester . . . . . . . . . . . . . . . . . . . 4
    Dwell meter . . . . . . . . . . . . . . . . . . . . . . . . 3
    Exhaust analyzer . . . . . . . . . . . . . . . . . . . . 6
    Fuel pressure gauge . . . . . . . . . . . . . . . . . . 4
    Hydrometer . . . . . . . . . . . . . . . . . . . . . . . . 6
    Tachometer . . . . . . . . . . . . . . . . . . . . . . . . 3
    Timing light . . . . . . . . . . . . . . . . . . . . . . . . 3
    Vacuum gauge . . . . . . . . . . . . . . . . . . . . 4-5
    Voltmeter, ammeter, ohmmeter . . . . . . . . . 4
Transmission lubrication and
    maintenance . . . . . . . . . . . . . . . . . 23-25, 36-37
Troubleshooting
    Alternator . . . . . . . . . . . . . . . . . . . . . . . . 8-9
    Brakes . . . . . . . . . . . . . . . . . . . . . . . . . . . 13
    Charging system . . . . . . . . . . . . . . . . . . . 8-9
    Clutch . . . . . . . . . . . . . . . . . . . . . . . . . . . 13
    Engine . . . . . . . . . . . . . . . . . . . . . . . . . 9-10
    Exhaust emission control . . . . . . . . . . . 12-13
    Fuel system . . . . . . . . . . . . . . . . . . . . . . . 12
    Ignition system . . . . . . . . . . . . . . . . . . 10-12
    Procedures . . . . . . . . . . . . . . . . . . . . . . . 7-8
    Regulator . . . . . . . . . . . . . . . . . . . . . . . . 8-9
    Starter . . . . . . . . . . . . . . . . . . . . . . . . . . . 8

## U

Universal joint maintenance . . . . . . . . . . . . . 26

## V

Vacuum gauge . . . . . . . . . . . . . . . . . . . . . . . 4-5
Valve lash adjustment (6-cylinder only) . . . . 43
Vapor saver system . . . . . . . . . . . . . . . . 114, 115
Voltmeter, ammeter, and ohmmeter . . . . . . . 4

## W

Wheel bearing lubrication, front . . . . . . . . . . 84
Wheel bearings, front . . . . . . . . . . . . . . . . . . 30
Wheel cylinders . . . . . . . . . . . . . . . . . . . . 84-88
Windshield washer fluid . . . . . . . . . . . . . . . . 15

# NOTES